# First-Person America

# FIRST-PERSON AMERICA

Edited and with an introduction by

## ANN BANKS

W · W · NORTON & COMPANY

New York · London

First published as a Norton paperback 1991

Library of Congress Cataloging in Publication Data
Main entry under title:
First-person America
Bibliography: p.
Includes index.
1. United States—Social life and customs—1918–1945.
2. United States—Social life and customs—1865–1918.
3. United States—Biography.
4. Oral history.
I. Banks, Ann.
E169.E56   1981   973.717′092′2 [B]   81-40092
ISBN 0-393-30781-6

Printed in the United States of America
W. W. Norton & Company, Inc., 500 Fifth Avenue, New York, NY 10110
W. W. Norton & Company Ltd, 10 Coptic Street, London WC1A 1PU

1   2   3   4   5   6   7   8   9   0

TO

MY GRANDMOTHER BLANCHE CARTTER BANKS

AND

MY GRANDFATHER JOHN A. DAY

# Preface
# to the Norton Paperback Edition

Ten years have passed since I last read these eighty stories, and the people in this book have changed. They have different things to make known now, fresh nuances to convey. The present has transformed them in unexpected ways, generally improving their luck. I'm struck by how many stories are threaded with optimism and good humor. The men and women whose narratives are collected in *First Person America* had endured a time of misery and struggle, yet showed few traces of despair. In large part, they took a friendly attitude toward the future, believing that change meant progress. This conviction often was coupled with an idealism concerning unions and an unshakable trust in the promise of technology—sentiments belonging to an era vastly more innocent and hopeful than our own. The inhabitants of this book have come to seem surprisingly enviable.

The men and women in *First Person America* told their stories in the late thirties with enough flourish to capture my attention forty years later. I loved their energetic clamor; their shrewd and spiky words. But how true were the stories? When possible, I tested the narratives against other sources—and found confirmation of even some of the gaudier tales. Yet it seemed more useful to ask instead: how were the stories true? I came to believe that the rich subjectivity of these rememberings was in itself meaningful and valid.

American historians have become more sophisticated in their approach to the workings of memory during the decade since the book first appeared. In 1989, the *Journal of American History* ran a special issue on memory, later published in book form as *Memory and American History*. In the introduction David Thelan wrote, "Historians have traditionally been concerned above all with the accuracy of a memory, with how correctly it described what actually occurred at some point in the past." That assumption, Thelan reported, is being challenged by scholarship in other fields. According to recent psychological research, remembering is a process of creative construction, not merely of replication. We don't retrieve our memories, psychologists now believe, we make them up. They further hold that a storyteller is not the sole author of his tale: he collaborates with his audience in shaping the story. Every story, in other words, is a conversation, even when only one person does the talking.

None of these findings would seem new or startling to the man most responsible for the stories in this book. Benjamin Botkin, the folklore editor of the Federal Writers' Project, wrote in 1945 that first-person narratives should be thought of as a collaboration between interviewer and informant. He was untroubled by the inevitable subjectivity of recollection, seeing it as a window onto the ways that people shape and reshape their identity. His perspective, confirmed now by research on how and why people remember, offers historians an additional framework for evaluating oral testimony. As Thelan wrote, "For our purposes, the social dimensions of memory are more important than the need to verify accuracy."

In editing *First Person America*, I entered into a collaboration with those who'd told their stories and those who'd listened. Although forty years had passed since the people in the book had sat down to talk, I tried to meet my partners face to face whenever I could. I managed to find a number of the Federal Writers who had collected the narratives, and I even located a few of their subjects. (After this book appeared, several more found me.) Most of the Federal Writers were surprised and pleased that their FWP work would at last see print. Several asked for advice on finding publishers for more recent writing, and wondered if their appearance in this anthology might open doors.

Today Federal Writer Stetson Kennedy credits *First Person America* with helping to focus attention on his long-neglected work. Although published successfully in Europe, two of Kennedy's books had never appeared in the United States. While on the Florida Writers' Project, he recorded a story of Ku Klux Klan terror; this horrifying tale so moved Kennedy that he later infiltrated the Klan as an undercover agent. A memoir of his experience appeared in London in 1954—and in the United States not until last year.(*The Klan Unmasked*; the London edition was entitled *I Rode with the Ku Klux Klan*.) Similarly, *Jim Crow Guide*, Kennedy's indictment of segregation, was originally published in Paris by Jean Paul Sartre in 1956. It finally found an American publisher in 1989. (Two other of Kennedy's works are now being republished in the U.S.: *Southern Exposure*, and *Palmetto Country*, a book based on his stint on the Florida Writers' Project.)

Among the most colorful tales in *First Person America* is that of a Key West rum runner who drew the line at smuggling aliens. In 1938 Captain Antonio (not his real name) told Stetson Kennedy that "me and the boys

gave Hemingway the stuff he used in writin that book—what'd he call it—
*To Have and Have Not.*" Ten years ago, Kennedy reinterviewed Antonio,
who elaborated on his Prohibition adventures: Instead of just telling
Hemingway about rum running, he'd taken him along to help salvage a
load stashed under ten feet of water at Sugarloaf Key. Antonio also
claimed to have made deliveries on the high seas to Franklin D. Roosevelt, who required his secretary to sample a bottle from every case before
accepting it. When *First Person America* was published, Kennedy put me
in touch with Antonio, who briefly considered appearing on television to
reminisce about his smuggling days. In the end, he declined. Having
lived a law-abiding life as a charter boat captain ever since Prohibition was
repealed, he chose to remain hidden behind his pseudonym.

Victoria Kramer wept when she reread the story she'd told forty years
before about the brutality of work in the Chicago stockyards. "It opened
up some closed doors," she told me. Yet she still took pride in having
been, as she'd reported to Federal Writer Betty Burke, "the first girl in the
Yards to wear my CIO union button." She hoped the stories in *First
Person America* would provide "roots for our kids," by preserving "some of
our thoughts and hopes and dreams for our children and grandchildren to
read."

I received many letters from people who said that this or that story in
the book reminded them of their Polish grandmother or their Irish aunts.
A few letter-writers claimed actual kinship. Robert Kress wrote from
California to correct an error concerning his wife's grandfather Samuel
Novelli. An Italian immigrant sculptor, Novelli was considered one of the
finest carvers in Barre, Vermont. The *First Person America* account
describes how Novelli carved the statue of Robert Burns, considered the
pride of Barre. According to Kress, Novelli also carved the memorial
statue of his partner Corti, who was killed in a local feud between socialists
and anarchists. The narrative attributes the statue to Corti's brother, but as
Kress wrote, "Corti did not have a brother, and it is such a beautiful work
of art, the real artist should get the credit."

The unpublished Federal Writers' Project manuscripts have had a
peripatetic history since the FWP was dismantled. When it became
apparent in 1940 that the Project's days were numbered, an effort was
made to salvage the vast quantity of material that had been collected.
(There also are numerous state repositories of Writers' Project material.
These are listed in a *Survey of Federal Writers' Project Manuscript
Holdings in State Depositories*, compiled by Robert Carter and myself,
and available through the American Historical Association, 400 A Street
SE, Washington, D.C. 20003.) The Library of Congress established an
editorial project to "collect, preserve and organize for use" the FWP

manuscripts. Little headway had been made on this task, however, when funds ran out in 1941.

At the time I read the life history narratives, they were stashed away, uncatalogued, in a dirty, airless chamber in the Library known as the Buzzard's Nest. After my description of these archival conditions appeared in print, the Library moved the papers from their grim setting to the safer, cleaner, and more convenient environs of the Manuscript Division. (Other Writers' Project material had been housed there all along—work that had been in book manuscript form at the time the Project ended. Also brought to the Manuscript Division were FWP papers left over from the preparation of the state and local guidebooks—material that had been crated, shoved from alcove to alcove, and finally relegated to a warehouse outside Washington.) A team of librarians spent several years organizing and inventorying the unprocessed papers.

Not long ago, I visited the Manuscript Reading Room to see the improved working conditions. Today nobody suggests donning a dust mask. Instead, a researcher wishing to peruse the life histories works at an ample walnut table resting on thick blue carpet. The material he or she requests, now filed state by state in pristine manuscript boxes, is wheeled to the table on a cart. These changes have helped spur a growing number of publications. Recent anthologies drawing on the life history collection include *Texas Cowboys: Memories of the Early Days*; *The First Franco-Americans: New England Life Histories from the Federal Writers' Project*; and *America: The Dream of My Life*, selections from New Jersey Writers' Project interviews.

I learned during my visit that the Library of Congress has additional plans for the Federal Writers' Project life history manuscripts. They will be included in The American Memory Project, an innovative effort to disseminate Library of Congress collections on electronic media. The collections, chosen because they illuminate facets of American history, include photographs, manuscripts, music, motion pictures, books, and sound recordings. Each will consist of primary documents accompanied by explanatory material. By the mid-1990s, the American Memory Project collections will be accessible at computer work stations in university and other libraries across the country.

For researchers who wish to consult the life histories, the benefits of this project will extend far beyond the convenience of not having to travel to Washington, D.C. As part of putting the collection into an electronic format, archivists are now at work on a subject index that will span all the life history manuscripts. A researcher interested in labor disputes, for example, will be able to consult the index for the location of relevant life histories. Using the American Memory Project computer, he or she can also try scanning part or all of the collection for specific words and phrases, such as "strike" or "union."

The American Memory Project will open the life history collection to researchers interested in a wide range of subjects. It also will ease the way for fresh interpretations of the material. As the present continues to reshape our understanding of the past, we can line up the stories to suit our amended purposes. A new host of collaborators can join those who already have taken an organizing hand.

Today, there is growing controversy over the role of government in fostering artistic and cultural activity. Many people are questioning the value of federal funding of the arts; it seems almost astonishing that the U.S. government once directly employed out-of-work writers. Yet the Federal Writers' Project cost the government $27 million—only one-fifth of one percent of all WPA expenditures. The Project's value as a relief measure and the excellent guidebooks it produced justified its existence. But in the rich vein of unpublished material, the Writers' Project also left a forgotten legacy—one that fifty years later is only beginning to be fully appreciated.

A.B.
New York City
1991

# Contents

# Acknowledgments

The Federal Writers' Project life history narratives are the product of a collaboration between those who were interviewed and the Federal Writers who did the interviewing. In attempting to understand the nature of that collaboration, I interviewed eleven former members of the Writers' Project who collected nearly half of the narratives published here. Their pleasure and surprise that work they did some forty years ago—work they had assumed lost forever—would at last appear in print, was a source of encouragement. The names of these men and women are listed in the Bibliography. Among them, I am especially grateful to Leonard Rapport, who freely shared his memories of the North Carolina Writers' Project, and to Stetson Kennedy, who wrote me many entertaining letters about his experiences on the Florida Writers' Project. I was also fortunate to locate a few people who had been interviewed by Federal Writers in the 1930s, and whose stories appear in this book. Victoria Kramer, a former stockyards worker and CIO organizer, remembered—and vividly described to me—nearly everyone in the chapter on meatpacking-houses.

For their help during the many months I worked at the Library of Congress, I am grateful to Joe Hickerson of the Folk Song Archive and Alan Jabbour of the American Folklife Center. The staffs of these two offices deserve my thanks, as well, for extending unofficial courtesies that made my life easier in countless ways. John Y. Cole, also of the Library, smoothed the way during the beginning stages of my research.

There are other institutional debts to acknowledge. I am grateful to the Institute for Policy Studies for offering a stamp of officialdom and students to teach during my stay in Washington, D.C. I also want to express my appreciation to the American Studies Center at Boston College, and to R. Alan Lawson in particular, for providing a wonderful office and a companionable atmosphere in which to work. Financial support for the work on this book came through the generous assistance of the Ford Foundation and the Rockefeller Foundation. My personal gratitude goes to Robert Goldman of the Ford Foundation and to

D. Lydia Bronte of the Rockefeller Foundation for their continued interest in this project.

In the course of my work, I have received the aid and guidance of many friends. I am grateful to Jerrold Hirsch for his critique of the introduction, and for our many conversations over the years about the Federal Writers' Project. Eric Foner and Alexander Bloom read successive drafts of the entire manuscript and provided valuable encouragement and counsel. Mara Liasson generously provided me with a copy of her unpublished thesis on the Federal Writers' Project, and Lyn Goldfarb took time from her own work to advise me about planning my research at the Library of Congress.

Several people offered useful critiques of individual chapters: Karen Lane of the Barre Ethnic Heritage Project; Dan Morgenstern of the Institute of Jazz Studies; John Hammond; Leslie Orear of the Illinois Labor History Society; and Delores Janiewski.

I owe a special debt to Helena Wall, for her friendship and wit, as well as for her remarkable abilities as a researcher and keen editorial eye.

I am grateful to Victoria Wilson of Alfred A. Knopf, whose editorial insight and high standards have made this a better book. My sister Jane, and my parents, Isabel and Richard Banks, all have taken an active interest in this project. Carol Baume gave not only friendship and support, but also the vegetable bin of her refrigerator as storage space for manuscripts. Finally I should like to thank Peter Petre for superb job of editing, and for helping me in many ways.

I have dedicated this book to my grandmother Blanche Cartter Banks and my grandfather John A. Day. I first learned the value of a good story by listening to theirs.

# Introduction

During the Depression the cries of peddlers filled the streets of New York City. Kingfish Smith of East 100th Street knew he needed "something extra" to sell his fish and vegetables. He hawked his wares and kidded his fellow peddlers in original songs set to popular tunes of the day. His best songs were inventions of the moment, inspired by the produce on his wagon that morning:

> I got vegetables today,
> So don't go away...
> I got oranges, tomatoes, nice southern sweet potatoes,
> I got yellow yams
> From Birmingham...
> I got greens
> From New Orleans.
> I got the greenest greens I ever seen.
> And I sure seen
> A whole lot of greens.

In the spring of 1938, Smith told two members of the New York City Federal Writers' Project how he composed his street cries and songs:

> On the street whatever comes to my mind I say it if I think it will be good. The main idea is when I got something I want to put over I just find something to rhyme with it. And the main requirement for that is mood. You gotta be in the mood. You got to put yourself in it. You've got to feel it. It's got to be more an expression than a routine.

Kingfish Smith's story of how he drew poetry from his workaday world was one of more than ten thousand first-person narratives collected during the last years of the Great Depression by members of the Federal Writers' Project. Eighty of these narratives are published here for the first time. They include accounts by an Irish maid from Massachusetts, a French-Canadian textile worker from New Hampshire's Amoskeag Mills, a Bahamian midwife from Florida, a patent-medicine pitchman from North Carolina, a Portuguese fisherman from Cape Cod, a Key West smuggler, a Chicago prostitute, and a Pullman porter from Harlem. Their stories of life and work during the 1930s are interwoven with reminiscences of ways of life long past by the time the Depression began. Many Americans in the Thirties remembered the nineteenth century as vividly as some people now recall the Depression years; more than one-third of the narratives in this collection describe earlier decades. People tell of meeting Billy the Kid, surviving the Chicago Fire of 1871, making the pioneer journey to the Western Territories, and fleeing to America to avoid conscription into the Czar's army.

The Great Depression today seems a distinct and unified era that began with the stock market crash of 1929, reached its depths in 1933 when one-fourth of the labor force was unemployed, was eased by the New Deal, and finally ended with America's entry into World War II. But for most of the people in this book, the Depression was not the singular event it appears in retrospect. It was one more hardship in lives made difficult by immigration, world war, and work in low-paying industries before the regulation of wages and hours. Though they spoke of living through bad times, those interviewed by the Federal Writers seldom mentioned the Depression itself.

Instead, people told stories about the everyday round of work and play, the details of survival. The life-history narratives are a compendium of knowing advice: how to get a job at Macy's, when it's safe to wear a union button, how to outsmart a tyrannical father or a dimwitted beau. As interpreters of their own history, people told stories they had chosen over time as giving meaning to their lives. The best of these stories offer insights born of years of living. As the critic Walter Benjamin wrote in his essay "The Storyteller," "counsel woven into the fabric of real life is wisdom."[1]

Although the country experienced a recession in 1938 and 1939, the harshest Depression years had passed by the time these narratives were collected. According to FWP director Henry Alsberg, the people interviewed belonged to the "less prosperous millions," but they were not starving, they were getting by. Federal Writers talked to few middle-class, white-collar workers, and even fewer of the destitute unemployed. Life histories collected by the Writers' Project concentrated on "resourceful, unembittered men and women coping with social disaster," as historian William Stott has noted.[2] The hard-working poor predominate, and they talk about general conditions from an individual perspective.

The fierce struggles to build unions had a profound effect on many of those interviewed. Anna Novak, a Chicago packinghouse worker and organizer for the CIO (Congress of Industrial Organizations), described the resistance to the union among some of the older religious women: "I tell them, 'Listen, don't you blame God for everything. Just because you're afraid to join the union and do something to keep your job safe and your children fed decently don't throw it on God. . . .' " Jim Cole, a black packinghouse worker, thought the CIO's biggest accomplishment was "breaking up the hate and bad feeling that used to be held against the Negro." He explained that his own union had many foreign-born workers whose English was poor, "but that don't make no mind; they all friends in the union, even if they can't say nothin except 'Brother' and shake hands."

Other narratives recall the dangers and uncertainties of work on construction projects and in granite sheds and steel mills. As Chris Thorston described his trade, "You ain't an iron worker unless you get killed." Yet for Michael Donegal, a granite carver, the chief hazard of his occupation, silicosis, was a lesser evil than unemployment: "Take away a man's job and you kill the man. Maybe the dust killed them, but being without work kills them inside—a worse way."

The Federal Writers who collected these stories were themselves victims of the Depression. The Writers' Project was based on the idea that unemployed writers, like unemployed carpenters, had a right to jobs.[3] Along with its companion Federal Arts Projects—Music, Art, and Theater—the Writers' Project was part of the New Deal's national work relief program, the Works Progress Administration (WPA).* At its peak, the Federal Writers' Project employed 6,500 writers and other white-collar workers for a salary of about $20 a week. Writers' Project offices in every state reported to a national headquarters in Washington, D.C. During the early years of the Project, the Federal Writers worked on a series of guidebooks which remain the FWP's best-known undertaking.

Federal Writers went on to gather the largest body of first-person narratives ever collected in this country.† These accounts were intended

---

* The name was changed to the Work Projects Administration on July 1, 1939.

† These accounts went under an assortment of names in the Writers' Project: life histories, living lore, industrial lore, occupational lore, and narratives. All of these terms were used to describe efforts to document real people telling their own stories in their own words. In the interest of clarity, I have referred to all first-person accounts as life-history narratives. The length of the narratives ranges from one to fifty pages of typescript, though most are between five and ten pages.

to be published in a series of anthologies that would form a composite portrait of America through the storytelling of people from various occupations, regions, and ethnic groups. But by the late Depression, the Federal Writers' Project, along with the other Federal Arts Projects, had become a convenient target for conservative attacks on the New Deal. In the wake of hostile criticism from the House Un-American Activities Committee, Congress decentralized and curtailed the Project in 1939. The Writers' Project came to a complete halt following America's entry into World War II. Its most innovative publication plans were abandoned, and the potential of the life-history collection was never realized.

Many of the narratives in *First-Person America* were meant for anthologies left unfinished when the Project ended. These included projected volumes on granite carvers, western pioneers, and tobacco workers, and a book of New England life histories to be called *Yankee Folk*. The two anthologies of Writers' Project material that did appear not long after the Project ended have been called classics of the documentary genre.[4] *Lay My Burden Down* was culled from thousands of interviews with former slaves, and *These Are Our Lives* was an anthology of life-history narratives of black and white southerners.*

The vast store of unpublished material—the hidden legacy of the Federal Writers' Project—has been gathering dust since it was deposited at the Library of Congress in 1941. Efforts at the time to process and organize the material—more than 150,000 pages in the Library's Folk Song Archive alone†—foundered for lack of funds. Undoubtedly the size and chaotic condition of the collection has discouraged potential users. Previous neglect of the Project's unpublished material was also due to the political and cultural climate of the postwar years, when many New Deal programs fell out of favor. As a result, these life histories were all but forgotten for forty years.‡

Most of the first-person narratives in the Library of Congress were

---

* Benjamin A. Botkin, ed., *Lay My Burden Down: A Folk History of Slavery.* Chicago, 1945. William T. Couch, ed., *These Are Our Lives.* Chapel Hill, North Carolina, 1939. A recent anthology of FWP life-history materials culled from the Southern Historical Collection at the University of North Carolina is *Such As Us: Southern Voices of the Thirties*, edited by Tom Terrill and Jerrold Hirsch (University of North Carolina Press, 1978).

† Several repositories of Writers' Project papers in state libraries and archives include life-history narratives. Some, but not all, of this material duplicates Library of Congress holdings.

‡ In contrast to the life histories, the narratives of former slaves gathered by the Federal Writers' Project have received considerable attention. George P. Rawick has edited a nineteen-volume facsimile publication of slave narratives, *The American Slave: A Composite Autobiography* (Greenwood Publishing Company, 1972). In addition, several anthologies of selected slave narratives have been published.

gathered under the direction of the FWP's Folklore Unit. The Folklore Unit favored interview methods that encouraged people to talk freely, "following the natural association of ideas and memories."[5] Life stories were to be "narrated as told by an informant . . . with all the flavor of talk and all the native art of casual narration belonging to the natural storyteller."[6] These instructions to Federal Writers were formulated by Benjamin A. Botkin, folklore editor of the Project in 1938 and 1939. Nearly all the narratives published here were collected during his term and reflect his views and interests. Botkin grew up in Boston and studied literature at Harvard and Columbia. By 1931, when he received his Ph.D. from the University of Nebraska, he had already collected regional folklore in the Southwest and edited a journal called *Folk-Say*.

Botkin developed his own unconventional approach to the subject of folklore. He had no interest in indulging "nostalgia for the old, the odd and the picturesque. . . ."[7] Folk materials, he believed, must be viewed "dynamically as part of the process of cultural conflict, change and adaptation." As folklore editor of the Writers' Project, he wanted to explore the rough texture of everyday life, to collect what he called "living lore." Before Botkin joined the Project, its folklore collecting had focused on traditional rural lore—superstitions, ghost stories—for use in the American Guide Series. Botkin shifted the emphasis to urban and industrial material. He believed that people's work lives, viewed in the context of their neighborhood and ethnic group, provided the richest source of folk material. "Folklore," he once said, "has a direct relation to the work men do and their attitude toward it. . . ."[8]

In gathering life histories, the Folklore Unit often collaborated with the FWP's Social-Ethnic Studies Unit, directed by Morton Royse, a sociologist. Royse's group concentrated on immigrants and the role they played in American life.* "We discarded the old patronizing attitude toward the immigrant," Royse wrote, "that of judging a group by the number of doctors, lawyers, and big businessmen it had produced. We assumed that every individual contributed, whether he slung a pen or a pickaxe."[10]

In the same spirit, Botkin wrote that the true measure of immigrant groups "as components of 'composite America' is in their participation in, rather than in their 'contributions' . . . to our cultural diversity."[11] Botkin and Royse hoped to change the view of American society as a

---

* In theory, the Folklore Unit dealt with "a body of lore in relation to the life of a group or community," while the Social-Ethnic Studies Unit focused on "the whole life of a group or community" in which folklore was only one aspect.[9] In practice, the distinction between the two ventures was frequently blurred: both stressed the collection of first-person narratives; and both drew on the same pool of FWP fieldworkers.

melting pot. The two men saw the nation not as an alloy but as a mosaic: a democratic, pluralistic community composed of many disparate elements.[12] The Writers' Project, they thought, could present that vision by assembling ethnically and occupationally diverse life histories. Each story would retain its individual integrity, yet would join with others to form a coherent picture of "a nation of nations."

The work of the Writers' Project was meant to instruct as well as describe. In the late Thirties many Americans were horrified by the rise of fascism in Europe and worried about possible consequences at home. Rabbi Stephen Wise, a founder of the American Jewish Congress, encouraged the Writers' Project to publish material sympathetic to ethnic diversity "as a way of preventing European hatreds from infecting our own country."[13] Botkin warned that those who collected folklore must beware of fueling reactionary notions of racial purity. It was necessary, he said, to distinguish "democratic and progressive folk consciousness from the regressive folk dogma of the racialists and nationalists."[14]

Botkin believed, with many intellectuals of his generation, that the artist should be a useful member of society. He suggested that writers could find a sense of community and social purpose by taking part in the group activity of folklore research.[15] Again and again he stressed the importance of the *process* of collecting narratives. The best results, he wrote, were obtained "when a good informant and a good interviewer got together and the narrative is the process of the conscious or unconscious collaboration of the two."[16] Botkin sought to implement this philosophy through specific instructions to Federal Writers. "Make your informant feel important," he directed. "Well-conducted interviews serve as social occasions to which informants come to look forward."[17]

Such advice was, of course, interpreted according to the temperament and inclinations of individual fieldworkers, as I discovered in conversations with several former Federal Writers. Stetson Kennedy, of the Florida Writers' Project, recalls that he established a comfortable atmosphere by interviewing people in their homes over a glass of beer. "Before tackling anything as personal as a life history," he says, "we naturally established a good deal of rapport with the person, before getting around to telling them their lives were so interesting they should be written down. Most people agreed and the more notes you took, the better they liked it."[18]

Frank Byrd, a black Federal Writer, became good friends with several of the Harlem residents he interviewed. "You can't just barge in and start asking questions of people who don't know who you are and how you feel as a person. You have to pass the time of day with them until you reach the point where you feel a warm relationship so that you can talk, so that *they* can talk."[19]

Federal Writers were encouraged to arrange interviews through community or work-related organizations, but that suggestion was often ignored in favor of chance contacts. Some writers interviewed their relatives; many more talked to friends or casual acquaintances. Jack Conroy acknowledges that the coal miner he interviewed (page 82) was his nephew. "I didn't like to mention that when I turned in the interview because I thought I might be accused of nepotism."[20]

Ralph Ellison was equally informal: "I hung around playgrounds; I hung around the street, the bars. I went into hundreds of apartment buildings and just knocked on doors. I would tell some stories to get people going and then I'd sit back and try to get it down as accurately as I could. Sometimes you would find people sitting around on Eighth Avenue just dying to talk so you didn't have to encourage them too much."[21]

Since the Federal Writers themselves were on relief, they were frequently accepted as sympathetic equals by those they interviewed. Betty Burke recalls feeling a bond of shared adversity with the packinghouse workers she talked to. "We were dirt poor ourselves and these people were, if anything, even poorer, so I was very close to them. I understood every word they said with all my heart."[22]

The Federal Writers often found that people were pleased to be interviewed. Telling stories of their work and lives strengthened their sense of their own past. Mrs. Anselmi, the widow of a Vermont stonecutter who died at thirty-two, was thankful for the chance to tell her husband Edo's story. "I don't mind talking about him," she told Federal Writer Roaldus Richmond. "If I could write, I'd put him in a book myself. A whole book about him."

People with all levels of writing ability found their way onto the Project. Since a major purpose of the Writers' Project was to provide relief, most applicants were required to pass a means test—although each state office was allowed to hire a few accomplished professionals not on the relief rolls. Stetson Kennedy had just graduated from college and was "ready to try anything" when he heard of the Writers' Project. "It so happened that the mother of a friend was high in the state office of the so-called 'white-collar division' of the WPA," he recalls. "That consisted of such units as the Federal Writers', Art, Theater, and Music projects. The purpose was to serve certain cultural needs of the public and to enable established—though unemployed—cultural workers to retain their skills, and young people to develop them. I didn't fancy a career in the furniture business, and on the other hand the Writers' Project

seemed made to order. With unemployment running around twenty
percent nationwide, my generation had slim pickings indeed."[23]

In addition to providing jobs for experienced writers and for begin-
ners like Kennedy, the Writers' Project served as a catchall relief agency
for the white-collar unemployed, such as clerks, librarians and school-
teachers. But sometimes men and women who had always wanted to be
writers used the Project experience to enter the literary world.

Black writers were among those who benefited most from the opportunity offered by the Project.[24] Novelists Ralph Ellison, Margaret
Walker, Zora Neale Hurston, Arna Bontemps, Richard Yerby, and
Richard Wright all served literary apprenticeships on the Writers'
Project. Wright had worked in the Chicago Post Office before becoming
a Federal Writer; he used the extra time the Project gave him to write
*Native Son.* Ralph Ellison, who joined the Project at Wright's instiga-
tion, says now that it encouraged him to think of himself as a professional
writer for the first time: "Actually to be *paid* for writing . . . why that was
a wonderful thing!"[25]

The Project sustained a considerable number of writers who
already had or later achieved national literary reputations. Among them
were Saul Bellow, John Cheever, and Conrad Aiken. *First-Person America* includes narratives collected by Ellison, novelists Nelson Algren
and Jack Conroy, and poet May Swenson. But the support of famous
writers is not the Project's only contribution to the world of letters.
Its purpose was not to produce "stars." As Henry Alsberg, director of
the Writers' Project, remarked, "We must get over the idea that every
writer must be an artist of the first class, and that an artist of the second
or third class has no function."[26] Many Federal Writers went on to
publish, but achieved only modest reknown. Of the forty-one Federal
Writers whose work appears in this book, more than half published
books after they left the Project.

Despite the subsequent literary accomplishments of Federal Writers,
the Project has been criticized for having failed to encourage creativity,
because its emphasis was on work relief rather than artistic output.
Project officials, however, believed that by providing a subsistence income
to a large number of writers, they were setting a precedent for government support of cultural life.[27] Although the priorities that govern federal funding of the arts have changed substantially since the 1930s, they
are still the subject of debate.* In a recent essay, the literary historian

---

* Since 1965, most federal support for the arts has been administered by the
National Endowments for the Arts and Humanities. The Endowments award grants to
a limited number of individuals and institutions each year on the basis of merit, without
taking into account financial need.

Daniel Aaron praised the New Deal's "hit-or-miss venture in the 'democratization of culture,' " as he called the Federal Arts Projects.[28] Jerre Mangione, a former FWP administrator, argued in his history and memoir *The Dream and the Deal: The Federal Writers' Project 1935–1943* that: "The simple act of providing writers and would-be writers with jobs that gave them a livelihood without unduly taxing their energies turned out to be the most effective measure that could have been taken to nurture the future of American letters."[29]

While only a few Federal Writers were allowed to do their own creative work on Project time, the Writers' Project experience offered more than just a meal ticket. Among those needy enough to qualify for Project jobs were a considerable number of people who had come from educated middle-class backgrounds. For them the Depression represented not simply the latest in a string of hardships, but a reversal of fortunes. Many of these newly poor men and women found collecting life histories a liberating and exhilarating experience; they were eager to put their skills to use documenting the lives of people who had always been poor. Poet Muriel Rukeyser later described such activity as "the key to the Thirties . . . the joy to awake and see life entire, and tell the stories of real people."[30]

Benjamin Botkin considered the FWP folklore work "the greatest educational as well as social experiment of our time." The Writers' Project experience, he wrote, could alter a writer's perspective by giving him or her "a social and cultural consciousness too often lacking in ivory-tower writing."[31] Along with the new outlook came new subject matter. Botkin shared the desire of adherents of literary realism to move "the streets, the stockyards and the hiring halls into literature."[32] The life-history narratives were "the stuff of literature," in Botkin's words,[33] and indeed, many Federal Writers' field research did influence their subsequent work. Mari Tomasi, who collected many of the granite industry narratives published here, wrote a novel, *Like Lesser Gods*, based on that experience. Sam Ross, who interviewed jazz musicians, recently published *Windy City*, a novel that describes the Chicago jazz scene as he knew it in the 1930s.

Stetson Kennedy's interview with Norberto Diaz about a gruesome Ku Klux Klan murder later inspired him to infiltrate the Klan as an undercover agent. He wrote about this experience in *I Rode with the Ku Klux Klan*. (Kennedy also interviewed a Key West smuggler who claimed to be Ernest Hemingway's principal informant for *To Have and Have Not*.) Passages in Nelson Algren's *A Walk on the Wild Side* echo his interview with a Chicago prostitute. And Ralph Ellison says that collecting folklore on the FWP "threw me into my own history. Once you touched the history of blacks in New York," he recalls, "you were deep into American history."[34]

Federal Writers learned from practicing the technique of collecting narratives as well as from the stories themselves. The life histories were gathered before the days of tape recorders, and the mechanical recording methods available were too expensive and cumbersome for any but a very few collecting expeditions. Instead, the life-history narratives were reconstructed from notes and memory. The FWP interviewer was encouraged to work at being "a good listener with a good ear for recording or remembering both what is said and how it is said."[*35]

Ralph Ellison was one who heeded Botkin's advice that Federal Writers should learn to listen for characteristic speech rhythms and the vernacular. In his Writers' Project interviews, Ellison began to experiment with ways of capturing the sound of black speech that he refined in his novel, *Invisible Man*. "I tried to use my ear for dialogue to give an impression of just how the people sounded. I developed a technique of transcribing that captured the idiom rather than trying to convey the dialect through misspellings."[36]

The Federal Writers' Project pioneered the collection of first-person narratives by people who would not otherwise have left a record. Benjamin Botkin called for an emphasis on "history from the bottom up," in which the people become their own historians. He believed that "history must study the inarticulate many as well as the articulate few."[37] The advent of tape recorders in the years following the 1930s has refined the practice of what has come to be called oral history and made it possible for Botkin's goals to be pursued more easily.

One widely read oral history—a book whose subject matter parallels this one—is Studs Terkel's *Hard Times: An Oral History of the Great Depression*, published in 1970. Terkel himself worked on the Illinois Writers' Project. More than thirty years later he asked an "improvised battalion of survivors," people who had lived through the Depression, to talk about how that grim decade had shaped their lives. Their retrospective accounts are colored by the intervening years—they are memories of the 1930s. In contrast, the people whose life histories are published here are voices *from* the Thirties. Their words reflect the perspectives and sensibilities of the decade in which they told their stories.

Both the Federal Writers' Project life-history narratives and *Hard Times* have a common antecedent. Ninety years before the Writers'

* *The Manual for Folklore Studies* emphasized accuracy. Federal Writers were directed to "take down everything you hear, just as you hear it, without adding, taking away or altering a syllable. *Your business is to record, not correct or improve.*"

Project, Henry Mayhew walked the streets of London interviewing the poorest people in Victorian England. The book that resulted, *London Labour and the London Poor*, was, claimed Mayhew, "the first attempt to publish the history of a people from the lips of the people themselves —giving a literal description of their labour, their earnings, their trials, and their sufferings, in their own 'unvarnished' language. . . ."[38] Mayhew hoped that by collecting first-person accounts of life among "the humbler classes of society" he could stir those in high places to improve conditions. Yet, like the impoverished rag-gatherers, seamstresses, and prostitutes of Mayhew's London, the men and women in *First-Person America* transcend their function as "evidence," historical or social. We see instead clear portraits of individuals who reveal in their words the richness and character of their lives. These vivid accounts belong to literature as well as to history.

Walter Benjamin has said that traces of the storyteller cling to the story the way handprints of the potter cling to the clay vessel.[39] The stories in this book bear the traces of several sets of prints. Benjamin Botkin considered the life-history narratives to be records of all the various factors that went into their making: the attitudes and values of the interviewers and informants, and the dynamic process of the interview itself.[40] This anthology, then, reflects my own attitudes and values as well as the process of sifting through over 150,000 unorganized pages of manuscript. I worked in a small windowless room, familiarly called the Buzzard's Nest, at the end of a labyrinth in the Library of Congress stacks, a room whose exposed insulation and crumbling manuscript pages made dust masks recommended equipment for researchers. Since the collection was without inventory or index, the only way to survey it was to work from the beginning to end. The material is filed in drawers labeled with geographical locations that are only sometimes accurate. First-person narratives are mixed in with traditional folklore and material derived from secondary sources. With two exceptions (tall tales collected by Nelson Algren and Ralph Ellison), this book is limited to first-person life-history narratives.*

The narratives published here were not selected because they were representative of the collection or of the Federal Writers who conducted the interviews. Predetermined criteria gave way before the sheer size of the collection; the eighty life histories in this book were chosen from some ten thousand. Certain stories communicated an unmistakable vitality that made itself felt across forty years. Each life history was the

---

* In the years following the Writers' Project, Benjamin Botkin included a number of the tall tales collected on the Project in his folklore treasuries.

record of a particular occasion: two people sitting down to talk—in a bar or a union hiring hall, on a front porch or at a kitchen table—one speaking, the other taking down the stories. Sometimes the speaker and the listener seemed to share a sympathetic understanding that encouraged moments of special insight. There were unexpected discoveries: familiar stories seemed to gain deeper meaning for the teller; old grievances found new resolutions. A Vermont farm woman came to forgive her parents for keeping her from school eighty years before. A Jewish peddler who had passed up his chance to prosper in order to raise his sister's children reaffirmed the choice he had made. For a stonecutter's widow, an unaccustomed feeling of pride surfaced as she recalled her struggles to raise her children alone. People spoke most expressively about what was most important to them. Reading such stories, I felt I could "hear the tones and the accents and see the facial expressions and bodily movements," as one Federal Writer described it.[41] It was this quality of immediacy upon which I finally relied in making my selections.

This anthology necessarily reflects the omissions and biases of the life-history collection, as well as its strengths. Few life histories depict either white-collar work or unemployment. Fewer women than men were interviewed. Federal Writers also seem to have been predisposed to interview those with exotic occupations or experiences. In addition, there may have been a temptation to tone down potentially controversial content in the political atmosphere of 1938, when the Project was under fire from the House Un-American Activities Committee. The material to be included in the state guidebooks at times became an ideological battlefield.* However, because the majority of life-history narratives were never prepared for publication, few appear to have been censored.† Of course, the Federal Writers undoubtedly censored themselves on occasion. Nelson Algren, who was a supervisor on the Chicago Writers' Project, urged Federal Writers to use discretion, "especially about the insertion of obscenity. This may be naturalism," he said, "but we aren't working here as individuals, we're working in a group observed by the society about it. . . ."[42]

---

* Stetson Kennedy recalls that on the Florida Project there was a major conflict "between those staffers who wanted to turn out 'touristy' guidebooks and others of us who were determined that the guidebooks would be in step with the literary realism of those days, and reflect as accurately as possible the quality of life in Florida without glossing over its more sordid aspects."

† Had they been published, it might have been different, as a memo from Frank Manuel, then New England regional supervisor, to the Washington office suggests. Concerned about the possible reaction to the eventual publication of life histories of Vermont granite workers, he wrote: "For the time being we are not indulging in censorship, although we are conscious that this job will ultimately have to be performed."

The diversity of the FWP life-history collection is reflected in the organization of this anthology. Chapters focusing on particular industries—meatpacking, jazz, tobacco, entertainment, granite—contain narratives collected by a single Federal Writer or a small group working together. Each of these chapters is preceded by an introduction that explains the historical background of the industry.

In the remaining chapters, narratives from many state Writers' Projects are grouped together. The life histories in these chapters are linked by threads of common experience. For example, immigrants from New York City to Chicago talk about tensions between preserving old ways and adapting to life in America. Pioneer women reminisce about the hardships they encountered on the frontier. Black men and women describe traditional ways of life in the rural South and the new urban culture developed by migrants to northern cities. Union organizers recall their struggle to enlist support among fellow workers in steam laundries, shoe factories, and department stores.

Life-history narratives are prefaced by headnotes that provide background information on the informant and the interview. When it was available I also included biographical information about the Federal Writer who collected the life history. The information in the headnotes comes from several sources. Many of the life histories were submitted with forms outlining the personal history of the informant, including education, ancestry, place and date of birth, family, community and religious activities, and special skills and interests. Some reports also included a description of the informant and his or her surroundings. The writers themselves provided additional information. I talked with eleven of the forty-one Federal Writers whose narratives appear in *First-Person America*. Their recollections of how they worked were a useful reminder that things weren't always done "by the book."

Several of the Federal Writers had formed lasting friendships with people they interviewed. This enabled me to locate a few of the people whose life histories are published in this book. Some of their retrospective comments have been included here. Additional information came from Project administrators.

Federal Writers were instructed to ask informants if they wanted their names used in the event the life histories were published. If the answer was no, Federal Writers usually provided a fictitious name. I have invented names for the life histories where none was provided.

The Writers' Project never fully resolved the question of dialect. There was a diversity of language as well as of experience among the people interviewed. Some were first-generation immigrants still struggling with English; others spoke with pronounced regional accents. But to convey these differences accurately in a written text required skill that the Federal Writers often lacked. FWP supervisors realized that dialect clumsily transcribed would seem patronizing and be annoying to read. In numerous memos, state and national FWP editors suggested guidelines for conveying "the flavor and movement of talk" without caricaturing the subjects.[43] The interviews were to be transcribed in a way that was "faithful to grammar and idiom, while avoiding phonetic spelling."[44] Such advice was not always followed. Some interviewers rendered 'was' as 'wuz'; one Federal Writer even instructed a Project typist to add the letter *a* to the end of all verbs in an interview with an Italian American. I generally bypassed such narratives in selecting material for this book, but a few were so compelling that I included them in spite of awkwardly rendered dialect; in these cases, I restored corruptions of spelling to standard English. In addition, I edited the narratives for the sake of continuity and readability, while trying not to distort the tone or content of the original version.

The Depression forced many Americans to redefine their goals for the future—to imagine a life that would be meaningful in the face of lean material circumstances. They looked to former times for heritage that could offer guidance.[45] As John Dos Passos wrote toward the end of the Depression: "We need to know what kind of firm ground other men, belonging to generations before us, have found to stand on. In spite of changing conditions of life, they were not very different from ourselves, their thoughts were the grandfathers of our thoughts, they managed to meet situations as difficult as those we have to face, to meet them sometimes lightheartedly, and in some measure to make their hopes prevail. We need to know how they did it."[46]

The life-history narratives collected by the Federal Writers' Project are themselves an expression of this impulse to discover a usable past, to learn "how they did it." The narratives reveal what people turned to for strength and where they looked for meaning: ethnic roots, family life, the spirit of community that came with shared hardships. Today, as we read the records of the Federal Writers' Project, we may agree with Dos Passos that "a sense of continuity with generations gone before can stretch like a lifeline across the scary present. . . ."[47]

By preserving a written record of personal stories, Federal Writers offered men and women the hope that their voices might be heard by an audience beyond their immediate circle of family and friends, and that their lives would touch people they had never met. Benjamin Botkin's ambition was to make the Writers' Project life-history narratives available to an "ever-widening public." It was not enough, he believed, to collect the narratives solely as archival source material for scholars. "We must," he wrote, "give back to the people what we have taken from them and what rightfully belongs to them in a form they can understand and use. . . ."[48]

The people in this book describe the world they lived in and what they made of it. As Botkin realized, personal recollection is subjective, shaped by "all the distortions of time, faulty memory and hearsay."[49] But the way people make sense of their lives, the web of meaning and identity they weave for themselves, has a significance and importance of its own. Botkin would have agreed with Studs Terkel, who wrote of the people in *Hard Times*, "In their rememberings are their truths."[50] The portraits that emerge from these life histories—of people, of the times they lived in—add the resonance of memory to the formal record of written history.

# OLD TIMES

# Mrs. M. F. Cannon

*Mrs. M. F. Cannon grew up on an Eastland County, Texas, stock farm. She was seventy-three years old when Federal Writer Woody Phipps interviewed her at the Masonic Home for the Aged near Fort Worth.*

I was raised in West Texas when it was considered the sure enough wild and woolly West. If I could remember all the things that happened to me, you'd be able to write a big book on it all. As it is though, my memory sort of fails me right when I want it to work, but I'll tell you all I can recall.

I was born on July 30, 1864, in Arkadelphia, Arkansas. Just as soon's I was able to be carried good and my ma was able to take a long trip, my dad set out for Texas on September 15, 1864. Dad's name was Eldridge Nix and he settled on what was known as the Nix Place. It was just outside Jewell, Texas, in Eastland County, and had about 160 acres in it. I suppose you'd call the place a stock farm because he farmed on a small scale, but he really worked cattle.

Now, the reason I didn't pay attention to anything in the way of business was because I was pretty spoilt when I was a kid. My mother died right after we got to Jewell, and my two sisters had the raising of me and all the household work too. They'd let me run loose after I got big enough to get away from the leash. You see, while I was too small to be depended on not to run off, they'd make a sort of harness that went around my shoulders and kept me tied to a wooden stake while they were in the dugout working. When we first came to that country, there were no houses and everybody lived in dugouts that were made by digging a square hole about ten feet by ten feet, then about seven feet deep, and running a long pole across the middle, about two feet higher than the ground level, then slanting the tarpaulin down so to let the water run off when it rained.

After we'd been there for about eighteen months, dad got together enough logs to have a house-raising. I was too young to have any fun at this one but you can bet I didn't miss many of them after I got big enough to dance and talk up for myself. Every time they'd have a house-raising after that, I'd be there. You see, the women folks would cook enough stuff to last a good-sized crowd of men for a couple days, then they'd tell everybody that there was to be a house-raising at So-and-so's place at so-and-so a time. Everybody knew they'd have a little dancing and eating thrown in with the work connected with raising the house, or rather, building the house, so they'd be on hand to help. Sometimes there'd be as many as fifty men there with their families and they'd make short work of putting up the house. They figured the quicker they got the house up, the quicker they'd get to dance, drink, and eat. I don't really recall just when I did learn to dance because the cowhands taught me to jig when I was really small. I was dancing with the men when I was going to school.

Dad gave me a little old Indian pony to ride to and from school, and I could really ride him. He was about the best pony I'd seen around those parts and he'd kick up on a frosty morning, but I'd stay with him. He got in the habit of getting loose from the rail when I'd tie him up at the school. No matter how tight I'd tie him, he'd always get loose. One day, he'd gotten loose and had strayed farther away than usual. By the time I'd found him, it was getting dark. I don't guess I was a hundred feet from him when I found him, but there were six old Texas Longhorn steers that found me at the same time. They'd run at me, snort, then run back. Was I worried? I'll say I was, but I kept behind trees and circled until I had the pony between me and the steers.

I'd forgot my rope and it was still tied to the rail so I took my bonnet and put it around his neck, then led him back to the rail. Since I always had to have somebody help me onto the pony and they were all gone, I didn't know how to get on him. I looked around for a stump but I couldn't see any, and it was getting darker all the time. There was an old graveyard by the school and there were tombstones in it that I could stand on to get on him, so I did it that way. You talk about scared. I was one scared kid until I got on his back; then I made him understand that speed was what I wanted. We were going ninety to nothing when I met my dad coming after me.

Now, back to the dances. The majority of them were square dances. After I'd got married and was a little older, I saw other kinds but I stuck to the good old square dancing. I met my husband at one of those dances and we got married when I'd only met him about five times. You see, if you'd go a long ways, you could go to a dance about once a month, but dad only took us about once every quarter so I really knew M. F. over a year before we got married.

Others that I recall meeting were Dink Logan, a good rider with a

A *pioneer woman of the Oklahoma panhandle, 1936. Photograph by* Arthur Rothstein.

pretty horse but I don't know whether I ever heard of his ability as a cowboy. I rated them according to how good they danced, and Dink could dance real good. We met at all the dances. Another that I recall was Dan Clawson. Old Dan couldn't dance but he could trot to beat the band. Then, Jim Thornton, he was a good dancer, and Steve and Temple Ellis. Let me tell you one on Temple.

One time he and his dad were going to the brakes after wood. They were just using the running gears, you know, no wagon bed, and when they got on top of a pretty steep hill, his dad told him to get some ropes and tie the wheels to the gears so they wouldn't roll and that way, the wagon wouldn't run over the team. Temple says, "Alright dad." He stood on the tire and held the wheel to keep it from turning, then when they got halfway down, he stepped off and let the wheels go. Well, the wagon like to have run over the horses and was going like a prairie fire when they got to the bottom of the hill, but Temple's dad handled them like a veteran and didn't have no trouble. Temple had to run real hard to catch up, but when the wagon was slowed down at the bottom, he caught up. His dad said, "What happened, Temple? Did the ropes break?"

Temple said, "No, I just wanted to see if you could ride it as fast as it would go."

Now, that was kind of a rough joke, but that's the way the cowboys joked. They lived a rough life and joked as rough as you ever heard. Why, a tenderfoot that lit on a ranch would almost get killed before he broke in to ranch life. The boys would lead him to one of their wildest horses and tell him it was tame, then let him get on the horse. The usual trick was to have the horse already saddled and ready to go before the poor fellow ever saw it.

He'd come out from the chuck wagon or wherever he was hired, and all he'd see was a horse already saddled and he'd been told they'd give him a gentle one before he tried the rough ones and he'd just mount it without ever a suspicion anything was up. The first time he knew otherwise was after getting the stormiest ride he'd ever had in his young life. The horse usually threw them after the first jump and the boys would be on hand to rescue him from anything else happening to him.

When I married M. F. Cannon, I was about fifteen-and-a-half years old. Cannon was a real man and wasn't afraid of Old Nick himself so he put it up to me like this. He said, "Now, we can live on your dad's place and take what he gives us, or we can strike out and build ourselves a place of our own if you've got the guts to stay with me."

Well, I'd lived a life of ease. That is, my sisters took all the bumps and nothing ever happened around the home place so I thought that in getting married I would have a home of my own, be my own boss, get up when I wanted to (I was a heavy sleeper and was hard to wake up), and just have things the way I wanted, so I jumped at the chance of getting off that way.

To start with, M. F. had been keeping his eye on me and had been saving money right along so he was in a better position to get married than anybody else, including myself because I didn't even know very well how to cook. Dad gave us two teams of horses, and a brand new Studebaker wagon to carry our stuff in.

The last I ever saw of my folks was after they threw a big dance as a farewell party for us; then we lit out. I won't ever be able to forget that trip. When we started out, we had good weather but we hadn't been long on the trail till a Blue Norther struck us. The second night out on the trail, we had to camp right out on the open prairie but we weren't worried because we had good stock and the best wagon money could buy in those days.

We went to bed that night and I went right off to sleep just like I always did when I was at home. I didn't know a thing till I woke up the next morning and M. F. told me what had happened. I'd slept through the worst wind storm that he'd ever seen and one that the old-timers that came out in the fifties [1850s] couldn't even beat. M. F. said that the wind almost blew the wagon over so he got out and dug holes in front of each wheel, then rolled the wagon forward and off into the holes. This way, the wagon would be harder to turn over or move any way. I'd slept all through this and woke up the next morning after the wind had gone down and everything was calm and peaceful.

About the third day on the trip, the wheels went to squeaking something awful. I thought we had been cheated on our pretty wagon with the pretty yellow wheels and red and green trimmings, but I didn't say anything to M. F. about it. I just kept quiet. When we got to a water hole, he watered the stock, then got a bucket and poured water on the wheels. He didn't seem satisfied with that so he dug some more holes and rolled the wagon off into them, then filled the holes with water. While the wagon stood in the water, he hunted for a pole and a block. With this, he used leverage, then had me turn the wheels so another part would be in the water. He did this until he had the entire wheel all wet and muddy. The next morning after we started out, he explained that the wheels had gotten dry and drawn up, and that the water would swell the wheels back out to where they wouldn't squeak anymore.

Well, it seemed like years before we got to that section of Texas known as the staked plains. We settled in Crosby County on a 220-acre tract and M. F. branded his sixty head of cattle with the MFC brand. I worked with the herd just like a man. Of course, I didn't ride a horse but I tended the cows that came fresh.

I never will forget one thing that happened to me while I was hunting one old cow's calf. You see, they'd hide their calves off where they figured you'd never find them, which was dangerous because they never got the right treatment and most of them would die. Well, I'd followed this old cow around for four days but she'd been giving me the slip. I finally let her out of sight, then followed her tracks through the sand. Now, there was still a few dangerous outlaws and rustlers in that country and I'd made a mountain out of a mole hill to where I looked for one to pop out anywhere. This condition stayed in the back of my head all the time but I got my mind set on the old cow's tracks and was going right along when I went through some bushes and bumped right into her. She had her calf and was suckling it at the time but I thought an outlaw had me so I tore out. The cow and calf went in different directions and we all had a good scare. She didn't find her calf till way the next day.

After we'd been on the place several years, we quit going to Crosbyton for rations and went to Amarillo twice a year for our grub. Contrary to the general notion, we didn't buy much stuff in barrels because a wagon would shake it to pieces. Barrels wasn't so good in those days either because they had wood ties instead of iron like they do nowadays. Well, we'd get about a dozen hundred-pound sacks of flour, a hundred-pound sack of coffee, half a barrel of syrup, a barrel of sugar, six sides of bacon, four boxes of dried fruit, and a hundred-pound sack of dried beans. We had plenty of wild meat and grew our beef and farmed enough garden stuff to care for us and some other places too, so you see, we had plenty to eat any time we wanted it.

We'd go to Crosbyton for the dances though. It was about sixteen to twenty miles there and M. F. would pick up all the women on the way that wanted to go. They'd hold a barbecue and dance for two days and nights there besides having the best fiddler I ever heard. His name was Fiddler Bill, and he could just make up tunes that beat anything by these long-haired guys that you pay to hear. Just a natural-born fiddler.

Now, about the cattle roundups and such, I went to several of the fall roundups before M. F. quit and went to carpentering. I met Jim Williams, who owned the SR Ranch and throwed a barbecue and a dance right after the roundup one year. It was held in Hank Smith's rock house in Blanco Canyon and lasted about three days and nights.

I remember when I went there, I saw thousands of cattle in the canyon. A little while after I got to the ranch house, I happened to be looking out the window and saw a wagonload of girls coming up the road. Now, they had to pass over a ditch that had some goat heads in it. You see, Hank had barbecued goats and throwed the heads into this ditch. Well, they failed to see this ditch and when the wagon jolted over it, three of them fell over backwards into the ditch. The first thing they saw when they sat up was these bloody heads sticking straight up out of the ground. Of all the screaming that came off, a hundred catamounts couldn't make that much noise. One of the boys had fixed the heads in that way, hoping to pull off a stunt about like that.

I met another rancher there that run some cattle on about one section of land. His name was Jim Thornton and he run the SD Ranch. I recall another foreigner I met there but I can't recall his name. He run the Z Bar L. You made the brand like this: Z—L. Then there was J. J.

Wallace who owned and operated the Triangle J with about a hundred head. You make his brand like this: △J. I also met several of the Swenson Ranch foremen but I don't recall their names. It was one of the big ranches owned by big easterners who lived in New York. They'd write the range boss to spare no expense to show the boys a good time after the roundup.

Well, I'm about run out of soap. One other thing, though, is the men M. F. usually played with at the dances. One was old Thomp Miller, he played the violin, and Al Patterson, who also played the violin while my husband picked the banjo. M. F. played for the dances and goings on till he died with the flu in Slaton, Texas, in 1918.

> Woody Phipps
> *Forth Worth, Texas*
> *n.d.*

# Mayme Reese

*Mayme Reese grew up near Charleston and moved to New York City as a young woman. She was fifty-seven at the time of the interview.*

We used to have quilting parties at least twice a year. Say there'd be three or four ladies who were good friends; one time we would meet at one house and one time at another. You'd keep on that way until the quilt was finished. If I was making the quilt, I'd set up the quilting frame in my house and the other two or three ladies would come and spend the day quilting. I'd have it all ready for the quilting to start. You'd decide before how you were going to make the stitches: if you were going to have a curving stitch, you'd sew one way; if you were going to quilt block fashion, you'd sew that way. I might have been sewing scraps together for a year until I got the cover all made. Then when my friends came, there wouldn't be anything to do but start working on the padding. If there were four ladies, each would take an end.

The ladies would come as early in the morning as they could. Sometimes you all had breakfast together. If you didn't you had dinner together and a little snack off and on during the day. If it was at my house

*Quilting, Hinesville, Georgia, 1941. Photograph by Jack Delano.*

and nobody was coming early enough for breakfast, I'd put something on the sideboard that everybody could reach if they got hungry before time to sit at the table. Sometimes there'd be sweet potatoes, some smoked pork, bread, maybe some syrup, and things like that. Then when you had dinner, there'd be the regular things everybody had at home. If somebody came way in from the country or a town eight or nine miles away, they'd have supper and stay all night.

Depending upon how many quilts you needed a year or just wanted to make, there'd be that many quilting parties for ladies who were intimates. If none of my friends were going to make quilts in a year, then they'd keep coming to my house maybe twice a week until we got it finished. If you worked right along and didn't stop to talk—course most of the time we stopped to gossip a little—you could finish a quilt in a day or two. That depended on the pattern, too. If somebody else was making a quilt, we'd go to their house and exchange labor till they got their quilt done.

Whenever we had a quilting party, the men folks had to look out for themselves. They ate cold food if they came in hungry in the day and if we finished working soon enough, they'd get their supper on time. If we didn't, they just had to wait. They didn't mind. If they fussed, we'd remind em about keeping warm in the winter.

Sometimes we'd take our quilts out to the country fairgrounds for exhibition in the fall. Each lady picked out her best quilt—the prettiest color, the prettiest pattern, and the best stitches—and took it to the fair to try to win the prize. It didn't make any difference if your prettiest quilt had been quilted by three or four other people; you already had the pattern and you'd already put the pieces together, so that much was your own idea. And that counted more than the help you got when you were putting it on the frame. Sometimes a church club would make a quilt and enter it in the name of the church. Even if they put it in the club's name, the club would give the money to the church if they won. Once I won the prize for my own quilt and once I was one of a group that won. The prize was most often five dollars, sometimes ten. One year they couldn't get the money together and they gave the winner some prize preserves, some pieces of fancy-work, and something else that had won first prize in other contests instead of the money. Course you'd rather have the money because everybody could can fruit and do tatting and crocheting and things like that and they could make their own things. But you couldn't act nasty about it. Anyhow, it didn't happen but once as I remember it.

Sometimes rich white women would hear that such and such a person had won the prize for pretty quilts and they'd come and ask that person to make them a quilt. Sometimes they'd make it and sometimes they wouldn't. If they did make it, they'd get around five dollars. Sometimes they'd furnish the scraps; most of the time, though, they'd buy pieces of goods and give it to the person who was making the quilt to cut up. They'd get different colors and say what pattern they wanted.

Some of the churches would have quilting parties. Not every church did that, but those that did had quite a few woman members come to quilt. They'd get some little boys to take the quilting frame to the church in the morning and then they'd go in the afternoon. I guess they'd quilt for two, three hours. Most of the time they'd be making the quilt to sell to raise money for the church.

Things like that were nice. Sometimes I wish I could go back to that kind of life for a while, but times have changed so. They won't ever be like that again. But I guess it's just as well. Nowadays, there are other things to occupy people's minds.

Dorothy West
*New York City*
1938

# Emma Ayer

*Emma Ayer lived in Camden and Charleston, South Carolina, until she moved to New York City at the age of forty. She was forty-seven at the time of the interview.*

Once or twice a year, around where I lived, most women with families would pack up for three or four days and go blackberry picking. My mother had some distant relatives in a little place called Ninety-Six [a town in South Carolina], not very far on the train from Camden. I remember the first time she took me to Ninety-Six when she went to pick berries.

She started getting ready about a week before we left. She boiled her Mason jars and boiled the rubber collars and she boiled the caps to fit on the jars. Then she packed about fifteen jars and collars and caps in a big basket and in suitcases so she could carry them without much trouble. Clothes didn't matter much. You had two or three gingham dresses and a pair of shoes and two pairs of socks and that was about all.

My mother took just me the first time I went. I was about seven then. I was the youngest and she thought she had to take me; she didn't want to take my brother and sister because she didn't know how much room the lady had where we were going to stay.

We got on the train and I guess we rode two, three hours—trains went slower then than they do now. Ninety-Six is a little flag station, just a little shed, really. When we got there, the woman's husband met us with a horse and buggy. There were two other women with their children at the house. I believe there were twelve or thirteen children in that house at one time. Miss Mary herself had seven children, I made eight, and one woman had two children, and the other one had two or three. It was always like that. More than one woman came to stay at a house during picking time. One time you went to this place, the next time you went somewhere else. And your relatives and maybe one or two of your best friends came to pick berries together.

We didn't do anything but play that first day. The grown folks got their jars together in the kitchen, and collected big pots and pans to put the berries in when they picked em. I guess they talked the rest of that day since they didn't see each other more than once or twice a year. When we got ready to go to bed, the girls were put together in the parlor on pallets to sleep, and the boys were put in the dining room. I know there were five of us girls sleeping on a pallet on the floor once. I don't know where the grown folks slept. I don't remember whether they slept on pallets; I guess not, since the children gave up their beds. I do know that sometimes as many as four women slept together in one room.

We got up early in the morning and had breakfast as soon as it was light. We had salt pork and hominy grits and hot biscuits and maybe one or two other things. Then the boys helped the women take the pans out and pile em on the wagon. One of the boys drove the mules, and two women sat on the seat of the wagon, and the other two sat in the back with as many of the children as could go. Sometimes the other children would want to go, and they'd hang on to the side of the wagon or behind it. If you didn't have room to go, you'd just walk along behind the wagon.

You'd take food along to eat in the middle of the day. Everybody would pick, the women and the children. You didn't put the berries in any special basket. You figured out how much everybody would get after you got back to the house. Everybody always got the same share. When you filled one big pan, you'd start filling another one, and you kept on till you'd picked as many as you could. Course the children ate more than they picked, and sometimes they'd run off and play.

The grown folks always carried utensils to hold enough berries to keep em picking till sundown. When they got through picking, they'd holler for the children if they had strayed off playing. More had to walk or hang on going back, because the pans would almost fill the wagon.

That night we wouldn't do much. Everybody was tired, and we'd have a big, hot supper, and then go to bed. Sometimes the children would make a lot of noise since so many of them were together, and the grown folks would have to come in and stop the fuss; but most of the time the whole house was quiet by nine o'clock and everybody was asleep.

The next morning the canning would start. They would put the wash pots out in the yard and start a fire. Most women had at least two washpots and some had three and four. They were heavy, old black iron pots about two feet deep, and they stood on three squatty legs about six inches tall—tall enough to make a hot fire under. They'd fill these wash pots with water and put the Mason jars in again to boil. Sometimes they'd let the big children take the jars out on long sticks. When they got through sterilizing the jars, they'd pour the water out and put some more in, and then put in the berries. They used the pots for different things. I think they made jam in them and started the wine in them, but I think they made the jelly in the kitchen. They worked almost all day. Then when they were ready to divide it up, one woman would fill a jar, then another one, and so on, till everybody had one jar full. Then they'd start again and keep on till everybody had two jars full. You kept that up till everybody had as much as everybody else. Course if there was a little left over, you'd eat as much of it as you could that night for supper and the rest you left to the woman whose house you were in. You didn't give her anything for letting you stay there except three or four quarts of jelly or jam or whatever you made.

Nobody ever went home the night they finished canning. They'd sit around and talk, and maybe decide where they'd go to can next time. You only went out like that to pick and can berries, or maybe watermelons if you were going to make watermelon-rind preserves. You canned peaches and apples and plums and things like that at home by yourself because you just bought whatever you wanted to put up.

Dorothy West
*New York City*
*1938*

# Nettie Spencer

*As a girl, Nettie Spencer decided against marriage in favor of travel and independence. Looking back in her seventies, she told Federal Writer Walker Winslow that she believed she had made the right choice. Spencer was a nonconformist from*

an Oregon pioneer family. As Winslow described her, "She
does not go in for fine clothes and when I interviewed her, she
had her feet in the oven and made no pretense at any of the
so-called social niceties."

I was one of a large family, so I was pretty busy just keeping out of the
way and going to school. All of our shoes were made by a man who
came around every so often and took our foot measurements with broom-
straws, which he broke off and tagged for the foot length of each member of the family. The width didn't make any difference and you could
wear either shoe on either foot—for a long time, too, for the shoes wore
well. Mother carded her own wool and washed it with soap she made
herself. She even made her own lye from wood ashes, and when she got
the cloth finished she made her own dye. Black was made from burnt
logs and brown from the hulls of black walnuts. I think she got her green
from copper, and peach leaves made the yellow. The red dye was made
from leaves she bought. The dresses were very full and lasted entirely
too long. Our styles weren't as bad as the men's though, for they took
a blanket, cut a hole in the middle of it, stuck their necks through, and
had an overcoat. They looked like Indians.

Most of the women folks wore calico and linsey-woolsey [a combination of linen and wool], and the men often wore jeans. Little girls wore
sunbonnets and shakers. Old ladies wore lace caps under their sunbonnets. Some of the better class were very prettily frilled with lace and
lavender ribbons, but not in this country community. One of the things
I remember most as a little girl were the bundle peddlers who came
around. They had bundles made up and you bought them as they were
for a set price. I remember that some sold for as high as $150. In these
bundles were all sorts of wonderful things that you didn't get in the
country very often: fancy shawls, printed goods, silks, and such other
luxuries. It was a great day when the family bought a bundle.

Our food was pretty plain most of the time and we didn't have any
salads like they do now. The menu for a fine dinner would be: chicken
stew with dumplings, mashed potatoes, peach preserves, biscuits, and
hominy. We raised carrots for the stock but we never thought of eating
them. Grandfather was eating peaches in St. Joe, Missouri, before he
came West and forgot and put a peach pit in his pocket and left it there
all through the trip. It was a variety that was later named after him and
became famous. We had cobbler often. Dumplings were another staple
and made to go with everything that had enough juice to boil them in.
We didn't have any jars to put up preserves in, like they do now, but we

used earthen crocks instead. The fruit was boiled with brown sugar—
we never saw white sugar and when we did we used it as candy—and
then put in the jars which were covered with cloth that was then coated
with beeswax. Another good cover was a hog bladder—they were the best.
Sometimes we had molasses pulls, and once in a great while we would
have some real striped candy. That was a treat!

Most of our medicine was homemade, too, and I think I can remember some of the old standbys. There was an awful lot of ague—
chills and fever—and it came, they said, from turning up new soil. Almost every pioneer community has had it. For that we used patent medicine mostly, but the standard was goose grease and turpentine. It was
supposed to cure everything. It was all you could smell in a schoolroom.
Of course, the old-fashioned mustard plaster was a standard remedy, and
then there were the teas. We had a tea for everything and most of the
herbs could be picked on the place.

There wasn't much social life on the farm, and I didn't pay any attention to it until I was older and moved into Salem and Corvallis. The
churches didn't have any young people's organizations and they were
dead serious with everything. Sermons lasted for hours and you could
smell the hellfire in them. We never had church suppers or the like
until way past my time. The only social thing about the church was the
camp meetings. That was where most of the courting was done. When
a boy would get old enough for a wife, the father would let him use the
horse and buggy for a trip to the camp meeting to get him a wife.

Most of these people came to church on foot over the muddy roads.
The ones who came by wagon used a hay-rack, and the mother and
father sat in a chair at the front while the children were churned about
in the straw strewn in the wagon bed. After a long meeting was out,
neighbors had a grand hand-shaking party, and then families often invited other families to dinner.

The big event of the year was the Fourth of July. Everyone in the
countryside got together on that day for the only time in the year. The
new babies were shown off, and the new brides who would be exhibiting
babies next year. Everyone would load their wagons with all the food
they could haul and come to town early in the morning. On our first big
Fourth at Corvallis, mother made two hundred gooseberry pies. There
would be floats in the morning and the one that got the girl's eye was
the Goddess of Liberty. She was supposed to be the most wholesome and
prettiest girl in the countryside—if she wasn't, she had friends who
thought she was. She rode on a hay-rack and wore a white gown. Sometimes the driver wore an Uncle Sam hat and striped pants. All along
the side of the hay-rack were little girls who represented the states of the

union. The smallest was always Rhode Island. Following the float would be the Oregon Agricultural College cadets, and some kind of a band. Just before lunch some senator or lawyer would speak. These speeches always had one pattern. First, the speaker would challenge England to a fight and berate the King and say that he was a skunk. This was known as twisting the lion's tail. Then the next theme was that anyone could find freedom and liberty on our shores. The speaker would invite those who were heavy laden in other lands to come to us and find peace. The speeches were pretty firey and by that time the men who drank got into fights and called each other Englishmen. In the afternoon we had what we called the "plug uglies"—funny floats and clowns who took off on the political subjects of the day. There would be some music and then the families would start gathering together to go home. There were cows waiting to be milked and the stock to be fed and so there was no night life.

Young women in Oregon didn't play much of a role in community life unless they were being courted. Our favorite magazines were *Godey's*, *Peterson's* and the *Bazaar*. Years later I saw the covers of the old *Godey's* magazine selling in Paris for a great price, and they tell me that people in high-class homes now use them as prints on the walls. All they meant in those days was that Oregon stores were two years behind with the styles. We used to get chromos [prints] with subscriptions to papers: some of them were pretty but I have seen farm houses where they covered one whole side of the room with them solid. Recently I saw a picture in the paper of a well-known pioneer woman holding up a little statue of Dickens her grandfather was supposed to have brought across the plains. If he did, he must have sent west for it, for I bought one off a peddler when I was a girl. That was our art then.

After I had gone to the Agricultural College for two years I went out and taught at a summer school in the country, for three months for thirty dollars. It was enough to pay my tuition the rest of the way through. I boarded with the parents of the children and it was pretty rough board sometimes. After I graduated I taught in Portland and roomed at the home of Judge C. B. Bellinger. I got fifty dollars a month to start, and then was raised to sixty. I think I was getting seventy-five when the depression of '93 hit, and they cut us twenty-five percent twice. It was a bad depression, but everyone had their own gardens and didn't go hungry. I left Oregon soon after this and went to Europe, where I taught school for several years.

Walker Winslow
*Portland, Oregon*
1938

# Lizzie Miles

*Superior, Montana, was still goldmining territory when Lizzie Miles and her husband moved there in 1891. Supplies were packed in from Virginia City and flour sold for as much as a dollar a pound at the store run by Miles's brother-in-law, A. P. Johnston.*

I came to Superior from Kansas in 1891. My husband, Adrian Miles, had gone on ahead a month earlier. Superior was situated at the mouth of Johnston Creek, across the river and a little west of what is now the Leib ranch. There were just three or four homes but seven saloons. A. P. Johnston's store was in the old Shamrock building, where the Corner Service Station now stands. Johnston ran a combination of store, saloon, and dance hall. It catered to the miners going through on the road, which then ran just north of the Johnston ranch, following the river bank. A saloon wasn't allowed at the Tunnel for a long time, but they finally got one. After celebrating there on pay days, the miners would get together a sleighload and go ripping and tearing about the country, having a high old time.

The first day we came here, Old Man Lozeau got Miles and me to work for him at his ranch. He was a Frenchman, but his wife was a quarter-breed Indian. She was fat and jolly, and I liked to hear her talk. She used to smoke a corncob pipe, the kind they made themselves. I'd often hear her call, "Lozeau, come build fire, Lozeau; that all you good for." They had a whole brood of young ones: Louis, Joe, 'Dolphe, Puss, Phonzine, and Mary. 'Dolphe used to fiddle for the dances. He'd get liquored up and play with his eyes shut, all night the same tune. Most of the miners at the dance drank up pretty freely, and before the night was over, they'd all be singing and having a gay time. "There'll Be a Hot Time in the Old Town To-Night," was the most popular tune, and usually it was a hot time.

The stub of the Northern Pacific was just completed in 1891. There were no passenger cars, just a common boxcar, with homemade seats of the sort they used in the old schoolhouse. It was rough, like riding on a lumber wagon. I came through on the road from Kansas, about the next week after the stub was laid. The Missoula agent didn't want to sell me a ticket at first; he didn't know if the road was put through here yet. When he found out Iron Mountain was where I was headed for, he said he was sure the track had been laid that far.

I was the first woman to walk across the first bridge across the Missoula River at Superior, the one the Iron Mountain Tunnel and Missoula County built. There was just the thickness of two boards to walk on, with a space between the planks. I was afraid to look down, for it seemed that any minute I must go through, into the river. Jimmy Harmon went ahead of me, packing my girl Laura, who was a baby then.

The Harmons were some of the early settlers of Superior. There were five brothers: Charley, Jimmy, Ernest, Bill, and Pete. I remember when they charivaried Charley Harmon, after he married Veronica Krupp. Everyone turned out for a charivari, with bells, whistles, and even saws. On this particular night, they had a big circle-saw, hauled in on their left shoulders. Billy Bonnett was one of those who carried it. He pounded it with a pipe with a knot on one end of it, and made so much racket we couldn't hear ourselves think.

Charley Harmon was too close even in those days to dig up a treat, but Jimmy Harmon had some apples and I had a cake. Mrs. Harmon had just come out here, was very religious, and not used to such carryings-on. She was nearly fainting. Bonnett was the sort to carry off things with a high hand. He went up to her and said, "Usually we get to kiss the bride." Mrs. Harmon turned white and red by turns. Charley spoke up timidly: "No, I don't think you'd better kiss my bride." Bonnett didn't, but he was the kind who would, if he had felt like it. Mrs. Harmon afterwards said, "Well, some may like this sort of thing, but not me."

I remember a Christmas tree we had once at the Thomas Hotel. Johnston had fixed up as Santa Claus, rigged out with a cotton beard. He came in by a ladder, on the third floor. In those days we didn't have electric lights, only coal-oil lamps and the colored candles on the tree. Johnston got too close to the candles, and his whiskers caught fire. Grandma Riefflin grabbed her plaid shawl, one she had brought from Berlin, Germany, and smothered the blaze with it. By that time, there was a regular stampede, everybody hitting for the stairs. A bunch of big men held them back, or some would have been trampled to death.

Soon after we came here Bill Beach wanted to hire Miles to work in the mine, and me to do the cooking, but he'd only pay next to nothing, so I wouldn't hear it. He was a big-bodied man with short legs. He wore his straight, black hair short around the neck and long everyplace else, with big whiskers tucked into his bib overall. I told him: "I'd like to take you by the whiskers and lead you around the country." He laughed, and answered, "You're the first woman I ever heard complain about a man's whiskers."

They had no scissors nor razors in the hills, and the men would come to town looking like a bunch of billy goats. Murray, "The Roller," was more like a shaggy dog than a man, what with his whiskers and long hair hanging down his shoulders. We called him The Roller because he'd watch for the miners to come from the hills and then roll them. He asked if he could camp on our place; he didn't do us any harm, so we let him. He rolled two big logs under a big tree, and slept between them. He was followed around by a ring-necked dog he called Bob. When he couldn't bum a quarter off anybody, he'd live on lambsquarter greens, eating them like spare grass.

He never bothered us at the ranch, and used to buy a quart of milk whenever he could steal a dime to pay for it. Mrs. John Connally, who ran the Northern Pacific Lunchroom, kept cows; Murray used to sneak up to them and milk into an old pail he kept. When he'd drunk his fill of the warm, unstrained milk, he'd call Bob to finish the pail. He carried a cane, with a spike at the tip, that he made pretty useful. Folks used to say, "There goes old Murray, sniping cigar stubs." They finally got tired of him and ran him out of town.

Mabel C. Olsen
*Superior, Montana*
*n.d.*

# Mary Patton Taylor

*The daughter of pioneers who followed the Oregon Trail, Mary Patton Taylor settled with her husband in Fossil, Oregon.*

Father and mother's married life began with a romance crossing the plains. Right away mother and father cottoned to one another, but grandfather had other plans. There was another young fellow in their train—they come with a big wagon train of sixty wagons in '48—that grandfather liked better'n Tom Patton, and that was a young man named Trullinger. When Tom Patton asked for mother, he was told to git out. He got all right, but mother was just as stiff as grandfather. She said, "If I marry anybody, it's Tom Patton," and when she said that, with her backbone up, I guess grandfather decided he might as well give in. Anyway, they were married.

*Williams County, North Dakota, 1937. Photograph by Russell Lee.*

Mother always said they had an awful good time crossing the plains.
When they come in '48 there wasn't any Indian trouble or anything,
and at night they used to have a lot of fun. All they danced then was
square dances, and after the camp was settled down for the night the
young folks would turn to and dance. Grandfather was religious and
awful strict. He didn't believe in dancing, so mother'd go to bed as
demure as you please, and as soon as she was sure grandfather was asleep,
she'd slip out and dance as big as any of them.

When my folks got to Oregon they settled in the Waldo Hills. They
settled on their claim just three days after they arrived. My grandparents
got here in September, and in November father and mother was married.
The only thing mother had to start housekeeping with was a plate. She
paid fifty cents for it, and she earned the fifty cents sewing three days
for a woman in the Waldo Hills. Father wasn't much better off than

mother. He wasn't twenty-one years old, and so he couldn't take a claim. And he didn't have any money, because all he made crossing the plains was his food and bed and fifteen dollars that he got for driving grandfather's oxen. But he wanted to get married, and, when he got there, he went to work for a man named Nicholas Shrum right away. He split rails for Shrum, and all he got was 37½¢ a hundred. Can you beat that? Just as soon as father had $2.25 he thought, Maybe that's enough to pay the preacher. When father and mother was married, father paid over the $2.25. He must have looked kind of poor about it, for right away Elder Simpson asked him how much money he had left, and father said that was all, and then Elder Simpson handed it back to him, telling him he needed it most. But father was gritty. He said, "If my girl's worth marrying, I'm willing to spend all I have to get her." And he made Elder Simpson keep the $2.25.

My father's parents had filed on a donation claim of 640 acres, and father hoped to get the one adjoining; but before he was old enough, a man named Center got it. That didn't discourage father any. He went to Mr. Center and asked him to take the claim a mile further on, so he could have the one next to his pa and ma. Center must have been pretty good-natured, for he moved along to the next claim. Father gave him a plug of tobacco, and everything was all right.

Everybody had big families in those days. There was nine in our family. We had good times, what with picnics and everything. I remember one Fourth of July there was six couples of us went in a wagon with four horses up to Silver Creek Falls to celebrate. There wasn't any roads then to speak of. We just rode across pastures and fields, and we come to a hill above the falls, and from there we had to climb down afoot. We had a picnic lunch and stayed all day. On our way home that night we stopped at a house and danced. There must have been twenty couples and we danced all night to the music of a first and second fiddle. Sometimes they made violins, or fiddles we called them then, out of corn stalks.

That picnic reminds me of another time I went to a celebration at Silverton with a beau. I couldn't get away from that simpleton all day long. I jest suffered tortures with him hangin around me every minute. I guess he was jealous and afraid I'd leave him in the lurch. Some things today are a lot better'n they were then. Folks ain't so prudish.

I remember, I guess it was the first wedding I ever saw, a young couple had just been married and they came to our house to stay all night. I guess our folks knew they was going to be charivaried, cause the men folks took the groom out to hunt coons and while they was gone the charivari party came. A lot of them had false faces on, and they shot off guns and beat tin pans and did everything they could to make noise. We only had one window and they would take turns peeking in. It was awful. I was just a little bit of a girl and I was scared to death. Father and the men heard the racket, so they hurried back. Then they invited them in, and father gave them a talking to.

I started knitting when I was six years old. Mother didn't want me to learn to knit, but I was set on it. Grandmother said if I would get her a couple of chicken feathers she'd teach me, and she did. Lands! I can remember how I used to sit there and kick the old cradle and knit. I think that's what ruined my form. There was always a baby in that old cradle.

Sara B. Wrenn
*Portland, Oregon*
1939

# Annie Lesnett

*As a young bride, Annie Lesnett followed her husband to the New Mexico Territory just before the Lincoln County War broke out. Beginning in 1876, rival cattlemen and political factions clashed in one of the bloodiest gunfighting conflicts in the Old West. The leader of one faction was the legendary outlaw, Billy the Kid, also known as William H. Bonney. Lesnett described the Kid's escape from the climactic "Battle of July 19" to Federal Writer Edith Crawford.*

I met my husband, Frank Lesnett, in Chicago, Illinois, when I was sixteen years old. He joined the regular army at Fort Stanton, New Mexico, to serve his enlistment fighting the Indians. He was discharged in 1875 at Fort Stanton. Early in the spring of 1876, Frank Lesnett and I were united in marriage. After a joyous honeymoon, my husband left me in Chicago, came west and settled on the Ruidoso, located at the foot of the White Mountains. He bought half interest in the Dowlin

Mill, and sent for me. I came by train to LaJunta, Colorado, and from there to Fort Stanton, New Mexico, on Numa Raymond's stagecoach, drawn by four horses.

My husband met me at Fort Stanton. He was driving two big bay horses to a Studebaker hack. We drove up the beautiful canyon toward the White Mountains by way of the Pat Garrett Ranch, which was located on Little Creek. When I arrived at our ranch I was happily surprised: it had a river called the Ruidoso running near the big two-story adobe house. There were tall pine trees and wild flowers of so many varieties and colors that I would not even attempt to name them. The ranch was beautiful! I was very happy in my new home, and to add to our happiness a son was born to us during the first year. The only thing to mar my happiness was that the Indians would go on the warpath, and the Lincoln County War was brewing. When Jennie Mae, my second child, was about nine months old, "The Kid" came to our house with a boy by the name of Jesse Evans,* and was introduced as Billie Bonney. Could this be the notorious Billy the Kid? I thought, surely not. He looked just like any other seventeen-year-old boy, and not in the least like a desperado. He was very fond of children, and liked Irvin and Jennie Mae at once. He called my little boy "Pardie" and always wanted to hold the baby. He would take the two of them for a ride on his gray pony.

The Lincoln County War, which was one of the bloodiest in the history of the West, had two sides, one for the Law and the other for Lawlessness. Almost every cattleman in the county was somehow involved. Strange as it may seem, the Kid, an outlaw, joined the forces for law and order.

The lawless side had driven the Kid and his band into the McSween home in Lincoln. As he talked to McSween, who was very religious and always carried a Bible with him, he held out a gun toward him. McSween pushed it away, saying, "I trust in the Lord, I know He will help me—bring me safely through." "All right, you trust in your Bible, but I trust in my six-gun," the Kid replied.

The McSween home was soon surrounded by the Murphy gang, and firing became very heavy. Murphy's men knew that they would never get the Kid and his band unless they could drive them out of the house. So they soaked a barrel with coal oil and rolled it down the hill to set the house afire. The house began to burn, but the battle did not stop. The Kid kept moving his men from room to room until they reached the last room. He knew that they would have to take a chance

---

* Outlaw Jesse Evans and Billy the Kid ended up on opposite sides of the Lincoln County War.

for their freedom. The only escape was to run across a thirty-foot space behind the house, roll under the fence, and go along the Bonito River.

He called his men to the back door and explained the plan to them. One by one they started for the fence, and one by one they fell, either dead or mortally wounded. At last McSween was to go.

"Run out of that door like a streak of greased lightning, roll under the fence, and hit for the Bonita River, then you'll see Mrs. McSween in the morning."

As McSween reached the door, he drew himself up every inch of his height and stepped quietly onto the steps.

"Here I am—I'm McSween," he called.

Fifty shots answered him—and his body was shot full of holes. Then there was a lull. They *knew* who was coming next. The Kid ran through the blazing door with a gun in each hand. He jumped from side to side as he ran and made a very elusive target. Not one bullet touched his body, though his clothes were ripped to shreds. His score was one dead and two marked for life—one shot through the jaws and the other lost the lobe of his left ear.

It is impossible to describe the horror of the deeds that were committed during the Lincoln County War. When one party met the other while riding through the hills they just opened fire, either pushing forward or retreating. If all the men were accounted for, their graves might reach from Roswell to White Oaks.

One evening when it was peaceful and quiet on the ranch, the silence was broken by a series of shots. I snatched Jennie Mae and Irvin from their beds and ran toward the river. As I ran past the great triangle used to call the cowboys to meals, I paused to give it several strikes; but this was not necessary, for the men—thinking that Indians had attacked —were already on their stomachs working their way toward the house. When the men got into the house and looked around, they found that a box of cartridges that had been on top of the mantel had been knocked by something into the fire. When I told the Kid about this, he asked me if I had a gun.

"Heavens, no," I replied, "I wouldn't know how to shoot even if I had one."

"Take this one," he said, holding one of his guns out to me, "and I'll teach you to shoot when I come back."

Poor boy never came back to our house. The next time I saw him he was a prisoner, guarded by Bell and Olinger. Olinger, knowing that I liked the Kid, invited me to the hanging. I turned my head and blinked fast to keep back the tears. Suddenly the Kid turned to me and said, "Mrs. Lesnett, they can't hang me if I'm not there, can they?"

It was just a few days after this that the Kid killed his two guards at Lincoln, and made his escape.

About two months later [on July 14, 1881], Pat Garrett killed him at Fort Sumner.

Edith L. Crawford
*Carrizozo, New Mexico*
*1938*

# IMMIGRANT
# LIVES

# Louis Kurland*

*Louis Kurland's immigrant journey—from Poland to Cuba to Key West—was not unusual: between the turn of the century and World War I, more than 3 million men and women left Poland, often because of religious persecution. Aliens without legal passports were often smuggled into the United States by way of Cuba as Kurland describes. (For another account of the smuggling of aliens from Cuba to Key West see page 45.)*

I sell fish. I begin to sell fish the day I come to Chicago. And I still sell fish. I had plenty of excitement before I come to Chicago.

I was born in a small town in Poland. I got married when I was nineteen, and when I was twenty-one—two years after the World War—I found out that I would be called to be a soldier. My wife did not want me to be a soldier in the Polish Army; she said better I should try to go to America. I could not get a passport because I was running away from military service. I knew a fellow who used to take people across the border, so I fixed it up with him that he should take me. This fellow had other men who wanted to go to America. It was two o'clock in the morning, it was January, and it was cold. We all met and we walked about a mile through a forest and we were in Germany. I paid the fellow fifteen marks [worth about $3.50 in 1921]. The three of us waited till morning and hired a wagon and drove to Berlin. In Berlin, we took a train for Amsterdam. Then we took a boat for Cuba.

In Cuba, the excitement started. I found a boardinghouse where I shared a room with two fellows. I wanted to get to Chicago where I had three brothers and many uncles and aunts. The only way I could go to Chicago was to be smuggled into America. After six weeks, I met a fellow who said he would take me to America for $150. I had enough money to pay this, so I told him all right.

One very hot night in March, this fellow came to the boarding-house and told me to get ready. He said I could not take anything, that

* Fictitious name.

it would take all night and all next day, and that I would have nothing to eat and nothing to drink. Not even a drink of water. Well, I did not want to stay in Cuba, so I went with him. He told me to walk a few steps behind him, and not to talk. He said he must get some more fellows who wanted to go to America. If I saw him go into a house, I should follow. I do as he say. He stopped in twelve houses, and soon thirteen fellows were following. It was a very dark night, but the fellow who had the boat must have had cat's eyes. He took our hands, one at a time, and put us in a small boat. Maybe there was a place for four men, and he put thirteen in and he was fourteen.

We lay in the boat like herring in a barrel. It was very hot and the heat from our bodies made it hotter. We were not allowed to take off our clothes. There was no room to move even an inch. We were not allowed to talk. The only sound was the noise from the engine of the small boat. We traveled like this all night and all the next day. The sun made it hotter. The fellow who was taking us went the longest way, so we did not meet any boats. That day was the worst I ever spent in my life. I am ready to go to hell, if I have to; it cannot be any worse than that day in the boat. About nine o'clock in the evening we got to Key West. The man pulled us out of the boat. We were more dead than alive. He laid us on the shore and washed our faces with the cool water. Then he gave us a little water to drink. He took us to a dirty boarding-house near the ocean where we got something to eat. But I could not eat. I only drank water. We slept on the floor, but the floor was heaven because we could move our arms and legs.

The next day we took a train for Jacksonville, Florida. We waited there six hours and then we took the train for Chicago. I'm telling you, when I saw my brother and uncle when I got off the train in Chicago, I cried like a baby.

Maybe you think my troubles was over? No, my troubles was just beginning. I found out that I could not become a citizen, and so I could not bring my wife and the children to Chicago. Well, the first thing was to make a living. One of my brothers had a fish market, so he gave me a basket of fish and told me where to go to sell them. The first day, I made two dollars. When I could speak a little English, I peddled fish in the high-toned places; I could charge a little more and I made a pretty good living.

My wife was writing me letters about how terrible it was in Poland. I sent her money every month. But it was terrible to have to keep quiet about being in Chicago. I could not get citizenship papers because I was smuggled in. And without citizenship papers I could not bring my family to Chicago. Then my wife wrote me a letter that one of our children died. I had plenty of troubles. I couldn't go back to Poland and I could not bring my family to Chicago.

Then a law was passed that all people who came to America in 1921 and before could get their citizenship papers.* I can tell you I got my papers as soon as I could. Then I brought my wife and my daughter to Chicago. And you can see, I still sell fish.

> Hilda Polacheck
> *Chicago*
> 1939

# Morris Horowitz†

*Russian-Jewish immigrants such as Morris Horowitz often started out peddling wares door-to-door. When Horowitz arrived, before the large Russian emigration of the 1880s, peddling wasn't a bad way to make a living. According to Oyser Blaustein, a popular late-nineteenth-century Yiddish writer, "When a peddler went out to the country with his goods people greeted him with pleasure" (quoted by Irving Howe in* World of our Fathers, *p. 78).*

How did I happen to become a peddler? When I came to Chicago in 1870, there was nothing else to do. I was eighteen years old. I had learned no trade in Russia. The easiest thing to do was to peddle. People coming to America today have a much harder time. There are better houses to live in and nearly everybody has a bathtub, but there are no jobs. In the old days, if you had a few dollars, you could buy some dry goods and peddle. But today you must know a trade or have a profession; otherwise you have no chance.

I went to live with an aunt and uncle when I first came to Chicago. They lived in a small four-room house on Fourth Avenue. They had four children but they managed to rent one room to two roomers. I shared the bed with these two men. The day after I got to Chicago my uncle asked me if I had any money. I told him I had ten dollars. He told

---

* This law was passed in 1929, and within a year 18,800 aliens had filed for citizenship.
† Fictitious name.

me to invest it in dry goods and start peddling. I peddled in Chicago till after the fire of 1871. There were not many stores, so I had no trouble selling my goods. I used to make from six to ten dollars a week. I paid my aunt three dollars a week for food and lodging and I saved the rest. I had the responsibility of bringing my father, two sisters, and two brothers to America.

It was the great fire of 1871 that made me a country peddler. I remember t 'e fire very well. It was in October. We used to go to bed early, becaus ' the two roomers had to go to work very early. We were getting ready o go to bed, when we heard the fire bells ringing. I asked the two men if they wanted to see where the fire was.

"Why should I care as long as our house is not on fire," one of the men said. "There is a fire every Monday and Thursday in Chicago." But I wanted to see the fire, so I went out into the street. I saw the flames across the river, but I thought that since the river was between the fire and our house, there was nothing to worry about. I went back to bed. The next thing I knew my two bedfellows were shaking me. "Get up," they cried. "The whole city is on fire! Save your things! We are going to Lincoln Park."

I jumped out of bed and pulled on my pants. Everybody in the house was trying to save as much as possible. I tied my clothes in a sheet. With my clothes under my arm and my pack on my back, I left the house with the rest of the family. Everybody was running north. People were carrying all kinds of crazy things. A woman was carrying a pot of soup, which was spilling all over her dress. People were carrying cats, dogs, and goats. In the great excitement people saved worthless things and left behind good things. I saw a woman carrying a big frame in which was framed her wedding veil and wreath. She said it would have been bad luck to leave it behind.

When we came to Lake Street I saw all the wagons of Marshall Field and Company [the firm was then called Field, Leiter and Company] lined up in front. Men were carrying the goods out of the building and loading everything into the wagons. The merchandise was taken to the streetcar barns on State near Twentieth Street; a couple of weeks later, Marshall Field started doing business there.

No one slept that night. People gathered on the streets and all kinds of reasons were given for the fire. I stood near a minister talking to a group of men. He said the fire was sent by God as a warning that the people were wicked. He said there were too many saloons in Chicago, too many houses of prostitution. A woman who heard this said that a fire started in a barn was a direct warning from God since Jesus was also born in a barn. I talked to a man who lived next door to

Mrs. O'Leary, and he told me that the fire started in Mrs. O'Leary's barn. She went out to milk the cow when it was beginning to get dark. The cow kicked the lamp over and that's how the fire started. There were all kinds of songs made up about the fire. Years after, people were still singing songs about it. You remember the song "Hot Time in the Old Town?" Well there was a song made up to that tune. These are the words:

> One moonlit night while the families were in bed,
> Mrs. O'Leary took a lantern to the shed,
> The cow kicked it over, winked her eye and said:
> There'll be a hot time in the old town tonight, my baby.

Since many homes were burned, many people left the city. Some went to live with relatives in other cities. A great many men became country peddlers. There were thousands of men walking from farm to farm with heavy packs on their backs. These peddlers carried all kinds of merchandise, things they thought farmers and their families could use.

There was no rural mail delivery in those days. The farmers very seldom saw a newspaper and were hungry for news. They were very glad to see a peddler from any large city. They wanted to hear all about the great fire. When I told a farmer that I was from Chicago, he was very glad to see me. You see, I was a newspaper and a department store.

The farms were ten, fifteen, twenty, and even thirty miles apart. It would take a day sometimes to walk from one farm to the next. I used to meet peddlers from all over. It was not an easy life, but we made pretty good money. Most of the men had come from Europe and had left their families behind. We were all trying to save enough money to bring relatives to America.

The living expenses of the peddlers were very little. The farmers' wives always gave us plenty of food. I did not eat anything that was not kosher, but I could eat eggs and there were plenty of them. There was fresh milk and bread and butter. The farmers always gave us a place to sleep. In the summer we slept in the hayloft. In the winter, if there was no spare bed, we would sleep on the floor. When the farmer had no extra blankets, we slept with our clothes on to keep warm.

I had a customer in Iowa and I used to get to his farm once a year. He had a nice six-room house, and it was one of the few places where I could have a bed to sleep in. When I got to the place after a year's absence, there was no house. The ground was covered with snow, and I could not even see the place where the house had been. As I was looking around, thinking that I was lost, my friend the farmer came out of a dugout. I asked him what had happened to his house.

"Oh, we had a terrible storm about four months ago, and the house blew away," said the farmer. "We are living in this dugout; it isn't as nice as the house was, but it's safe and warm. Come on in."

I had never been in a dugout and I was surprised to see how nice the farmer and his wife had fixed up this hole in the ground. Seven people were living in this dugout, but they made room for me. The farmers were very lonely during the long winters, and they were glad to have anybody come to their homes.

After carrying the pack on my back for two years, I decided to buy a horse and wagon. Many other peddlers got the same idea. I used to meet the small covered wagons as they drove about the country. I had now been peddling for five years and had saved enough money to bring my father, brothers, and sisters to Chicago. By that time a great many new houses had been built and we rented a four-room house on Maxwell Street. My oldest brother started peddling. One of my sisters started working in a clothing factory, while the other one kept house.

After my father had been in Chicago a few months, he wanted to go to Burlington, Iowa, to see a friend who had been his neighbor in Russia. When he got there, he met this friend's daughter and decided that I ought to marry her. So I went to Burlington, met the girl, and I agreed with my father. The young lady and I were married in 1875. I rented a small house near my father's home and we furnished it. I believe we had the first rug in the neighborhood. We were very proud of our first American home. It was the beginning of a good life. I stayed home for a week with my young wife. It was my first vacation since I had come to America. Then I started off again in my wagon. During the fifty years that I peddled, I always went home for all the Jewish holidays and when a baby was born. I would stay home a week and then was off again.

Many of the men who carried packs on their backs and in covered wagons became very rich. They learned American business ways. Some of them opened small stores which their wives looked after while the men were on the road. When the stores showed a good profit, they would quit peddling. Some of the largest department stores in the country were started by men who peddled with packs on their backs.

I never got rich. My wife and I raised six children. When my sisters and brothers got married, my father came to live with us. Then one of my sisters died and her children came to live with us. Then my wife brought her parents to America and they lived with us. Then we wanted our children to have an education, so we sent them to college. There

never was enough money left to start any kind of business. But I feel
that we made a good investment.

Hilda Polacheck
*Chicago*
1939

# Manuel Captiva

*Cape Cod fisherman Manuel Captiva told Federal Writer
Alice D. Kelly that he never stayed long on return visits to his
native Azore Islands because "it's awfully old-fashioned back
there." In background notes, Kelly commented that she had
known the Captiva family since she was a girl and that she was
"still Miss Alice to the old-timers."*

I wouldn't never be happy without I had a boat under me. In the
Old Country, we was all fishermen, me and my brothers. My father
fished, and his father too. Some dragging, but mostly with hooks. That's
about all they do back there. I could work as good as a man by the time
I was fourteen. I come over here when I was nineteen. The way I come,
we had folks over here. They write to my father, tell him there was
good money over here. My old man come over and my mother and us
four boys. Then we send for other people. That's how we all come.

My boy's a good fisherman. Portuguese boys do more like the old
man. Some of em get these ideas to go to high school. Don't do em no
good, as I can see, but don't do em no harm either. Lots of these
Americans tell me their boys is in the city. Got jobs here, got jobs
there. Me, I like to have the boy on my boat. Then I know where he is,
what he's doing. The boat will be his. It's good for him to know how
to handle her.

On land the Portuguese and Americans don't always get on so
good. But we fish together all right. It's different out in the boats.
There's the same rules for everyone. The rules for a captain and crew
are the same everywhere, and we all want the same things: a good catch
and a good market. We get on good on the sea.

They find out we're good fishermen. Anybody'll tell you they ain't
no men can fish better than the Portuguese. We can always get jobs on

*A Portuguese drag trawler fishing off Cape Cod, 1942. Photograph by John Collier.*

the boats. I wouldn't want to work on land all the time. Lots of the men do when they get older, but not me. I wouldn't never be happy unless I had a boat under me. I'm a good fisherman. Maybe I wouldn't do so good with a regular land job.

The Yankees fish to get money enough to go ashore, run shops maybe, or do business. The Portuguese fishes because he wants to, because he doesn't want no boss. One time I had a good job on a yacht. Good pay, the best of everything, but I didn't like it. Rather be independent, not say this "Yes sir" and "No sir" all the time. The Yankees they don't mind. They run stores, they work for bosses, and they don't care.

It's a good life and there used to be big money in it. Not no more, though. Now the middleman gets everything and they don't pay the prices anyhow. Sometimes you might as well throw away the catch. It don't keep forever. Give it away or throw it away if you can't sell it. I think the government don't know the conditions of fishing. We make a big lot of money some seasons, then for a long time we're broke. We got to get good prices.

You won't find many nowadays got much of anything saved. We most of us belong to one of these burial insurance societies. But the vidows of most of us wouldn't have much if we went. That's why a .nan's foolish not to buy a house if he can, even if he has to have a pretty big mortgage. And that's why it's good to own your boat. The Portuguese aren't as good for business as the Yankee fisherman.

I do dragging. We drag with big nets along the bottom. I don't go out nights much no more, but I got accommodations on my boat so's eight men can sleep on board. She's a sloop—that's one mast. My new engine's beautiful. Raises my profit. Used to cost ten, twelve dollars a day to take the boat out. Now costs only two, three.

I got a good crew, too. I'm captain. Then I got engineer, and cook. And my boy fishes. We fish on shares; I get most because the boat's mine. I don't know nothing else, only fishing and the sea. I never think about drowning any mor'n you think about the danger in the streets. Sure, the women worry, I guess. They used to get down on the beach and yell and pray when there was storms and the boat was out late. But the women always worrying about something, anyway.

My wife worries sometimes about the boy. I tell her he's better off at sea than running around with all these wild crowds. Ain't drowned yet, nor I ain't drowned yet. She wouldn't really want me to come ashore. Her people was fishing folks too. She knows I wouldn't be no good on land.

My boat can hold twenty-five thousand pound. We don't often get that much. Sometimes we do, though. One time we went out seven-thirty, eight o'clock at night. Nine o'clock we come back in—full. Twenty-five thousand pound this silver perch. Made a thousand dollar that one night. We go out nights when we hear the fish are running good. We don't have no regular plan where we go, but no boat ever goes alone. We start out, try all the places where we know fish come sometimes. Then we come back, one boat comes up. The Cap says, "You had a good catch?" If I say, "Yes," then likely he'll say, "Jeeze, I didn't get nothing. I'm coming with you tomorrow." Or if I didn't do so good, next day I go out with a crowd that's got a good catch.

We start about three, four in the morning. It's dark, and boy is it cold! We go outside the harbor, not far—couple of hours, maybe—and start fishing. It's light then and there's coffee on the stove. Everybody feels good. I got a beautiful stove on my boat. We cook chowder, oyster stew, make coffee—everything. And plenty of room.

My great-grandfather he was Spanish, and he was took prisoner by the Moors. After two, three months he escape. He comes to Portugal and settle down in little village near Lisbon. He was young fellow, very handsome, good fisherman. He had scars from Moorish prison. He was brave and also he told big stories, how he escape and kill Moors and everything. So everybody they call him Captiva. That means "prisoner." So that's the name we had since then. People say the Captivas got to be brave because of my great-grandfather. When I first tell the children, they won't believe me. But now they do. First they laugh and say, "Some more stories!" The Old Country, she's far away. And they think they know more than their old man.

It's the schools does it. They used to keep sending word home— have so much milk, so much orange juice. Must brush teeth. I never brush my teeth in the Old Country. Nobody did. And I got fine teeth. I send back word to the teacher once. I says, "Tell em I know them when they was little. Their fathers was fishermen just like me. They never had no orange juice and no quarts of milk." But they laugh. Say times is change. I guess so.

The young people over here, they have a good time. Back home the old folks was strict. Too strict. Young people was all the time running away. My kids they bring their friends home. That youngest girl of mine, she's always after me dance with her, go out places. Kids ain't afraid of the old folks no more. I think that's a good thing. Look at the Fisherman's Ball. It's for the families. My wife was there and my girls. My girl, the youngest one, she likes make me dance with her. She says, "Don't be behind the times, pa." She's a great kid.

We're the Portuguese pilgrims. We made the Cape. We built it up. Us and the American fishermen. We make Gloucester too. I was up there a couple of years. I fished all over, out of Chatham, out of Gloucester, everywhere. When we first come here there wasn't nothing but sand and a few houses and docks and boats. We used to dry the codfish out on the Dunes. There'd be pretty near miles of it spread out. The whole place stunk.

There was fishermen all up and down the Cape then. The old whalers went out then. And fishing off the Grand Banks was a goldmine. You'd get so much you couldn't load it all. Times you'd be up two, three nights cleaning, up to your knees in it and half frozen.

Then the artists come down. They must have painted a hundred miles of nets and boats and docks. And then the writers heard about it, and the summer people. But we started it. Even now they'll ask you to take them out in the boats and they ask questions. Fishing seems exciting to them.

Alice D. Kelly
*Cape Cod*
1939

# Philippe Lemay

*Philippe Lemay's people left a bankrupt Quebec farm to come to the United States in 1864. After the Civil War hundreds of French-Canadian families joined the southward migration, and by the turn of the century one-third of Quebec had moved to New England. Most of the French Canadians went straight into the textile mills. The Amoskeag Company of Manchester, New Hampshire, where Philippe Lemay rose from bobbin boy to overseer, was the world's largest textile factory in the early twentieth century. The 1922 strike that Lemay described was precipitated by the company's announcement of an increase in working hours and a 20 percent wage cut.*

When we landed at Lowell in 1864, there were very few French Canadians. Many more came after the Civil War was over. I was only eight years old, but that didn't stop me from going to work. My first job as a textile worker was in the Lawrence mill, Number Five, where I worked as a doffer [a worker who removes filled bobbins from spindles] for about three years. In 1872, when I was sixteen, our family moved to Manchester.

Here I started in a card room* as roping and bobbin boy, but I wanted to be a fly-spinner, making cotton into thread, ready for the weave room. It wasn't until 1875 that I got my chance. How I landed in Number One spinning mill of the Amoskeag, where no French Canadian could be hired before, is a story in itself.

Each spring and fall, it seems, the older immigrants had a touch of homesickness. Most of them still had farms in old Quebec, so they

---

\* The card is the machine that untangles the cotton or wool fiber in preparation for spinning.

*The spinning room of the Amoskeag Manufacturing Company, c. 1900.*
*Courtesy Manchester (New Hampshire) Historic Association.*

went back to Canada twice a year. They had to make many sacrifices to save up enough money to pay railroad fares and other necessary expenses. While there, they visited friends and relatives, but their principal reason was a serious one. At heart, they were still farmers like their ancestors, and they wanted to get something out of those farms, some of which had been in the family for many generations. In the spring, they attended to ploughing, harrowing, and sowing; in the fall, to the harvesting of the crops.

While they were absent from the mills, other hands had their chance to work. That's how I got into spinning. The overseer was out sick and the second hand hired me. When the boss came back, I was giving all my attention to my work and not losing a minute. But the overseer didn't look pleased when his assistant told him my name. He wanted to know why I had been hired when he didn't want any Frenchman working in his mill. The second hand said he'd discharge me right away and I felt that my dream of becoming a fly-spinner was coming to an end quickly. I kept on working. The boss looked at me, seemed to think twice before he spoke, and then said: "Don't do it now; wait until Smith comes back to work."

Smith did come back and I was out of a job, but not for long. The

boss was sorry to let me go, that was plain. He took my address and said
he'd let me know as soon as he needed me. He had changed his mind
about hiring French Canadians after he had seen one of them work.
The very next day he sent for me and after that I had a regular job in
the Amoskeag. That same boss hired many of my people, and that is the
point I want to bring out in my story.

Later, I was transferred to Number Four mill. One day, another
overseer tried to get me, and when I spoke of leaving, the boss of
Number Four wouldn't hear of it. To keep me, he offered me extra pay
if I would do the work of a sickly operative who had to loaf at times,
and more extra pay if I wanted to take the place of a third hand once
in a while. I accepted, and as long as the arrangement lasted I got two
dollars a day and a little more. I was finally given a regular job as third
hand, quite a promotion for a French Canadian at the time. In 1881
I was made second hand, and in 1901, overseer in Number One
spinning mill.

It was a big event when I was appointed overseer of the One and
Eight spinning mills. There was to be a vacancy very shortly. I knew
about it and, convinced that no one would say a good word for me,
I decided to speak for myself. I asked the super if he wouldn't give me
the chance. He was so surprised that he couldn't speak for a long time,
or so it seemed to me. He was looking at me as if he had been struck
by thunder and lightning. What! A Frenchman had the crust to think
he could be an overseer! That was something unheard of, absolutely
shocking. When he recovered enough to speak, he told me he'd think
it over, turned his back on me, and walked off. He was certainly upset.

The next day, he came to me and, with a doubting expression still
spread all over his face, said he'd try me for six months. But I didn't
want six months, I answered back. I wasn't going to clog up that
spinning department. Either I was the man for the job, I said, or I
wasn't. One month: that's all I wanted to show what I could do. The
super seemed to be wondering again but answered it was all right with
him. So I became the overseer of Number One spinning, where I had
made my shaky debut in 1875.

That was another step ahead for the French Canadians, but this
time it was an awful scandal. The sad news didn't take long to spread.
Americans and Irish were mad clean through. The Irish, it seemed,
were afraid that we had come to take their jobs away from them in the
mills and tried hard to send us back to Canada by making life impossible for us in America. They looked at me and spoke to me only
when they were strictly obliged to, but there was no more friendship.

I, a Frenchman, had jumped over the heads of others who thought themselves the only ones entitled to the job of overseer. Here was a sin that could not be forgiven, and what was the world coming to, anyway?

Later, several other French-Canadian textile workers got well-deserved promotions. One of my own second hands was a boss just three days. Then he came back to his old job with me after telling the superintendent that he'd be happier and healthier that way. "An overseer has too many worries," he said. So my friend had the distinction of being the first French Canadian to refuse an overseer's job.

I liked the people who were with me in the mills and I sympathized with them. I helped them as anybody else would have done in my place. Didn't I, when I was a boss, hide some who weren't quite sixteen, when inspectors visited the mills? If boys and girls were big and strong enough to work, even if they were a little under the legal age, I gave them a chance to keep their jobs. I started working in the Lowell mills when I was only eight years old, and I could understand. Their parents were poor and needed every cent they could get. So I'd tell these younger workers to keep out of sight until the inspector had gone away. There was no harm to anybody in that, and it did a lot of good. Besides, the law wasn't so strict in those days.

That strike of 1922 was really a terrible thing. It lasted nearly ten months and was the worst thing that ever happened. It was bad for the city, its merchants, tenement owners, business in general. It destroyed Amoskeag's trade. The company never recovered from the blow and kept going down until it had to close its doors [in 1936]. But my sympathy goes first to all the workers, for they suffered the most. They lost all their savings, went deep in debt, and lived on canned beans while the hope of winning the fight was kept dangling before their eyes. They were told almost every day by the strike leaders to be patient and tighten their belts because victory was in sight. But there was no victory, only defeat for all concerned.

As an overseer, I couldn't join their ranks in the union nor help them in any way, but neither could I be against them. As a boy, a young man, and a middle-aged man with a family, I had worked long hours for anything but high wages. I knew what it meant to be poor, what sacrifices must be made if you want to lay something aside for a rainy day. The workers wanted more pay; I would have given them a living wage if it had been in my power to do so, every worker having a right to that. They wanted shorter hours; I would have given them a reasonable work week if I had anything to say about it. Even as a second hand and an overseer, I never forgot my humble beginning and always considered myself a textile worker. Those strikers were textile workers too, and I was sorry for them.

Louis Paré
*Manchester, New Hampshire*
*n.d.*

# Herman Kirschbaum

*Herman Kirschbaum, an unemployed fur worker, was interviewed in Manhattan's Union Square, a traditional gathering place for the jobless and a center of mass protest.*

My father was a rich man. He had hundreds of acres of land and the biggest house in a little town near Libau in Russia. We always had plenty of everything. I never knew what it was to go without anything I wanted. My father was in with all the big gentiles and traded with them. He was Jewish but not very orthodox and everybody liked him. He always made plenty of money.

Naturally he was up to everything that was going on in business and cashed in on it. But for all that, I didn't like it. I never did like it; my home was too strict. Not enough freedom. For *me*, anyway.

Everything had to be just so. That was the way the gentiles did. So that's the way *we* had to do. My father wanted the good opinion of his neighbors. If I went out with a girl, my father said people were talking about me. As if *I* gave a damn what they said! But the folks cared and I was blamed for it. If I took a little too much drink, the folks complained. The gentiles didn't do that way. The gentiles did this and the gentiles did that. It got on my nerves. It was too cramped there.

So when I was fifteen I ran away from home.

From my father's desk, in the big front room, I took some money and ran away. I took a good deal. Plenty. Enough to last a long time. I had no passport, but in Europe with money you can do anything. I bought one. I went to Belgium and then got a boat out to London. I had no trade. I didn't know how to do any work. A rich man's son doesn't learn a trade. I didn't even know the language. But I had some money and that's what carried me through.

Well, in London I met an English Jew. He told me that America was the place. At home I had always heard that America was no good. A place for gangsters and lawlessness—only bad people went there. And it was the same way in England. They all cried down America. In fact, all over Europe everybody believed America was a bad place. But this English Jew wasn't fooled. He knew. And he put me wise. I couldn't talk English, but we got along together in Yiddish. "America's the place," he told me. "Suppose we go in together. You help me and I'll help you. You got money, you can't talk English. I ain't got enough money, but I know the ropes. I want to go to America too. You help me with the money and I'll get the passports and arrange everything." Well, I paid for the tickets and we landed in New York. That was in 1912. Prices were very low then. I still had a little money left. For fifteen cents you could buy a whole meal. I'll never forget those meals! I walked into a restaurant on Rivington Street. It was the corner of Eldridge. I remember it as well as yesterday. I should drop down dead if I didn't for fifteen cents buy a four- or five-course meal! I had soup—a big meat order, and good!—dessert—and then tea, coffee, or milk. And on top of that, they gave you a big soda [water] order—you know, at the soda fountain—if you wanted it. Free, mind you. And if you gave the waiter a nickel tip once a week, he was your friend for life. He would give you the best in the house. To a waiter a nickel was a lota money in them days. Believe me, when I walked outa that restaurant, I felt as if I had eaten something! I thought New York was the best city in the world. I still do. I went to that restaurant, regular, for a long time.

At that time six dollars a week was good wages. If a man got eighteen, he was a prince. That was in 1912, as I say, when I first landed here. I was sixteen years old. But if I live a million years I'll never forget those old days on Rivington Street! At that time, that section was the old ghetto—that is around in Seward Park, a little farther down. There was plenty of Jews there. I thought I had never seen so many Jews! As a matter of fact, I never had. And friendly! New York was a wonder city. Everything was cheap and I still had a little money. Less than fifty dollars, to be exact, but I was a prince while it lasted.

My friend, the London Jew, had friends in Boston and he went there shortly after and I sort of lost track of him. Well, my money didn't last forever. I had to go to work. I had no trade. One day I began selling shoelaces on Broadway below Fourteenth Street. A little later I got a chance to learn the fur business and jumped at it. I was in the manufacturing, or assembling, branch of the industry. That is, the putting together of the furs and the cloth into the finished garment. Inside of two years I was getting fifty or sixty dollars a week. I was sitting pretty. It went a little to my head. It was the war that did the trick. The war created a demand for American products. Up jumped prices. And up jumped wages. There were no more fifteen-cent meals on Rivington Street. They were charging forty-five and fifty cents for the same thing now.

I moved up to Riverside Drive and went in for culture. I wore expensive clothes, smoked high-priced cigars, paid high prices for food.

But, as I say, the Depression came. Everything has a catch in it.

Now I'm on relief.

And that, gentlemen, is how I happened to be in Union Square, on the bright summer night of September 19, 1938, and enjoying the hospitality of Uncle Sam, of whom I had never even heard in my home; instead of lingering there, like a barnacle still, in a village near the present city of Libau.

I am not there. I am here.

And that's why.

B. Hathaway
*New York City*
1939

# Captain Antonio\*

*Like Hemingway's Harry Morgan, who wouldn't "carry anything to the States that can talk," Captain Antonio smuggled liquor across the Florida Straits from Cuba to Key West but didn't like to fool with aliens. He had plenty of stories about those who did, however. Federal Writer Stetson Kennedy became a close friend of Antonio's and attests that he was indeed Hemingway's "principal source of material for* To Have and Have Not *and may well have been the model for the principal character." According to Kennedy, Antonio still lives in Key West in retirement, after having spent most of his life as a charter boat captain. "After all," Kennedy points out, "smuggling in liquor in Prohibition days was regarded as something of a social service, so there was no reason for him to pull any punches."†*

---

\* Fictitious name.
† Stetson Kennedy to author, September 2, 1978.

Me and the boys gave Hemingway the stuff he used in writin that book —what'd he call it—*To Have and Have Not*. Hemingway's all right. Ever now and then he comes around and drinks and cusses with us. But he put a lot of bunk in that book. All that stuff about monks—you know, Chinks. There were some Chinks smuggled, but they were handled out of Havana and landed up the Keys—never at Key West. Most of the people smuggled were Cubans, Spaniards, Mexicans, some Slovaks. I brought my wife and her sister in from Cuba. There was one man in Key West who smuggled monks, but Hemingway didn't know about him. Nobody but me knew about him. There was stories that he smuggled monks, and dropped em overboard. He'd leave Havana with a load of em, and land in Key West all by himself. But nobody never proved nothin.

Once when I was crossin to Cuba I seen a monk hangin on a light buoy. Most of the boys runnin aliens tied em up in sacks so they could throw em overboard easier. I was sittin around the sub base in Key West one time and a boat full of monks came in and tied up at the dock. The smuggler had tried to toss em overboard, but one of em had a gun and shot him dead. So the monks just piloted the boat on into Key West. They was put on the next boat and headed back to Cuba.

I mean them aliens caught hell. I heard guys in Cuba tell about takin on loads of em, collecting in advance, and then landin em round on the other side of Cuba. Another time the customs picked up a bunch of em marooned on an island in the Bahamas—they was half starved to death. Once I seen a bunch of monks walkin down the road up at No Name Key. They'd been wanderin around I don't know how many days, looking for New York City. You know Mexicana? He brought in a load of Cubans and landed em at South Beach. They all carried a bunch of fishin tackle. The customs was busy watchin up the Keys, so Mexicana just loaded em all in his car and drove right down Duval Street.

I never did like to fool with aliens. I sold my boat to Garcia. He rents it out to fishing parties now. Me and Garcia used to run in good loads—Scotch, rye, gin, rum, champagne, wine. Key West was one of the few towns in the country where you could get stuff that wasn't watered.

Me and Garcia had a good reputation—could practically guarantee delivery. That gave us good business. We always went around and got up orders and collected in advance before we made a trip. It ain't but eighty miles over to Cuba, but that Gulf Stream gets mighty rough for small boats. I've crossed the channel in a storm with only a coupla inches freeboard. We moved at night. Sometimes the customs pushed us so close we had to drop the load overboard. Then all they could hold us for was running without lights. When they would get on our trail we'd make a run for shallow water where we could lose em, or at least drop the load and pick it up later on. Used to hate to have to throw stuff over in deep water. A good friend of mine got drowned tryin to save a few extra bottles.

The damned pelicans—hijackers—bothered us more than customs. Them pelicans knew the water good as we did. We never knew when they was watchin us hide a load under water. That's why we call em pelicans—they'd wait till we was gone, and then they'd dive down and bring up the load.

One time me and Garcia unloaded out at Cow Key because there was a customs boat in Key West. We hid the stuff in the grass, and Garcia took the empty boat on in to Key West. Cow Key is a good fishing place, and the next day a coupla strange fishermen landed to cook lunch. I give em a few kegs of wine to keep quiet. They hadn't been gone long when the customs boat swung out of Key West and headed straight for me. I didn't have no boat, so I just waited for em to land. You know what happened? The customs marshal got me to slip the whole load into his garage.

Nobody never tell you about Cockeye Billy? He had a reputation. He could swim like a fish, and that's how he made a lot of his getaways. He'd high-ball for shallow water, snake through the channels, and head up into some mangrove swamp. In some of those creeks we had pockets cut outen the mangroves and he would run his boat into the pocket and pull down the mangroves behind him. He even had cut pieces to scatter over the top of the boat to keep the customs airplanes from spottin it in the daytime.

But if they cornered Cockeye he'd dive overboard, swim under water, and come up way back in the swamp. He was just like a fish in the water. One night the customs caught him a coupla miles off shore and shot it out with him. Cockeye dropped overboard and never came up. Nobody seen him since. The government men saw blood on his boat and reported he'd got drowned or the sharks had got him.

Ever now and then some of the boys up on the Keys gits drunk and say they seen Cockeye in Tampa or Miami. But he wasn't that good a swimmer.

Stetson Kennedy
*Key West, Florida*
1938

# THE YARDS

Chicago
1939

*It was stupefying, brutalizing work; it left her no time to think, no strength for anything. She was part of the machine she tended, and every faculty that was not needed for the machine was doomed to be crushed out of existence.*

—*The Jungle*, 1906

Thirty-three years after Upton Sinclair published *The Jungle*, with its grim account of Elzbieta at her sausage machine, Estelle Zabritz told Federal Writer Betty Burke about operating a power machine in the Dry Casings department of Armour & Co. [Casings are the guts used to make sausage coverings.] In the spring of 1939 conditions in the Chicago stockyards were still "really awful," but the spirit of the workers was no longer crushed. "It was an exciting time when the CIO [Congress of Industrial Organizations] was organizing," Zabritz recalls. "We were young and daring and willing to do things."*

Betty Burke interviewed packinghouse workers at a critical time in the industry's labor history, just as the CIO came to the stockyards. The militant new union organization met with immediate enthusiasm. Its rapid progress in the yards was founded on events that had profoundly affected the meatpacking industry during the previous three decades, events still on the minds of the men and women Burke talked to in 1939. During the first quarter of the century, the packinghouse workers lost three bitter strikes, and on one occasion management imported trainloads of southern blacks to swell the ranks of strike-breakers. In addition, meatpacking was one of the earliest industries to mechanize; by the 1920s, work in the packinghouses was increasingly unskilled and semi-skilled. All these developments seriously undermined the Amalgamated Meat Cutters and Butcher Workmen, an American Federation of Labor union. Earlier, the Amalgamated had attempted to organize along industrial lines, but a series of defeats left it enfeebled. By the 1930s, it

---

* All quotations from Estelle Zabritz are from an interview with the author, February 1978.

still had failed to attract largely unskilled black and female workers. In contrast, the CIO, led by United Mine Workers President John L. Lewis, actively promoted rank-and-file organizing industrywide. The path was smoothed for the CIO's approach to labor organizing by the 1935 Wagner Act, which guaranteed collective bargaining and the right of employees to elect representatives. It became illegal to fire or blacklist workers for union activities.

Stories in this chapter testify to the CIO's ready acceptance in the yards. Within six months of Betty Burke's interviews with packinghouse workers, the CIO's Packinghouse Workers Organizing Committee (PWOC) won a crucial contest in its drive to organize the industry: in a November 1939 election, the workers at Armour & Co. chose the PWOC four-to-one over the Amalgamated.

One important element in the success of the PWOC was the union's emphasis on minorities and women, an emphasis paralleled by Burke's interviews with female, black, and Mexican-American workers. The PWOC took a militant stand against racial discrimination and included a greater number of women in union work. The PWOC was also sensitive to the non-economic concerns of packinghouse workers, and willing to fight for better working conditions. These had not improved significantly since the publication of *The Jungle*; in 1942 meatpacking still had the highest accident rate in the country among consumer industries.

From the start, the PWOC included a substantial left-wing element. One of the women interviewed by Burke, Victoria Kramer, was designated by the Young Communist League to organize within the industry. Kramer has discussed how she helped start the PWOC in the book *Rank and File* and in the film *Union Maids*. For the film and the book she used the name Stella Nowicki, and Nowicki and Kramer are just two of the names by which she was known in her organizing days. "I was blacklisted under my real name for union activity at Armour's," she recalled recently.* "I went right back to work in the same department under a different name. In the end, I must have had about five different names." When she wasn't blacklisted, she was shifted from department to department to break her seniority. "Every time I went to another department, I saved the names and addresses; and when the NLRB [National Labor Relations Board] election came along, I was able to make contact with all those people. So in their zeal to break my seniority they gave me a wider audience."

---

* All quotations from Victoria Kramer are from an interview with the author, March 1977.

Now a secretary in Chicago, Victoria Kramer is still in touch with friends from Back of the Yards, as the neighborhood around the packinghouses is called. Her connections led to contemporary interviews with Betty Burke and Estelle Zabritz. For each woman, reading the FWP interviews forty years later freshened painful memories. Even though Kramer has spoken frequently about packinghouse conditions in the Thirties, she wept when reading an interview that described hands blistered from handling scalding-hot meat. Some things, she explained, had simply been too painful to remember.

For Betty Burke, rereading the interviews she conducted "brought back how hard times were Back of the Yards."* Burke went to work on the Writers' Project when no one else in her family could get a job, so she didn't feel much better off than the people she interviewed. Burke's empathy for the packinghouse workers made her especially sensitive to the contradictions in the lives of the women she met. They were "a curious blend of real tough and stereotyped feminine, trying always to pretend that they were not really all that tough. But they *had* to be tough, both to live Back of the Yards and to work there. They really had to be strong women. But they were also very much influenced by Catholicism and its teachings that women ought to be in the house taking care of their children, and there they were out working and their children God knows where. Well, they had all kinds of troubles, all kinds of troubles."

Burke was already "all for the CIO" when she started interviewing packinghouse workers. "My dad was a socialist, so that gave me the background for it. And I read *The Jungle* when I was eleven or so, and that influenced me very strongly." Burke found strong union members the most articulate and willing to talk, and she met many of them through the Industrial Department of the YWCA. "I just made friends with people and then went on to interview them," she recalls. She took extensive notes during her interviews and tried to record the language verbatim. Burke was strongly influenced in her work by novelist Nelson Algren, her superior on the Chicago Writers' Project.† "He gave me carte blanche and he also gave me the idea that the truth is first, no matter what it is."

---

* All quotations from Betty Burke are from an interview with the author, February 1978.

† See pages 90 and 177 for work done by Algren while he was on the Writers' Project.

# Mary Hammond*

*Mary Hammond was born and raised Back of the Yards. She was twenty-four and had already worked in the stockyards for about ten years when she talked to Betty Burke in 1939. By then she had finished eighth grade by attending night school—after working a ten-hour day—three hours a night, three nights a week for four years.*

*Swift & Co., where Hammond worked at the time of her interview, had slightly better working conditions than the other packinghouses and also the most firmly entrenched company union.*

I'm in the Sliced Bacon. That's supposed to be the lightest, cleanest place to work. They wouldn't take on a Negro girl if she was a college graduate. There's plenty of them doing all kinds of dirty jobs in the yards, but Sliced Bacon, oh, that's too good to give a colored girl.

The work is very simple but very fast. They brought a lot of new machinery in. The man who makes all that detailed machinery [run] is only a worker. He gets paid a little more, and the girls who lost their jobs because of his junk, Jesus Christ you couldn't count em. Once I went up to that guy on the floor, and I asked him how much the machinery was stepping up production. You should have seen the superintendent rush up and tell him not to talk to me and for me to mind my own business and get back to my table.

Here's the psychology of a girl at the yards.† She tries to forget she works in the yards after work. She'll tell people she works in an office; at best, she'll say she's an office worker in the yards. She'll go around with everyone except yards girls. That's the single ones; married ones are different. Of course the union has changed that attitude to a certain extent. But Swift's beat the union to the draw. They raise the wages before the union got established there and so the workers think Swift's is the nuts. They fail to realize that if it hadn't been for the

\* Fictitious name.

† Attached to the transcript of Mary Hammond's remarks was an unsigned note from an FWP supervisor expressing doubt about the authenticity of the narrative's diction. Specifically, the memo questioned whether a stockyards worker would use a phrase like "Here's the psychology of a girl at the yards." When Victoria Kramer read this editorial comment forty years later, she was so offended by its implied condescension that she penciled in her own reply beneath: "Yes she would. I knew her."

union they wouldn't have got that in the first place. And if the union don't catch hold there, they'll get cut so fast they won't know what struck em. I used to think Swift's was the cream. They pat you on the back and make out you're just one of the family, a great big happy family. Lots of the girls go for that. Then they start laying them off right and left and even then some of these girls will say, "Well, they were nice about it, they said they were sorry to have to do it." In Swift's now, if a married couple works there, they lay off one of em.

Reminds me of Wilson's. Boy, what a craphole! In '34 they had me going like a clock ten and twelve hours a day. I used to get home so tired I'd just sit down at the table and cry like a baby. That's where I was blacklisted. Some spy found out I was friendly to the union. It took me a long time to catch on to why they kept laying me off. They broke up my seniority that way and then finally they wouldn't put me back at all. I didn't waste my time fooling around with the foremen and the small-time guys around the office. I went to see the head employment manager. I asked him how it was that I wasn't put on when I knew other girls in my department were working. He just looked at me awhile, then he said, "We've got the girls in that department like this," and he clenched his fist. "That's the way we'll keep them. You couldn't do a thing with them, even if you had the chance—which you won't have. Of course, you can go out and sit in the employment office and wait. Come every day if you want to." That's all he said, didn't mention union organizing, not in so many words, but I knew I was through as far as Wilson's was concerned.

My brother worked in the Hog Kill for eight years, and work's getting so scarce they're starting to cut into the eight-year seniority bunch. He was lucky; they just transferred him to Beef Kill. In 1919 my brother walked out with the others and while he was walking through the yards a watchman called out, "Who goes there?" Well, my brother was damned if he was going to report to a squirty watchman and so he didn't answer. The watchman shot him in the leg, put him in the hospital for a year. You'd think that'd teach him something, but it didn't. He never joined the union. He's just a suckhole for the company. He sticks up for Swift and Company like he owned the damn place. That's all right, though. We can get along without guys like him.

Betty Burke

# Estelle Zabritz

*"Nowadays I wouldn't even think of going to work in a place such as that," Estelle Zabritz said recently. Not long after her Federal Writers' Project interview, Zabritz left her job in the yards, to stay home and raise her children. She was twenty-three at the time, and Betty Burke described her as "a beauty" who got along well at the yards because the foremen mistakenly believed her to be dumb as well as beautiful. "They would come and cry on her shoulder all the time about the union and she would be so solicitous and sympathetic and indignant about it all—she who had a CIO button stowed away in her purse since the first day the union came to the plant," Burke wrote in her background notes.*

*Zabritz told Burke that young girls who worked in the packinghouses were reluctant to admit it. Forty years later, she reflected further on the conflict between working in the yards and fulfilling traditional standards of femininity. "You were kind of ashamed of working in the yards, especially when you went out with boys. Maybe it was because it was so smelly and dirty and wet, and then of course the clothes you wore weren't that glamorous. When you're sixteen or seventeen you think that's awful."*

I'll tell you how I got to working in the yards. I wanted to finish high school but we had a lot of sickness and trouble in my family just then; my father got t.b. and they couldn't afford to send me anymore. Oh, I guess if I had begged and coaxed for money to go they would have managed, but I was too proud to do that. I thought I'd get a job downtown in an office or department store and then maybe make enough to go to school. Me and my girl friend used to look for work downtown every day. We lived right near the yards, but we wouldn't think of working in that smelly place for anything.

But we never got anything in office work and a year went by that way, so one time we took a walk and just for fun we walked into Armour's where they hire the girls. We were laughing and hoping they wouldn't give us applications—lots of times they send new girls away because there's so many laid-off girls waiting to get back, and we really thought working in the yards was awful. Lots of girls do even now, and some of them even have the nerve to tell people they don't work in the yards.

*Estelle Zabritz (center) and two friends outside the Dry Casings department of Armour & Co. in 1938. "I worked in a dry area,"* Zabritz recalls, *"so I didn't have to wear boots like the other girls, just heavy wooden shoes. We all wore waterproof aprons while on the job."*

They'll meet other girls who work there, at a dance or some wedding, and they'll say *they* don't. But you always know they're lying, because their fingernails are cracked and broken from always being in that pickle water; it has some kind of acid in it and it eats away the nails.

Well, in walks Miss McCann and she looks over everybody and

what did she do but point at me and call me over to her desk. I guess she just liked my looks or s( nething. She put me to work in Dry Casings. You might think it's dry there, but it isn't; they just call it that to distinguish it from Wet Casings, which is where they do the first cleaning out of pig guts. The workers call it the Gut Shanty and the smell of that place could knock you off your feet. Dry Casings isn't that bad, but they don't take visitors through unless it's some real important person who makes a point of it and wants to see. Lots of those ritzy ladies can't take it. They tighten up their faces at the entrance and think they're ready for anything, but before they're halfway through the place they're green as grass. The pickle water on the floors gets them all slopped up, just ruins their shoes and silk hose. And are they glad to get out! They bump into each other and fall all over themselves, just like cockroaches, they're so anxious to get away and get cleaned up. We feel sorry for them, they look so uncomfortable.

I operate a power machine in Dry Casings. It's better where I am because the casings are clean and almost dry by the time they come to the machine and I sew them at one end. Mine is a semi-skilled job and I get good pay, piecework, of course. On an average of from twenty-three to twenty-seven dollars a week. In my department there aren't so many layoffs like in the other places. I was lucky: I only got it three times in the five years I was there. I think they sort of like me, Miss McCann and some of them.

But the first week I was there, you should have seen my hands, all puffed and swollen. I wasn't on sewing then; I was on a stretching machine. That's to see the casing isn't damaged after the cleaning processes it goes through. That pickle water causes salt ulcers and they're very hard to cure, nearly impossible if you have to keep working in the wet. The acids and salt just rot away a person's skin and bone if he gets the smallest scratch or cut at work. Most of the girls in Casings have to wear wooden shoes and rubber aprons. The company doesn't furnish them. They pay three dollars for the shoes and about a dollar and a half for the aprons.

My husband got the hog's itch from working there. He can't go near the yards now but what he gets it back again. He used to have his hands and arms wrapped up in bandages clear up to his elbows, it was so bad. The company paid his doctor bills for a while till it got a little better, but they broke up his seniority. They transferred him to another department after he had worked three and a half years in one place, and then after a couple of months they laid him off because they said he was new in that department. They just wanted to get rid of him now that he was sick and they had to keep paying doctors to cure him. Finally he got a job outside the yards so he said to hell with them.

Betty Burke

# Betty Piontkowsky

*Betty Piontkowsky told Betty Burke that she hadn't been outside the yards district in three years and didn't care to go. Piontkowsky, who was twenty-four, had worked in the stock-yards off and on since she was thirteen.*

Kid, I always worked at Armour's. Some of them places in the yards ain't worth a s - - t. Armour's ain't so bad. Some departments, like the one I work in, the Lard Refinery—it's pretty clean. I operate one of those big automatic carton machines. These machines are up on a high plat-form, and after I feed the empty carton and wrapper into a machine it comes out on a belt and the carton's packed with lard and goes down on the floor by belt to the check girls. My machine is fixed for a rate of sixty cartons a minute. We used to stitch the boxes, but now there's a great big machine and all the boxes are glued automatically. Lots of girls are out on account of that machine doing their work.

They got a new rule now. They won't take no women over thirty. You got to go through a doctor's examination if they lay you off more than sixty days, every time, even if you're an old-timer. There was a big, fat woman in our department; we used to call her Mama. She was laid off once and when she came back they wouldn't take her. Miss McCann— she's in charge of hiring all the women—come out with her ass stuck out and said, Mama, don't you know it's for your own sake we can't take you back. Why, you might have a heart attack at work and then the com-pany would be held responsible. You shouldn't be working at this anymore."

You should have heard Mama. She was so mad! She started yelling and hollering about how she was good enough to work there four months ago and how she was only fifteen pounds heavier than when they laid her off last. She was a 215-pounder, but there was nothing wrong with her. She was stronger than most of us, like an ox. She didn't have no weak heart. But old piss-in-the-face McCann just didn't want her anymore and she wouldn't take her back. Mama called her every name she knew in Polish before she went.

I worked in the refinery this last time until I was more than five months gone. It didn't show so much then. If they knew I was that way they wouldn't let me go to work. I got a bad eye lately too, my luck. My machine needs good eyes, else I could get a hand mashed easy. It's a good thing we get fifteen minutes morning and afternoon relief. We have half-hour lunch. One minute late and we get docked half an hour.

I remember when they had fights in the yards over the unions. Some of the men got stabbed. Jesus, they had cops all over the place for a long time. It was kind of exciting. But I didn't know what it was all about anyhow. Didn't care to know, either.

Betty Burke

# Victoria Kramer*

*When she was seventeen, Victoria Kramer left the Michigan farm where she was raised and headed for Chicago. She went to work at Armour's for 37½ cents an hour and boarded with Herb March and his family. March later became district director of the PWOC; he encouraged Kramer to join the Young Communist League and to take a leading role in organizing the union.*

I've lived in *some* dumps near the yards. Once I stayed in a basement around Forty-fifth and Ashland that was five feet below street level. Around that neighborhood you don't know what a bathtub is. You have to take showers in the parks around there. There's two parks that have them that I know about. But you've got to wait for hours for your turn, and in winter nobody wants to walk blocks in icy weather or snow and then have to take a chance on getting pneumonia coming home. People come home from working in the yards and they're dead tired and then to have to travel to take a bath—well, naturally, they don't, not in winter, anyway.

* Kramer is known as Stella Nowicki in the book *Rank and File* and the film *Union Maids*.

*Victoria Kramer at a CIO state convention where she was a delegate from the Packinghouse Workers.*

My work right now is taking the casings, the intestines, and I string them over a pipe and grade the different sizes with a gauge. Then I run water into the casings and it drains off on the floor. We all wear rubber boots and big long aprons of rubber. Wet departments like mine are no good to work in. You get rheumatism in no time at all, and that really cripples lots of people in the yards. If you get crippled up like that, they're supposed to pay you something like one-fourth of your weekly pay for one year—that's only if you've been working steady for two years. The company's doctor treats you, but they can't cure rheumatism if you really get it bad. So if you can't work after the year's up, it's just too bad: they'll *never* take you back then.

They've got hot-air pipes overhead in my department. Gets you so sleepy you can't see straight. Last week I was working away there and getting sleepier and sleepier till I hardly knew what I was doing. All at once a casing burst and I got myself drenched with cold water. That woke me up fast.

They have sick insurance, you know. It takes at least twenty-five dollars a year from your pay. If you don't get sick you're just out that much, and if you're laid off you'll never get it back either. But the thing that burns me is the way they break your seniority. They'll lay you off just before your two years are up. That gyps you out of your chance for a vacation with pay because you've got to work there two full years in order to get that. Or they'll lay you off for a couple of months and then rehire you. That means you've lost your seniority, because if you're laid off for more than fifty-six days then you have to go through all the red tape at the hiring office and begin as a temporary worker again—though you might have worked in the yards off and on for years and years.

I was the first girl in the yards to wear my CIO union button. I was dumb, though. I shouldn't have done it till we had some others willing to wear them too. You think I didn't get fired on account of it? I sure did. But then the union got my place organized and they got my job back. I quit after it was almost closed shop. They aren't very well organized yet where I am now. But it won't be long. The union's on the job. They'll be coming in.

Betty Burke

# Anna Novak

*Anna Novak was "a good Catholic," according to Betty Burke's background notes, "but criticizes certain activities of the Church freely, probably due to husband's influence, his cynical attitude, and his advanced political views." Novak's statement that "lots of the priests say 'The CIO is against religion and the Church'" tells only one side of the story. The strongest forces in the Back of the Yards community were the union and the Catholic Church. Although some priests initially resisted the CIO, individuals from each group eventually worked together. In July*

*1939, a PWOC mass rally featured as speakers both John L. Lewis and Bishop Bernard J. Sheil, one of the first major church leaders in the Chicago area to support the CIO.*

I've had eight years of the yards. It's a lot different now, with the union and all. We used to have to buy the foremen presents. On all the holidays, Christmas, Easter, Holy Week, Good Friday, you'd see the men coming to work with hip pockets bulging and taking the foreman off in corners, handing over their half pints. Your job wasn't worth much if you didn't observe the holiday custom. The women had to bring em bottles, just the same as the men. You could get along swell if you let the boss slap you on the behind and feel you up. I'd rather work any place but in the stockyards just for that reason alone.

I tried to get out a couple of times. Went to work for Container Corporation. Used to swing a hammer on those big wooden boxes. My husband wouldn't let me keep on there; it got to be too much for me to handle. I had to have work, so I went back to the yards. I worked in the canning rooms at Armour's. In summertime they're full of damp and steam so dense it's like a heavy fog and you can't breathe. In winter the steam penetrates your clothes and turns cold and clammy on your skin; your hands and feet simply freeze. You should see the rash the girls who have to handle poisoned pork get. And the acids from cans gets you so you can't stand up. You don't know what's the matter with you, but you can't work to save your life.

When the union came they made me steward of the girls in my department. Then because we were getting somewhere with the union they thought they'd scare me, so they laid me off a couple of times and broke up my seniority that way. Then after I got through testifying at the National Labor Relations Board they laid me off for good. I used to come up to old lady McCann and ask her why I couldn't get back. I'd say, "Haven't I always done good work, haven't I been a steady worker?" And she'd say, "Yes, Anna, you're a good worker, and an experienced girl; but you see now that your seniority is broken, I can't do anything for you." And all the time I'd be sitting there talking to her I'd know she was giving me the horse laugh. That dame got many a shiner from girls for her mean tricks. There was a time when she couldn't step out of her office without an escort because girls and women she'd laid off would wait for her right outside. I mean hundreds of them. Everybody has it in for her, because they all know what it's like to go through her mill. But when it comes to getting work she's God Almighty as far as Armour's is concerned. No woman gets in or out of Armour's without her say-so.

Here's one thing the union changed while I was in Armour's. They have some kind of honor system: the white girls in Armour's usually get better work if they work fifteen years. A little easier job, you know. What do you think they give the colored girls who work that long? They give them a black star pasted on their time cards! They hardly ever get a chance at anything but the dirtiest, wettest jobs, that even the white men can't stand or just wouldn't take. And that star is an easy way for the bosses to spot the colored women so that they won't accidentally give a good job to one, in some emergency. The union is putting the heat on that particular practice. The colored girls come into the union easy, and at union meetings now they stand up and have their say.

The Polish girls and the Lithuanians, they're the hardest to get in. You know how it is. There'll be a bunch of Polish and a bunch of Liths working and the foreman will play them against each other, and they'll fall for that stuff. They'll be so busy calling each other names, lousy Lugans or dumb Polacks, that when the time comes to get together, they can't, they're so used to fighting. The big reason, though, is that they're ruled by the priests and lots of the priests say, "The CIO is against religion and the Church!" They tell the Polish women, "You have no business going to union meetings, you should stay home and be concerned with raising a family of good Catholics." Around here they always yell about the married couples who have no children. They don't want to give them absolution. Raise children, raise children, raise children, that's all they know. But how to feed the children—that they don't know.

I have a time down at work with some of the women, especially the older ones. They'll say, "If God wants me to be happy, I'll be happy; if He wants me to be laid off, it's His will, and I must accept it and not doubt Him." I'll say, "Listen, don't you blame God for everything! Just because you're afraid to join the union and do something to keep your jobs safe and your children fed decently, don't throw it on God!"

Sometimes I'll be up early in the morning, and just sit down at the window and watch old ladies, seventy years old and more, going to work in the yards, so bent over and shriveled up and sick it makes you want to cry just watching them. The bosses make it so miserable for them, too. They should give them the easier jobs if not a pension for them after they get so old. Instead, they'll set an old woman to work at a high truck and have her bending over, taking heavy cans out of it, all day long. They'll be so gray in the face after a day's work, almost dead-looking. They have to sit down there on the floor and rest for half an hour after work before they have the strength to get up and go home at night. Sometimes some of us change jobs with them for a while if the foremen aren't around, but when they catch us we get bawled out. They want to make the old ladies quit, see.

I've been working at Agar's for eight months now, since Armour's put me on the blacklist. Our union contract expires in July and we're negotiating for another one with them now. I was appointed steward by union membership vote. Agar's isn't so bad now. Half the plant was organized before I got my job, but did we have to crawl to get the others in. Now what we want is a good contract and if they won't bargain, all we need to do is tie up the killing floor and Agar's will close up tighter than a clam. They can't afford that. And we've got the plant with us solid.

In the departments where there's salt water on the floors, every month it would do for a pair of shoes. It eats the leather out. We got after the government inspectors and the company, and the union made them keep sawdust on the floors after that. When we kick about things like that and talk about the union, we make the boss mad. When he gets good and mad and he knows he can't stop us from talking, he hollers, "Every dog gets his day and when I get mine!" And we just laugh and say, "Oh, the dogs have their day now, you had yours ten years ago, before the union came." Does he get sore!

Once I was working nights and it was one minute to eleven—we were supposed to start at eleven. The girl next to me was waiting, and she had her thumb in the dry cornmeal machine bin, picking at something. At the other end of the room was the girl who turned on the machinery switch when it was time to start. Well, that lousy foreman thought he'd rush work, and so he came up to the machine starter and hollered, "Alright, shake your fannies! It's eleven o'clock!" She pressed the switch, and this other girl at the end of the room screamed. Her thumb was cut clean off—because of a man so eager to push company production that safety restrictions meant nothing to him if he could chisel even a minute of the girls' time. It's things like that the union is here to prevent and to see that when some worker does meet such an accident she won't be thrown out on the dump heap, maimed and thrown a little compensation sop that wouldn't last a year. The companies can't get away with that anymore. People know more.

Betty Burke

# Jesse Perez

*"Jesse Perez was really pro-union," Victoria Kramer recalls. "All the Mexican workers were. They would talk about the Mexican Revolution; they just had an immediate sense of what the union meant." Perez eventually became a beef boner, which was the most skilled job in the plant.*

I started in as laborer. Got 62½ cents an hour. I get laid-off slip from fellow who has to leave town, that's how I get in employment office. Now I work as beef lugger, carrying the beef on cutting floor. Work is heavier than laborer, make 72 cents hour.

The bosses in the yards never treat Mexican worker same as rest. I was first to wear CIO button; ever since I start wearing the button they start to pick. I can butcher, but they don't give me job. They fired me on account of CIO union one time. I started to organize the boys on the gang. I was acting as steward for CIO union. We had so much speed-up and I was advising the boys to cut the speed. So when I start telling the boys we have a union for them, almost all join right away. We talk all the time what the union going to do for us, going to raise wages, stop speed-up. The bosses watch and they know it's a union coming.

So every day they start saying we behind in the work. They start speeding up the boys more and more every day. The boys ask me, what you gonna do? Can't keep on speed-up like this. We told bosses we working too fast, can't keep up. The whole gang, thirteen men, all stop. Bosses say, we ain't standing for nothing like this. Four days later they fire the whole gang, except two. We took the case in the labor board and they call the boys for witness. Labor board say we got to get jobs back, boss got to promise to put us back as soon as they can. That time was slack, but now all who was fired got work.

Now the bosses try to provoke strike before CIO get ready, before the men know what to do. Foremen always try to get in argument about work, to make the boys mad so they quit. We know what they do, we don't talk back, got to watch out they don't play tricks like that.

Betty Burke

# Jim Cole

*According to Jim Cole, the CIO provided a common ground for black packinghouse workers and those from European immigrant backgrounds. His interview also illustrates how women become lost to history. As he heard the story—and as he repeats it—the PWOC was started by twelve or fourteen men in the back of a saloon in 1937. That historic meeting was indeed attended by fourteen men—and also three women, one of whom was Victoria Kramer. "Men just don't see the women," said Kramer when she heard of her exclusion from Cole's account.*

I'm working in the Beef Kill section. Butcher on the chain. Been in the place twenty years, I believe. You got to have a certain amount of skill to do the job I'm doing. Long ago, I wanted to join the AFL union, the Amalgamated Butchers and Meat Cutters, they called it. They wouldn't let me in. Never said it to my face, but reason of it was plain. Negro. Just didn't want a Negro man to have what he should. That's wrong—you know that's wrong.

Long about 1937 the CIO come. Well, I tell you, we Negroes was glad to see it come. Sometimes the bosses or the company stooges try to keep the white boys from joining the union. They say, "You don't want to belong to a black man's organization. That's all the CIO is." Don't fool nobody, but they got to lie, spread lying words around.

The people in the yards waited a long while for the CIO. When they began organizing in the steel towns and out in South Chicago, everybody wanted to know when the CIO was coming out to the yards. Twelve, fourteen men started it first part of 1937, meeting in back of a saloon on Ashland, talking over what to do. Some of my friends are charter members. I got in too late for that.

Union asked for fifteen extra men on the killing floor, on the chain. Company had enough work for them, just tried to make us carry the load. After we had a stoppage, our union stewards went up to the office of the company and talked turkey. We got the extra help.

I don't care if the union don't do another lick of work raising our pay, or settling grievances about anything. I'll always believe they done the greatest thing in the world getting everybody who works in the yards together, and breaking up the hate and bad feelings that used to be held against the Negro. We all doing our work now, nothing but good to say about the CIO.

In my own local we elected our officers, and it's the same all over. We try to get every people represented. President of the local, he's Negro. First vice president, he's Polish. Second vice president, he's Irish. Other officers: Scotchman, Lithuanian, Negro, German. Many different people can't understand English very well and we have to have union interpreters for lots of our members. But that don't make no mind; they all friends in the union, even if they can't say nothin except "Brother" and shake hands.

Betty Burke

# Elmer Thomas

*Elmer Thomas was recording secretary of his local and a very active union member. He was thirty-two at the time of the interview and had worked on the killing floor for twelve years.*

Time I started, there was lots of Negro workers who had been in the yards since they were brought from the South to help break the big strike. They put me on as a laborer on the killing floor. That was in Beef Kill, but they soon had me transferred to Sheep Kill. I used to try handling a knife to do some of the butcher jobs, when the foreman wasn't around. That's a trade, and I wanted to learn it so I'd have a better chance to keep a job there. They'd let me pick up the trade, helping them on the job. Foreman, he come over once and see I knew how to handle a knife so I got a butchering job as soon as there was call for that. What I do is cut off sheep's head after it's been dressed. I been doing that particular job more than twelve years now. I know fellows, told me when they started in the yards and tried to learn to butcher, white men on the floor didn't like to see it. They'd do almost anything to keep them from learning, throw anything they could lay hands on at them, knives, sheep-fat cups, punches—that's tools we work with—anything. The white butchers hated the Negroes because they figured they would scab on them when trouble came and then get good-paying, skilled jobs besides. Well, that was a long time back—with the CIO in, all that's like a bad

*The processing line at the Hormel meatpacking plant in Austin, Minnesota, 1941. Photograph by John Vachon.*

dream gone. Oh, we still have a hard row, but this time the white men are with us and we're with them.

You take porkpacking. Jobs like that, they're clean, easy, light. You won't find Negroes working there. They won't give them such jobs. When they raise a gang—that's a term they use in the yards when there's new men being hired—you can bet you won't see any Negroes coming in. Like in '33, they were hiring young white boys, sixteen and eighteen years old, raw kids, didn't know a thing, but there were plenty of colored boys waiting for the same chance who never got it. Hank Johnson* said just the other night he'd bet there hadn't been a Negro hired in Armour's in seven years. He knows what he's talking about. Of course, they lay off Negroes who are later rehired. But if they haven't worked there before, they don't stand a chance. I remember one time I was fired. I was doing my job and the work was coming too fast so I had to let some of it go on by. Well, the boss was drunk and he come by, asked me why I didn't

---

* Henry Johnson was a leader of black groups in the PWOC as well as assistant national director.

keep up, and I told him. He was too drunk to listen, just got mad and said, "Get to hell out of here." I see there was no use arguing with him like he was. Just picked up my coat and hat and walked out. Three days later they called me back to work. I thought they'd take away my vacation time for that, but they didn't. Never will know why they didn't break my seniority on account of it.

Guys would tell about when they worked for the church.* A man would finish his work and go punch the time clock. Then he'd have to come back and work without being paid for the time he was putting in. Never had to do that myself, but sometimes the foreman would make us work five, ten minutes overtime. Finally we stopped that. At that time they had those big sheep-fat cups hanging on the chains. We'd see they were working us past supper hour. Man farthest away from the foreman would whistle and all the guys at work would start hollering s-o-u-p and whistling and banging the cups around, working all the time, you know. So they couldn't fire us all and we made so much racket they quit that particular chiseling after the first few times.

There's an old man, he pulls fat off the carcass and stows it in the fat cups. He's been on the killing floor for thirty years, and been stone blind for twenty years. Don't know how he lost his sight. He can get around on that floor as well as anyone of us with eyesight. Knows every man on the floor by the sound of his voice. He does his full share of work, and better than most, at that. I was working with him six months before I found out he was blind—he gets around that good. He don't need but a man to take him home at night and bring him to work mornings. Guess after you been working thirty years at one job you don't need much else except habit to keep going. Some guys come to work so drunk they can hardly walk, but they can do their work. They've been doing the same thing for so many years, they can do it sleeping.

They have a credit union in Armour's, keeps a lot of people out of the CIO. If you want a loan from them you have to have a good record. Well, some colored fellow tried to get a loan. They knew he was a union man, so they made it hard for him. Told him to get some worker with a bank account in the credit union to vouch for him. Fellow went and got Charlie. Charlie'd been in the yards a long time and he happened to have some money there. He walked into the office and signed them papers, and them in charge of the loans with their eyes popping like a fish out of water. Manager was so upset he asked Charlie to step into his

---

* The expression "working for the church" derives from Gustavus Swift's founding of a Methodist Church in the stockyards neighborhood. Unpaid work was referred to satirically by packinghouse workers as their contribution to Swift's church. (I am indebted to Leslie Orear for this information.)

private office. He said to him, "You really mean you want to sign for that man, and he a colored man! I hate to think a white man would want to take on that responsibility." Charlie—he's Irish—looked at this manager and grinned. He said, "Well, sure now, I do appreciate that bit of advice, seein you ain't chargin nothin for it. But that black boy's my friend. He works with me. He's a union brother and I guess maybe you're surprised to hear that I'm with the union, too! So just save that advice of yours for somebody don't know no better." Walked out of there and slammed the door. You think that colored fellow didn't get his loan? He got it. Manager couldn't do a thing. He really spoke his piece out of turn that time. Got a union man mad that time, and got himself told.

Betty Burke

# INDUSTRIAL
# LORE

# Henry Mitchell

*Henry Mitchell was born in 1884 on the Penobscot Indian
Reservation on Indian Island, Maine. He worked for years in the
Old Town Canoe Company factory before he was laid off. "I
went to the manager, but it was no use. When a man gets to
be over fifty they toss him out in favor of a younger man. This
is the machine age, and I suppose employers think that young
men can keep pace with machines better'n older men."*

I don't remember exactly when the Old Town Canoe Company was
started. Al Wickett was the superintendent in the canoe shop when I
went to work there. We went to work at six-thirty in the morning and
worked a ten-hour day. They introduced a piecework system about the
year I went to work and although the hours were long, we made good
pay. Thirty-six to forty dollars a week. That was too good to last, of
course, and after five years of it they began to cut the pay. It was really
Sam Gray's [the owner's] fault but we always blamed the French Canadians. They came in here by the carload. Sam knew he could get them
for less money and he did. A lot of the Indians lost their jobs, but, of
course, he had to keep some of us. There was a picture of an Indian on
the outside of their catalogue, and the book told about how the patient
Indian craftsmen constructed the successors to their birch-bark canoes.
Sightseers used to come in and sometimes one of the women would
say, "Oh, I want to see the Indians." Sam would lead them around
to where a few of us were working and say, "Here are a few of them
right here. We would never be able to run this place without them, I
assure you."*

Sam put Brown, the efficiency man, in here. He was a young fellow,

---

* The FWP guide to Maine perpetuated this myth in its description of the Old
Town Canoe Company factory: "The presence of Indians working with modern equipment recalls the romance that hovered over the silvery birch craft so skillfully fashioned
by their forefathers. . . ." (*Maine: A Guide "Down East,"* p. 295.)

just out of college, telling old canoe-makers how to go about their work. It was funny but Sam never got around to the point where he could see the joke. Brown was responsible for some worthwhile innovations here: he recommended blowers for the basement and ventilators and exhaust fans in the color room. But any dumbbell could have told Sam about the need for those things long before Brown came here. Sam should have known about it himself.

After Brown got through turning things upside down everywhere else, he got around to Hymie's room, the filling room. They used to fill a canoe and let it dry slowly for four or five days longer. That, of course, was as it should be. However, Brown must have been reading up on ceramics, for he says to Hymie, "Have some drying bins put in here. Ten days to dry a canoe is unheard of! We've got to speed it up a lot." They got the bins built and all fitted up with steam pipes, and they shoved the canoes in. It took only four hours to dry them in the bins. There was some talk about Sam appointing Brown general manager and handing him a few blocks of shares.

They got a big order of five hundred canoes from Macy's that year and they broke all records getting them out. It was all due to the drying bins that Brown thought up. About two months after the last canoe was shipped, they commenced to come back. They had warped and cracked ribs and splintered gunwales. Some of them had places where big gobs of paint a foot across had dropped off. There was 275 came back out of 500.

Sam, I guess, was sorry that the old custom of burning people at the stake had died out among the Indians, or he would have turned Brown over to us with orders to give him the works. As it was—laws being what they are—the best he could do was fire Brown without ceremony.

Robert F. Grady
*Old Town, Maine*
1938

# Nelson Walton

*Steelworker Nelson Walton and Federal Writer Sam Ross became friends while Ross was researching a novel on the 1919 steel strike. The novel was never published, but Ross recorded*

*for the Federal Writers' Project Walton's stories of his com-*
*pany's attitude toward worker safety. Walton, Ross recalls,*
*was a crane operator and a militant CIO member.* *

I don't know how true this story is. I have been hearing it for years. A guy fell or was pushed off one of the bridges into a ladle. He goes pouff into nothing. Then the company buried the guy with the steel until the family got over the accident, or until they moved away. After that the company dug up the metal and used it in making steel.

The last fatal accident we had was on the mold yard crane runway. There were three cranes on the runway: two slag cranes and a mold crane. Some molds were needed in a hurry and the foreman sent the mold-crane operator down to get the craneman from one of the slag cranes to relieve him on the mold crane because he was faster. The guy thought he'd ride on the center crane instead of walking. Before the crane stopped he jumped off. It was pretty dark in the place and as he jumped he was crushed to death between the crane and the columns that support the roof of the building. Next day the company issued orders that no craneman can get on or off moving cranes.

The ladles in the pits are big—175 tons. They are hooked up into the cranes by hookers in the pits. We had an old fellow, pretty well along in years and not as husky as he used to be. The hook got away from him and swung back from the ladle and hit him in the chest. That didn't kill him right away, but a few days later he died. The company doctors went over to examine him. They said the man had died from heart trouble.

For years steel has been made with soft ore, raw lime, scrap steel, and a small amount of scrap iron. That made up about forty percent of the total charge. The hot metal added made up about sixty percent of the charge. A week or so ago the bosses got a brainstorm and decided that ore was more expensive to use than "cinder," which was nothing but old slag they had thrown away and which they dragged out of the lake. Now this cinder is porous; it's fine when the weather is dry, but holds a lot of moisture in damp weather. The bosses overlooked that. They started a charge with cinder in dry weather and it worked fine. But yesterday was the second of two damp days and the cinder they charged yesterday absorbed a great deal of moisture. So when the metal was poured on top of the partial melt in the furnace it trickled down to the

---

* Interview with Sam Ross, February 1978. For other narratives collected by Ross, see The Jazz Language.

cinders. It created a tremendous force of steam, and two furnaces were blown up. What a noise!

Sam Ross
*Chicago*
1939

# Hank Sims

*Hank Sims, goldminer and drifter, took up the family line of work—his father was a Forty-niner who followed the gold rush. Sims, who was eighty-six, reminisced freely about his journey-man's skill at outsmarting crooked assayers and detecting salted mines. But when Federal Writer Walker Winslow asked about the lingo of hard-rock miners, Sims told him, "You'll have to pan it out of my talk." Sims's insistence that he was in the poorhouse was his own fancy: he actually lived in the Odd Fellows' retirement home in Portland, Oregon.*

When I talk I am liable to do some tall running off at the mouth. I am a miner and for forty, fifty years I have been traveling a shaft straight into this poorhouse. You can't call that very good mining. Most miners is fools, and I'll bet you that for every dollar lifted off the bedrock in this country two was put back on it. Miners is liars, too—honest liars. If you question a miner's word about his claim you might as well question his daughter's virtue. That's the way they stand by their lies.

I am a hard-rock man and I learned my business at Kermit, California, up in the Feather River country. That was a big diggings, and some of the best of the old hands was there. I learned the business from the ground down. You don't learn from the ground up in my business. I could timber and cut my own steel before I was twenty-five. We didn't have none of them hardware-store drills in those days. The boss handed you a bar of steel and said, "Cut er up." To be a timber man you had to be a first-rate rough carpenter, and like as not you had to fell your own timber right on the ground. A man had to know his business, and a fore-man could tell a greenhorn like reading beef from a poor ox. You didn't ask the foreman how to do anything. He'd just say, "Go ahead, and if it don't suit me I'll let you know."

Gold miner. One of the few remaining residents of Bannack, Montana, in 1942. Photograph by John Vachon.

No one ever got fired in them days. All you had to do was criticize a man and he quit. There was none of this sucking around like you have now, and a man didn't hang onto his job like a priest to a parish. Every once in a while we just drug down our pay on principle, and went down the road to a new job. They'd call us hoboes now, I guess. But in them days we was known as Overland Johns, and by God, I knew every creek and cow between here and Mexico, and right back up to Alaska. In them days if you were a mining man there wasn't any other way around. People didn't like the homeguard, and if you stayed in one place very long that is just what you got to be. If a man kept moving he had to keep on his toes, and that made good mechanics of us old-timers. People hired the drifters.

I'll give you an example of how we got our jobs. I drifted into Cornucopia one night on the late stage, just shaking the smell of Portland off myself, and I dropped into a small blind pig [an illegal drinking establishment] to warm myself a little. I'm not much of a drinking man, but the bartender there could see that I was an old Overlander, and he was an old-timer himself. He grinned at the sight of me. We didn't have much to say, but when I got up to leave for the hotel he calls me and says, "Looking for a place, old-timer? You go see So-and-so in the morning. He wants a man." Then he asked me my name, and I told him and went on to bed.

The next morning I went around to see the guy he told me about, and he asked me a hell of a lot more questions than he had any business asking about: where I had been and who I'd worked for. I told him as much as I thought he ought to know. I could see that the job was in highgrade and that he wanted to know just who he was hiring. He was just about to tell me it was no go when here comes the bartender and he says, "Say, So-and-so, ain't you hiring this man? This is Hank Sims. He don't amount to nothing and never will, but he is a hard-rock man from way back, and so tight in his mining it would take a ten-pound sledge to drive a drill in him, and so honest it would take a pinch bar to pull it out." "You're hired," says So-and-so to me. Well, I handled some of the steepest highgrade you ever did see for that man. I have seen the time when we pulled down a stand of it that would run six hundred ounces of silver to the ton, and maybe three hundred gold, and I don't think that the man ever watched me. He trusted me, and that highgrade was the kind you carry in canvas so none of it will leak out. That bartender's word was better with him than a deacon's.

Highgrade ore is the kind that is rich enough to steal the way it is, and the men who steal it are known as highgraders. A man could be honest as hell until he saw a clump of highgrade, and then all his princi--ples would leave him. I had a Swede working with me that just couldn't leave highgrade alone. He was an honest man up to a certain point, but with that ore there was too much of a strain on it for him to stand up under. The shaft ran back into the mountain and this highgrade clumped out every so often. The way you do with that stuff is leave it hanging so the boss can watch it. He can measure a bunch of it that way and there is no running off with it. One day we ran around a hanging of extra-rich stuff and finished cleaning up around it just at quitting time. I went out of the shaft and left the Swede standing there looking at the highgrade, and then pretty soon I heard a crash. He couldn't stand it any longer and he had knocked it down. We went on down to the bunkhouse together, and an hour later along came the foreman, and he says to the Swede, "I am going to have to lay you off—you are a good miner, but I got to let someone go and it might as well be you. I'm going down the hill tonight, and I want you for company." You couldn't leave him and that loose highgrade in the same county, and the super knew it. He didn't blame the Swede, and he walked clear to town with him to keep him honest. Now I've been too damned honest. People used to call me Honest Hank

Sims. They ought to have said, "There goes Honest Hank Sims on his way to the poorhouse."

Besides highgrading, there was a lot of salting and crooked assaying went on in the early days—still does, I guess. I saw a lot of it—some of those highbinders brought ore samples clean from Mexico to salt an Oregon mine with, and any man that had ever worked this country would know it was foreign ore, but people are prone to be fools—that's why we got places like this. I didn't open my mouth about it many times for the chances are that the man who was mining on a salted claim had just as much chance as he would anyplace else. If he had to be digging a tunnel it didn't make much difference where, just so it was mining country. What was worse was the crooked assayers. You'd take your samples to them and they'd pitch them out the back door and tell you what they had been paid to tell you—that your ore was worth, say, seventy, eighty dollars a ton. You take them a piece of highgrade and they'd tell you the same thing. There was a way to get around that, though, and I showed more than one man how to do it. You'd take a half dozen samples and put them in six numbered envelopes and then take a half dozen envelopes that were empty, and when you got in the office of the assayer you split the samples between the envelopes and told him you were going to have the government check on him, but that you wanted a hurry-up assay. You'd scare the Jesus out of him that way and he would be as honest as he was able. Most assayers were drunkards and had the jimmies so bad that they didn't know what they were doing.

You would think that mining your life away was enough of a gamble, but no. A miner wouldn't have it that way. He had to sweat out hole cards right along with his other prospecting. Sometimes they'd hit, but not very often. I saw one poor galoot of a Cousin Jack—that's a Cornishman—come into one place with not enough clothes on him to flag a handcar. He walked up to the wheel and put his last dollar on the double—he was drunk, and it pays thirty-six to one—and damn me if he didn't hit the pay dirt. It wasn't a very big joint and the limit would have been ten dollars under ordinary circumstances, but Cousin Jack was drunk and the dealer knew that there wasn't no double O's coming up twice in a row, and so he says, "Leave her lay, Jack." He did, and here comes the old double O again. The house only had eighteen hundred dollars, and he took it all. In three days I saw Cousin Jack, and all he had was the jimmies and no breakfast. The next time I saw him he was bull cook [a general flunky and cook's helper] in a Mormon camp—happy as hell; said that as soon as he made a stake he was going out prospecting. A real miner never goes prospecting until he has to earn his grubstake the hard way. He'd no more take money he made mining or gambling and do that than a priest would shave with holy water.

I guess that if a man has miner's blood in him, he can't never make it on top of the ground. He's like a mole: he can tell his way around by the kind of rock he's in, but the wind don't make no sense.

Walker Winslow
Portland, Oregon
1938

# Fred Harrison

*Although Fred Harrison had worked at several factory jobs, he felt he was cut out for the hard life of the mines. "You can't keep a groundhog out in the sun long," he told Federal Writer Jack Conroy. Both from the coalmining country of northern Missouri, Conroy and Harrison were friends and distant relatives. Harrison was the model for the character of Ed Warden in The Disinherited,\* Conroy's autobiographical novel, which begins in the Monkey Nest mine where his father and two brothers died.†*

I began in the drift mine when I was twelve. According to law, you must be sixteen before you start, but there's also a provision that a miner can take his son in to work with him. Many a boy begins in the mine when he's nine or ten. Of course, he can't do as much as a man, but he can pick up chunks and put them in a car being loaded, and he can fetch prop-caps [supports used to hold up the roof of a mine] when his old man is putting in a narrow cutting or using the riddle.

One of my first jobs was to shake the riddle. The riddle is a coarse sieve through which the fine coal is sifted, the fine stuff falling to the ground to be shoveled separately into a car. This fine coal is sold later as "slack" at a lower price than the coarser lumps, which the man holding the sieve tosses into another car. The riddle man usually sits cross-

---

\* Jack Conroy, *The Disinherited* (New York, 1933).
† Interview with Jack Conroy, February 1978.

*Bertha Hill, West Virginia, 1938. Photograph by Marion Post Wolcott.*

legged, and for the greenhorn it's an extra-tiring job having to sit there and feel the shock of each shovelful of coal thrown into it. At first the shock tingles up from your hands to your shoulders like an electric charge, and afterwards your arms get numb for a while until a dull ache spreads all through your arms and back. Some riddlers prefer to kneel, but this is pretty tough on your knees. You can wear canvas knee pads, of course, but they're heavy to pack around and a lump of coal can find a tender spot right through them, anyhow.

The miners that work in the big up-to-date mines don't know what it is in the drift mines. These go back at a slight downward slant into the heart of a hill with a coal vein in it. The roof is usually much lower, and it keeps getting lower as the mine burrows further back under the hill, for the veins are shallow to begin with and soon dwindle away. You just can't afford to take out a lot of rock and dirt just to get a small layer of coal. So you crawl along on your belly and push a little low car before you or pull it behind you. Mules or donkeys are usually used to haul out the small cars, and a mule driver has to be a pretty tough and bold man. Mine mules get plenty rambunctious, and may kick the daylights out of you if you don't watch them. When you pass one in an entry, it's best to squeeze tightly against his hindparts so he can't lift his back legs at you.

The air is bad most of the time and it makes you sleepy and gives you a headache. Large mines have a power-driven fan to drive out the foul air and pull in the fresh. Worst of all is the "black damp" that forms in damp and abandoned places. It can kill you before anybody can help you out. You strike it mostly when you break into old works.

Drift mines are usually located in a valley, and nine times out of ten that means there's a small stream nearby. Water gets into the entries and sometimes has to be pumped out before you can go back to work in the morning. Every drift mine has a hole called the "sump" dug at its lowest point for the seepage to drain into. Every greenhorn in a mine is sent all around the place looking for "the key to the sump."

There is a good deal of waste material after the coal is loaded. Soapstone falls from the roof, and there are sulphur streaks in the coal itself. The streak has to be picked out if it is too big, for the weigh boss gives you a dirty mark for every lump of soapstone or sulphur-filled coal you send to the top. When the dirty marks tally too much, you hear about it. Some of the waste material is thrown into the places just mined out, and this part of the mine is known as the "gob." Miners throw scraps from their lunches into the gob and the place is always overrun by rats that fight and squeal in the dark. When I first went into the mine I was terrified at the thought of the rats, and so were other boys beginning in the mine. One of the standard threats of veterans to green boys is: "Look alive, or I'll throw you in the gob with the rats."

The first day a new boy is in the mine, the other lads who have been working awhile put him through a hazing ordeal. His pants are taken down and coal dust smeared on his body. If it's an old-fashioned place where the lard-oil lamps are used instead of carbide, a little lard oil is used to make the coal dust stick better. Spanking with a shovel or a pick handle ordinarily forms part of the initiation, too.

Nowadays some of the mines are so spick-and-span that you can almost wear white gloves at work. You handle a mining machine instead of swinging a pick. When I started in, a man had to walk maybe ten miles with his pit clothes on and the coal dust still all over him. We washed in wooden tubs, and now some of the mines have shower baths. Only trouble is that a machine can pick coal faster than a man and when it ain't working it don't have to eat.

Jack Conroy
*Chicago*
1939

# Jack Hartley*

*The Oklahoma City oilfield, where Jack Hartley worked when he was interviewed, extended far inside the city limits; there were oil wells on the lawn of the state capitol and within yards of the governor's mansion.*

*Federal Writer Ned DeWitt came to the Oklahoma Writers' Project after working as a newsboy, soda jerk, truck driver, and rig-builder.†*

In Endlington, Pennsylvania, where I was born, we didn't know there was anything but oil—oil and gas. We smelled it all the time, had rigs all around our house, used crude for syrup on our pancakes, and had so darned much in us we had a good grade of wax-free oil for blood. There wasn't anything but oil to think about or work in. Maybe that's why I been following it all my life.

My daddy was superintendent for the Ohio Oil Company in Pennsylvania, and when we got big enough my four brothers and me followed right along behind him, working in oil. When I was sixteen I went to work as a roustabout,‡ and two years later I was a driller. We didn't know anything but standard [cable tool] drilling then, and I got to be pretty good. I followed the tools from Pennsylvania on out to California and back, and made all the booms of any size at all. In 1908 I made my first trip down into Oklahoma and went to work for a contractor on a Phillips well. The Phillips Oil Company drilled its first wells in that field, and I worked on most of them.

I dressed tools, roughnecked, roustabouted, or done anything that had to be done when work got a little bit slack, but mostly I drilled. I'd had my fingers nipped on the tools and had plenty of scars and bruises on me already, but I had my first accident up there near Bartlesville, Oklahoma. One day I noticed the water in the boiler was getting low; I don't know why the boilerman hadn't tended to it, but he hadn't. So I climbed down off the rig and turned the water pump on. When the cold water hit those boiler tubes they couldn't take it. The whole thing blew up right in my face. It blew me about sixty feet right straight up in the air and more'n a hundred feet away from the rig, and just scared the

---

\* Fictitious name.

† *Economy of Scarcity: Some Human Footnotes* (Norman, Okla., 1939).

‡ *Roustabout* and *roughneck* are terms for common laborers.

*Moore County, Texas, 1942. The oil well was being drilled with a portable rotary drilling outfit. Photograph by John Vachon.*

By God out of me. I didn't get hurt, though. It just lamed my side and hip and bruised me up pretty bad. I was in the hospital about a week, and then they turned me loose and I went back to work.

I worked around up there in Osage County till 1910, I guess it was, and then I went out to California where there was quite a bit of oil play going on. I dressed tools out there and pushed gangs, and then I left and followed the tools and drilled in Hobbs, New Mexico, Smackover, Arkansas, and some more towns in California. Three Sands, Oklahoma, was a good field to work in, because the formations were soft and you could really pound a hole down in a hurry.

The booms at Healdton and Cromwell and Kiefer were about the worst I ever saw. Old Bag Town at Healdton wasn't nothing more'n a bunch of tents, with chippies, gambling, and everybody else and everything else a man could think of to snake a nickel. Cromwell was a tough place to work in, but I don't believe any of them could hold a light to old Kiefer. There was a little old crick run through the field there, and for years after they'd quit drilling there'd be a body come up to the top, and people'd find out it was some worker that'd been hijacked and his body thrown in the crick. Must've been a couple of dozen workers killed like that. Wages was pretty good—I was making fifteen to twenty dollars a day myself—and a man that flashed a roll wouldn't likely be eating his breakfast with the boys next morning. They wouldn't find out what happened to him till years after, when there was a big rise in the crick, big enough to float his body up out of all that sludge.

I was up at old Big Heart in 1913, and I got married there. Old Big Heart was where Barnsdall is now. That Big Heart was a pretty live town itself; most of the outlaws in that part of the country holed up there, and until the Barnsdall Company cracked down on em there wasn't much peace there, what with them drinking and fighting and carrying on all the time.

I drilled for the Barnsdall around there for a while. I damned near got burned up one night. We was burning black dogs—kerosene drilling lamps that look something like bombs—and there was so da..in many gas pockets in the sand that when we hit a big one it blowed all the lamps out. I told the boys to go on working and I'd light em up again. I climbed up there and struck a match easy as I could. I didn't get but a few of em lighted till they hit some more gas down in the hole, and whoosh! That whole damn rig went up like a blowtorch. I jumped, but not quick enough because I got burned some. I was in the hospital a week or two, and when I got out they told me they'd had to abandon the well because the rig burned down and the drilling tools were ruined.

But the company didn't worry about just one hole; they had plenty more. They'd buy up land, 160 acres at a time, and put sixteen rigs on each one of them quarter-sections. I've seen the time when there'd be a thousand rigs in one field all lit up at night, and the ground shaking like an earthquake with all them bits pounding at it.

I do everything; I been head roustabout, switcher, pumper, gauger —damn near everything they had. Most of the roustabouts have been with the company a long time, like me. Back some years ago, lots of the companies hired college kids to work roustabouting, but there ain't so much of that anymore. A man's got to be next to his job now: he's got to know what he's doing. They used to send out a gang-pusher with a bunch of men, but now they just send out one or two roustabouts who know what to do without having a straw boss tell em.

My company's moving out of this Oklahoma City field; it's about played out and they don't figure this stuff'll last much more'n nine months. There ain't enough gas pressure left now to blow your hat off.

I kind of hate to leave Oklahoma City though, because of the accommodations around here. It's easy to find a place to stay, a good place too, and the rent's cheap as it can be when you compare it with lots of towns like Seminole, and some of them Texas towns. I don't guess me'n my wife ever lived in a regular house till we moved up here to Oklahoma City. We just kind of jungled up [stopped at a hobo camp] wherever we could and tried to live through it, and when that boom was over we went through the same kind of a deal again. My oldest daughter was born in a shack-tent in Osage County. We had an old tent I'd bought in town—that was all I could buy. The lumber companies couldn't even get hold of enough lumber to sell to the rig-builders. Well, I set up that tent, then got some scrap lumber and built a little shack outfit on the end of it. We cooked in the shack part and lived in the tent. And my daughter was born there.

My wife don't like for me to tell things like that. She says people'll think we been living like a pack of dogs or something. But I tell her, "Hell, Frances, that's the way we did live, and why not tell it?" But she don't like it. Just like she don't want me to cuss anymore. I never did much, not around home anyway, but I did let it out some when I'd get a bit stuck when I was drilling or something like that. But she says, "Boogie"—that's what everybody calls me: "Boogie, you let somebody that don't know you hear you cussing like you do and they'll think you're just a common tough oilfield worker." I just tell her, "Frances, goddamn it, that's the way I always did talk, and there ain't no use of trying to change me now. You was satisfied with me when we lived in Seminole and Shidler and around like that: what's the matter with me now?"

I guess she's like most women about things like that: she don't know that cussing kind of relieves a man and grows on him till he don't even notice he's doing it. I don't cuss anything like I used to, though. Her and the girls—I got one, twenty-three, that's married; and then one sixteen, in high school; and then another one, thirteen years old—kind of cured me. I guess I was kind of put out when all of em turned out to be girls, but that was just at first. Now I wouldn't trade any one of em for a whole damned houseful of boys.

My oldest daughter has got a boy and he stays over here all the time: won't leave at all. She just lets him hang around, cause he likes me to fool with him. I'm always getting him a train or something, and then both of us'll get down on the floor and play with it till my wife almost goes crazy listening to us. I call him "Jacko." I don't know if he'll be working in the field when he's as old as I am or not; it's good work, nothing wrong with it, and I wouldn't keep him from it if he wanted to. But course the wife and daughter will probably decide for him—less me and his dad get together first.

There ain't but three in my family left in oil now. My daddy got him a farm down in Texarkana, Texas, and settled down, and two of my brothers got killed in the war. One's in the Illinois fields on rotary rigs, and the other's pushing rotary tools down there at Ada. One of my brothers, one that's dead, had nine strings of tools working down in Mexico before he got killed: he had more sense'n the rest of us because we're just keeping our end up and that's about all. If Jacko does go in the oil game I hope he gets calluses on his hands from a pencil instead of tools.

Ned DeWitt
*Oklahoma City*
*1939*

# Chris Thorsten

*Chris Thorsten was interviewed about the dangers of iron work in the early days at the union hall of the International Association of Bridge, Structural Steel and Iron Workers. In 1911–1912, out of 124 deaths among members of the union only 15 were due to natural causes. The remainder were caused by accidents.*

I been in this racket thirty-two years. I remember one job, it was the Parcel Post Building, Forty-third and Lexington Avenue. I worked straight through five days and four nights. I was with the hoisting gang. The only time we got off was two hours for breakfast, one hour for lunch, one hour for supper, and one hour at night. Then I went into the saloon and went to sleep. They couldn't wake me with a sledgehammer. I felt kind of ashamed of myself that I couldn't take it, falling asleep and all that. We was loading thirty-two-ton girders. That was a good job. We made money in those days.

I was on a job once and my friend George Morgan got killed. We're just sitting there joking. He was tying on a safety railing on the scaffold and a beam rolled. The next morning we had to go over and work where he fell down. I had him in mind and I got stuck between beams and landed in the Good Samaritan Hospital.

Now take that Sixth Avenue El job. Plenty of men get killed there. The first man gets killed standing on the railroad tracks down by Canal Street. They dropped a whole load of steel. Friday another man gets killed. They can't get union men to go down there. They're rushin it: a man don't have time to watch out for himself. There'll be plenty of men killed before this job is over.

Men get hurt on all the jobs. Take the Washington Bridge, the Triboro Bridge, plenty of men hurt on those jobs. Two men killed on the Hotel New Yorker. I drove rivets all the way on that job. There was an airplane factory across the way. The motors were running and you couldn't hear a thing. I was leaning over the rail and I got caught between the beam and the rail. A collarbone broke and all the ribs in my body and three vertebrae. I was laid up for four years.

You ain't an iron worker unless you get killed.

Arnold Manoff
*New York City*
1938

# Highpockets

*Highpockets was an efficiency expert's dream, an imaginary factory worker who bent every muscle toward helping the company. Nelson Algren's story about the perfect, tractable employee is a proletarian version of the traditional tall tale, a form invented by members of the Chicago Writers' Project. Algren, who had already published* Somebody in Boots, *was one of the major contributors to an unpublished manuscript of Chicago industrial folklore. The best of these tales were in-*

*tended for a FWP collection, A Tall Chance to Work, which*
*was never published.*

When Highpockets first came into the mill room, he was walking like a man stepping over cornstalks. We knew he was a hillbilly from way back at the fork of the crick. Them guys raised on pumpkins and yaller crick water is anxious to work and get ahead; a jitney looks as big as a grindstone to them.

The time-study man had made it hard enough on us before Highpockets come, but afterwards—oh, man!—afterwards, it was hell on wheels. The time-study man, that mother-robbing creeper that watches you from behind dolly trucks and stock boxes, he's always trying to figger a way to get more work out of you at the same pay. He'll even ask you if they ain't some way you could do a little more than you are. He never expects you should say yes, and that's why it almost knocked him off the Christmas tree when Highpockets told him he reckoned he could do a sight more than he was. He was tending a milling machine that worked pretty fast, but it only took one hand.

Next thing we know, by Jesus, the time-study man was having the millwright put in another milling machine for Highpockets' left hand, and be damned if he didn't turn out twice as much work as before. The time-study man has got real fond of him by this time, and hangs around watching and admiring him. Trouble is, he started in on the rest of us, wanting we should do something about them idle left hands of ours.

Still, the time-study man ain't satisfied with Highpockets' work, because that cornfield canary is so husky it looks like he ain't taxing his strength a particle. Next, there's a block-and-tackle business fastened to Highpockets' right leg, and he's pulling stock pans off one conveyor onto another slick as you please. He's happy as a meadowlark in a plowed field of fat worms, and by quitting time he's as fresh as a daisy and skittish as a yearling bull.

"Take it easy, buddy, f' Christ's sake," we say to Highpockets every time we pass by him on the way to the can or water cooler. We say it low, so's the time-study man won't catch on, but might as well talk to an eight-wheeler that's lost her airbrakes on a downhill grade. These cornfield canaries ain't got sense enough to pound sand in a rat-hole or pour water out of a boot when it's got full directions printed on the heel.

It goes from bad to worse, with next a band fastened to Highpockets' left leg, and be damned if he ain't jerking empty fender hooks off another conveyor and piling them in a dolly box, neat as apple pie.

It looks bad for us, that's the God's truth, and beginning to look worse. The time-study man goes around saying: "He's true blue. He's the kind of man that gets ahead, got the company's interest at heart. Yes, sir, that kind of man *gets* somewhere around this plant. You birds that get full as ticks every night, booming and whoring around and coming in here next morning half-crocked, you get your hands in the company's pockets halfway to your elbows."

We thought Highpockets was speeded to full steam finally, because he's got a little bar in his teeth and with this he's jerking his head back and forth and this runs a brush back and forth over new stock coming in and knocks the dust off it. He's finished, we said, he *can't* do no more. He's doing all he can, and that's all a little red bull can do, boys. He's going like a blind dog in a meathouse, and it's REACH (right hand) REACH (left hand) KICK (right leg) KICK (left leg) PULL (teeth), REACH REACH KICK KICK PULL. He goes so fast you can't see him for steam.

"He's true blue! He's true blue! The kind of man that gets somewhere in this plant," the time-study man says, as he wiggles back and forth in tune with Highpockets' motions and whispers something in his ear. We know he's asking him if they ain't lost motion somewhere. This time we feel swell because about all Highpockets can really say is: "Gee, you got me there, boss, I give up."

All of us keep going at the same old merry-go-round, but we cock an ear to hear what Highpockets has got to say. This time the time-study man's got him where the wool is tight.

The sweat is falling off him like Niagara Falls. Here he goes, lickety-split, never misses a stroke: REACH REACH KICK KICK PULL REACH REACH KICK KICK PULL REACH REACH KICK KICK PULL. . . .

He was true blue, that cornfield canary was, and a credit to the human race. The kind of a man that *gets* somewhere in this plant. He grins game as a fighting cock and chirps right out loud:

*"Sure, if you want to stick a broom someplace, I think I could be sweeping the floor!"*

Nelson Algren
*Chicago*
*n.d.*

# MONUMENTAL STONE

Barre, Vermont
1939 and 1940

The granite of the Vermont hills is one of the hardest common stones in the world, the dense gray of a thundercloud. It makes fine monuments. Rough granite blocks quarried from Millstone Hill overlooking Barre City have been carved into memorials for parks and cemeteries across America: commemorative statues of poets and Confederate generals, of beloved spaniels, and Victorian children in high-button shoes.

The exceptional quality of Barre granite, and the comparatively high wages for the men who worked it, drew quarriers and carvers from the stone centers of Europe. Beginning in the 1880s, waves of men from Aberdeen, Saragossa, and Brescia made their way to Barre, where a sign in the railroad station welcomed them to "The Granite Center of the World."

The Federal Writers' Project state guidebook noted the "fast and lusty tempo that sets Barre apart from the rest of Vermont."* Barre's ethnic diversity contributed to this reputation for vitality as well as its unusual political mix. Immigrant stoneworkers brought with them a variety of radical persuasions. The political concerns of the townspeople of Barre extended well beyond the town boundaries. In 1912 granite workers and their families took in children of striking millworkers from Lawrence, Massachusetts. A decade later the Sacco-Vanzetti case aroused sympathy, and a benefit play at the Barre Opera House sold out three times over. In the 1930s, Barre workers, worried by the threat of fascism in Spain, donated enough money to send the Loyalist forces an ambulance.

Each immigrant group kept its own identity, forming musical societies and political clubs, reading newspapers in the language of the Old Country. Italians were widely acknowledged to be superior sculptors. From the northern provinces such as Tuscany and Lombardy, many of the Italian carvers had practiced their craft at the Carrara marble works where Michelangelo's stones were quarried. Italian carvers of excep-

* Vermont: A Guide to the Green Mountain State (New York, 1937).

tional promise studied sculpture at the *Reale Accademia di Belle Arti di Brera* in Milan.

The fine hand-carving that these artisans perfected was largely a memory in 1940 when the Federal Writers' Project documented Barre life. By then, pneumatic sandblasting tools had replaced the chisel for most of the lettering and ornamentation. Still, the granite workers paid tribute to the artistry of the hand-carvers, and their greatest achievements endured in the cemeteries of Barre.

The fine memorial stones often marked the graves of granite cutters who had died too young, victims of silicosis caused by years of breathing air misty with stone dust. The mayor of Barre told a Federal Writers' Project interviewer, "Our beautiful cemeteries are full of stonecutters who died in the prime of life." Technology introduced to the granite sheds during the first twenty years of the century was responsible. The new cutting machines not only made craft skills obsolete, they also created a more serious health hazard by increasing the amount of stone dust. "Sometimes the air was so full of dust you couldn't see the man next to you," one granite worker recalled. By the late 1930s, suction equipment that carried off the dust was in general use, but it was too late for those men whose lungs were already clogged. The immigrant sons shunned the sheds like death, according to the mayor: "They've seen too many funerals in the family. And they know what caused those funerals."

Federal Writers Roaldus Richmond and Mari Tomasi—assisted briefly by John Lynch—spent more than a year in Barre collecting over one hundred life histories from granite workers of every nationality. They also interviewed widows of granite workers, as well as other Barre citizens: the mayor, a bootlegger, a farmer. Tomasi was from a local Italian family, which "got us into a lot of houses," Richmond recalls.\* Their best interviews came from repeated contact and association with the subjects, rather than from single meetings. "Sometimes we couldn't even take notes because people didn't feel so free. But we tried to make it verbatim, and often one of us could fill in what the other didn't remember. We'd usually write it up right after we'd talked to somebody, so it was pretty authentic."

The Barre interviews were intended for a Federal Writers' Project study, never completed, called *Men Against Granite*. The FWP super-

---

\* All quotations from Roaldus Richmond are from an interview with the author, May 1978.

visors in charge of the study thought the interviews particularly successful. The historian Frank E. Manuel, then New England director of the FWP, wrote in a memorandum that the Barre project "holds forth extraordinary possibilities."* Morton Royse, who directed the Social-ethnic Studies Unit of the Writers' Project, recalls forming a positive opinion of the granite study during a field visit to Barre. "I'd go around myself talking with the quarry people and the stonecutters. Then I'd check the interviews to see if they sounded right based on what I had heard."†

# Miss Wheaton‡

*Miss Wheaton had lived for seventy years in the Georgian brick house her father built. By 1940 it was the only remaining residence on a street crowded with office buildings, department stores, gasoline stations, and taverns.*

My great-great-grandfather on my mother's side was Barre's first settler. That was in 1786. My great-great-grandfather organized the first church in Barre, and he was one of the committee to give us Elmwood Cemetery.

Living here on Main Street I've seen Barre grow and change color, you might say. So many foreigners rushing to the sheds and quarries brought color and varied interests to what was a staid, sleepy valley town. I wouldn't like to say they made Barre "wild"; I prefer to say "progressive and cosmopolitan." But it suffered the usual growing pains that every progressive town experiences.

Granite has put Barre in an enviable position in the state. Seventy-five percent of our people own their own homes. Being on Barre's Main street my home would make a fine location for a business block. I have been offered close to a hundred thousand dollars for it. But I won't sell. Never. It's my home.

Mari Tomasi

* Frank Manuel, "Report on a Field Trip to the Vermont Writers' Project," November 7, 1939, Library of Congress Folksong Archive.
† Interview with Morton Royse, January 1978.
‡ Fictitious name.

# Dave Bernie

*The owner of the manufacturing shed where Dave Bernie*
*polished granite monuments was a skilled carver himself.*
*Probably three-quarters of the sheds in Barre were owned by*
*men who began as granite cutters and continued to work at*
*their trade. Since a granite cutter owned the essential tools—*
*hammers, chisels, and drills—even a recent immigrant might*
*become a shed owner-operator.*

I work in the shed. It's pretty good, but my brother is the one makes
the money. He's on the road—a salesman. A good man on the road
makes ten or eleven thousand dollars a year, maybe better than that.
You don't make nothing like that in the sheds. I'm a polisher and I get
eight-fifty a day. That'd be pretty good if a man worked every day. I've
been luckier than some. I work most of the time.

We got a good shed to work in. We got a cement floor instead of
dirt. Some of the sheds are pretty cold and damp, but ours is O.K. The
lights are good and it's cleaner than most sheds. The suctions suck
the dust away from the cutting tools, you know. Of course, polishing
you don't get no dust anyway. But the way it is now, the other fellow
don't get nowhere near so much dust either.

There's seventy-five manufacturers in Barre City. On the Hill, up
round Websterville and Graniteville, there's six quarry companies. The
Hill is where we get the stone from. Them quarries are big, hundreds
of feet deep. That Hill is all cut up with quarries and piled with
grout. You see it from some places, it looks like the ruins of an old fort
or something. The towns on the Hill look just like mining towns.
Wooden houses thrown together fast and not kept up too good. But
you'd be surprised at the insides of some of them homes. Furnished
good with everything, comfortable, clean, nice to live in. There's money
up on the Hill. But I wouldn't care for quarry work. I'd rather be in
the sheds than down in them quarries.

In the shed when the stones get to me they've been sawed to about
the right size and smoothed down by the surface cutters. I put the
polisher on them. It's a big machine, a big disk you move around the
face of the stone. You use different abrasives in order, one after another.
It's slow work; everything in the granite business is slow. After the
machine, sometimes the edges and corners are finished by hand-
polishing. You can't get it all with the machine. After it's all polished,

Workers at the Anderson-Friberg Company manufacturing plant,
Barre, Vermont, 1932. Rough granite was brought from the quarries to
the manufacturing plants, where it was sawed, carved, and polished.
Courtesy Aldrich Public Library.

the stone goes to the sandblast room or the hand-carvers and letterers.
They all get the same pay, eighty-five a day, except some of the best
carvers and letter cutters get more. They used to get a lot more, the
good ones did.*

But like I told you, guys on the road make the money. Today the
money is in selling, no matter what the line of business is. You don't
need to know nothing to sell either. You just got to have that gift of
gab. Lots of nerve and plenty of gab. Nowadays they don't sell so many
big mausoleums anymore, but they still sell some big pieces. My brother
sold Mrs. Palmer—remember Palmer Method Writing they teach in
the schools? Well, it was that family. She wasn't interested at first. She
didn't intend to buy nothing. But my brother used to be a draftsman.

---

* During the years when each memorial stone was individually carved, the best
artists could earn $25 per day.

He sketched the stone all out for her, showed her just what it would look like. She got so interested she ordered it off him. He didn't need to work no more that year.

If they was going to cut that table in stone, say, and the company figured it was a three-thousand-dollar job—they add ten percent to that, and that's the salesman's commission. You see, they get a nice cut even on a small job. You ain't selling magazines when you sell granite! But it burns me up to think of some of them dumb bastards knocking off over ten thousand a year. My brother don't make that much. He did once but he don't now. But he still makes a good living all right.

The granite workers get along all right with the other people in the city. The old-timers used to keep more to themselves. It was natural to do that way at first. But now they mix right in like anybody else. Lots of the younger ones have gone into business here, and lots of them are doctors and lawyers now. Their folks came over to cut stone, and the money they made in granite started the sons off in business or educated them to be lawyers and doctors. Naturally the granite people are a class by themselves like any people who work the same trade. But they ain't cut off from the rest of the people anymore. Maybe some of the big shots think they're better than the stonecutters, but the stonecutters feel the same way about them, too. Stonecutters are pretty proud and independent, and they don't kneel down to nobody.

You see it in the sheds. Lots of the owners and all the bosses started out cutting stone themselves. It's different from most kinds of business. The bosses don't bother you much. They leave you alone to do your work. They don't try to drive a man; they know it ain't no use. Stonecutters won't stand for it. In the sheds every man knows his work and does his job. He don't need nobody standing over him, and the bosses know it.

We work eight hours a day, five days a week. That gives us forty hours a week, and my week's pay is $42.50. It ain't enough either. But it's more than you can get in any other line around here. It ain't bad in the sheds. The noise is the worst thing. It's a hell of a racket with the saws grinding back and forth. You know it takes an hour to saw four inches into granite. The drills are going all the time, and them big cranes smashing overhead. You get a vibration from the air-pressure machines. At quitting time when the noise stops, your head feels funny inside, the ringing stays in your ears. But you get used to it.

Roaldus Richmond

# Alfred Tornazzi*

*Shed-owner Alfred Tornazzi studied sculpture for eight years at the Reale Accademia di Belle Arti di Brera before coming to the United States. Tornazzi carved the monument he described as his masterpiece around the turn of the century. A statue of a little girl wearing a dress trimmed with delicate eyelet lace, it still stands in a Montpelier cemetery.*

I didn't start operating a shed of my own right away, although I could have. I wanted to learn more of this country, the way the sheds did business. I did carving for a shed in Barre the first year. The second year I went out to our western granite states. I found you could do better, more delicate work with the hard Barre stone, and I learned that it rated high in eastern markets and was quickly becoming known further west, so I decided to settle in or near Barre.

My brother, who had come to this country two years before I did, suggested that we start a shed of our own. It went under the name of Tornazzi Brothers. We've had our ups and downs, but we've made money and we've put out plenty of memorials that we're proud of.

My favorite memorial and what I believe is my masterpiece is one of my very early statues. It's called *The Little Margaret*. It stands in the Green Mount Cemetery in Montpelier. There's a story to that, too. I won't tell the customer's name, although you can easily find out by going to the cemetery and looking at the memorial. This customer wanted me to carve a statue of his little daughter who was dead. I'd never seen the girl. Her family produced a full-length picture of her and asked me to make the statue identical in clothing, posture, et cetera. I said it would be difficult since the picture was a poor one, and faint, but I'd do my best. I completed it, and was justly proud of it. The parents liked it, too. I remember the mother cried and said it looked real. But in spite of their satisfaction, they hated to pay the price agreed upon. I admit it was a steep price, but it was good work, and hard, and they could afford it. Well, the father came to me one day. He pointed to the picture and said, "Look, you promised to make the statue exactly like this picture. You didn't. On the memorial there's a button missing on one shoe. Since they aren't identical you should lower the price." It made me mad. I'd been very careful in carving those shoes; they were

* Fictitious name.

"The Little Margaret," Green Mount Cemetery, Montpelier, Vermont.
Photograph by Terry Gips.

those old-fashioned, high-buttoned shoes the girls wore at that time,
and since the picture was so dim I'd been careful to make sure of each
detail. "They *are* identical," I assured him, and proceeded to prove it.
A magnifying glass held over the picture showed that sure enough one
button was missing on the shoe. Well, the short of it is the man stopped
quibbling and paid the price I'd asked.

Mari Tomasi

# Michael Donegal[*]

*Michael Donegal and his wife, Mary, left Aberdeen around the turn of the century partly because "Mary was part Irish and her family had no wish to see her married to such as me."*

I learned the stonecutting trade in Scotland when I was in my teens. But Mary and I was both of a mind to get away to a new country and from America came letters telling of this great country with all its jobs. They said a carver like myself would make a fortune in no time over here. Well, whether I believed it or not, over we came.

Barre was swarming with stonecutters from Italy, Spain, Scotland, and Ireland. It was a wild, unsettled time, and many rough men came to work on the granite. Some sent back home for their families and settled down here, steady and good. Others had no thought of settling down, but came only for the big money, the drinking, the good times. The people born here blamed us all for what the bad ones did. But we had our trade to work at, our steady money coming in, our own countrymen and friends. So we did not mind it so much. And it changed as time went on. People mingled more and became friends.

I was a fair enough carver, so they say. But I was never with the best of them. The best ones came from Italy. No better workmen maybe, but with more of the artist in them, more of the inspiration. Like the old-time sculptors, they were. One of the finest, a slim fair Italian, a statue cutter—he died at thirty, or younger. He had beauty in himself; he could put it into the stone. All of the best ones are gone now. The last real one, the best one left, had to stop working a time ago. They do everything by machines now. It still needs workmen of skill, but not the artists. They are gone, once and for all.

It's the way things change, that is all. Everything changes the same way. Machines take the place of men, and men go without work, and hungry. That is the curse of the world today—the machines, and everywhere men out of work. That makes for unhappiness and misery and trouble. Take away a man's job and you kill the man. Maybe the dust killed them, but being without work kills them inside—a worse way.

Roaldus Richmond

---

[*] Fictitious name.

# Anthony Tonelli*

*Anthony Tonelli learned the trade of stonecutting in Viggiu, Italy. Silicosis was not an occupational hazard there because the stonecutters worked on marble—softer than granite—in open-air sheds. Tonelli expected to send all his children to college. "At least that will take them away from the sheds," he said, "and after they get out of college they won't want to work with granite. I have planned that."*

The life of a stonecutter is fifty years. No more. Every one of them, they all die in their fifties, they are through before that. I am near fifty. I die soon. I expect it. You got to expect it when you work with granite. You can get up any morning and go to work and say to yourself, "I am going to die very soon"; when you see your kids, you can say, "Yes, I am going to leave them soon." And other people are saying, "I am going to retire because I am in my fifties and I want to enjoy life a little," but you say, "I can not retire. I am in the granite business and it will retire me." But I hate like hell to leave my family when I am fifty. Just beginning to live. No children of mine will ever go into the granite sheds. Too much dust. I want them to have fresh air, and good jobs. I don't care what they do, so long as they keep away from the dust of granite.

I have seen big, strong, healthy men come to work. They have laughing eyes, they show they love life, they enjoy themselves. They are good workers. They have strength and knowledge of the job. Skill. And they don't last long. And this keeps up for many years. People grumble. The grumble increases. People lose their heads. I see children with tears in their eyes as they follow the casket to the grave. The big strong men do not last long against stone dust. They die and people cry and the family starves for a while, but all the time I keep saying, "The problem will be solved, this dust will end in the sheds," and they say, "You are a fool, dust will stay here forever, you can't end dust." I laugh now. It is coming to an end but nobody says to me, "You are smart, you tell us years ago that dust problem, this silicosis will be over with." No, I am not smart. I think a lot. I see improvements in every line.

I say the scientists are brilliant. They study when we are not thinking of them. They solve disease when it has killed millions, and

* Fictitious name.

they make autos and they get better every year. Look at the children. They get better care. Doctors know more. Why wouldn't they end this big problem of ours? It has caused a lot of suffering. Everybody in the granite business has been sad because of dust, deaths in all families, but now it is near the end. You will see men work longer in the sheds. They will not grow old so fast.

I have gone to work in the morning and after a little while in the shed I couldn't recognize my own body. It was covered from head to foot with dust. Of course we have to breathe that dust in. That is what does it. We give our whole strength, our hearing, our hands, our sight, the eyes, everything we possess to the business. We give our lives, our family, we give everything we have and love, and then what do we get out of it? Just a little money. Granite cutters have always been under-paid. You can't get around it. You go in there and die young. Do you see any of them rich?

You want to know what I do? I am a letterer. I have responsibility. If I cut one little piece from a stone, just when it is nearing completion, that spoils the whole works. It is all destroyed. And I get the gate. I can't take any chances getting drunk with all that at stake. It takes everything I got, everything. After a day in the sheds I am no good for anything, or for anybody. I guess most men wouldn't like it. You got to be strong. How many men can stand it? By the time you become good at your trade, you are ready to die.

John Lynch

# Frank Cardini*

*During Prohibition, according to Roaldus Richmond, Barre was known for bootleggers like Frank Cardini, who ran whiskey from Canada into the United States.*

Only suckers work for a living. I know because I tried it. I worked in the stone sheds. My brother Dante is still in there. I tell him he's fish but he don't listen. The poor bastard can't help it anyway. He's married and got a family. He figures he's got to stay in the sheds. I guess maybe

* Fictitious name.

he has got to. He shoulda known more than to get married in the first place. Only suckers get married.

I was a lumper for a while. You have to chain the blocks so they can be moved. You got to be goddamn careful with them chains or somebody gets hurt. If them chains slip it's too bad. I seen a guy lose a leg one day. A pal of mine, Sierra, was killed the summer after he got out of high school, working in his old man's shed. He was a swell ball player, a swell guy. He was going to college that fall if that stone hadn't clipped him. They was loading a truck when it fell. It crushed all the lower part of him from the waist down. The hell of it was it didn't put him out right away; he was conscious while they was getting that block off him. I'm glad I wasn't the guy that chained that stone.

I wasn't cut out to work steady. What the hell is seven, eight bucks a day? Chickenfeed. I could make more chips shooting craps and playing poker. I quit one day. The night before, I made about ninety bucks shooting craps. I was up all night and I didn't feel much like working that day. The boss started riding me in the yard. I don't take that stuff from anybody. Especially not when I got ninety bucks in my pocket. The boss told me to hurry it up and I just looked at him. A guy had a match out lighting a cigarette. I took a dollar bill outa my pocket, lit it from the match, lit my cigarette with it. The boss went crazy. I took a long time doing it, see? The boss said, "You're fired, Cardini. Get your time and get out." I laughed at him. I told him: "You can't fire me, you prick! I quit already." So I walked out and I never went back.

That was during Prohibition, and all the boys was running booze. My brothers, the older ones, had a gang bootlegging. They had a bunch of big old Packards and Caddies. There was dough in that racket all right, and it was fun to bring it in. Times was good then, everybody had money, everybody was spending it. This always was a good spending town. You know how stonecutters are, they're all spenders and they all drink. Granite was going good then and there was plenty gold in Barre.

We ran mostly ale. We got it in Canada for five bucks a case and sold it here for fifteen or twenty. You could load a lot of ale into those big crates we had. We kept five or six cars on the road at the time. We sold everybody in Barre and Montpelier from the poolroom crowd to the town big shots. We was sitting pretty them days. Now things aren't so hot here. After Repeal we tried running alcohol into Canada but it wasn't so good, and if you get caught up there you never get out of the can. Right now all I do is run a poker game and sell a little beer. No money in beer, but the game pays me pretty good. I get a drag on every pot, sure, and I win plenty of pots myself. I got a nice place here, and a blond to keep house for me. I've settled down but I ain't married. Only suckers get married. We got a bad name in this town but it don't make no difference. We're getting by all right. We always got along on our own; we always will. I been flat, I been down-and-out, but I always came back. Nobody helped me neither. I came back myself. And I'll always come back like that. The sonsabitches can't keep me down.

I'm doing all right. I got a new Ford sedan and it's paid for. If I want to make a run to Montreal or New York I can do it. I make enough to get by on, but it don't come easy no more.

Roaldus Richmond

# Angelo Bertacci*

*The pride of Barre was a statue of the poet Robert Burns presented to the town by the Scots in 1899. The monument was executed by a pair of Italian carvers whose artistry was legendary. As Angelo Bertacci recounted, one of these men, Elia Corti, was later accidentally shot when a fight broke out between Socialists and Anarchists at a public meeting.*

Rhind from Edinburgh designed that monument. He felt bad not to get the contract to carve it, too. He died without seeing the finished piece. The two men who carved it I knew well. Elia Corti did the carving on those panels in the base. Delicate carving, it is. Beautiful. But you got to go close to see how beautiful. They are scenes from Burns's poetry. His business partner, Sam Novelli, carved the statue. Great carvers, those two.

Corti I knew well. We were friends. He came in my store a lot. Just a small, thin fellow. People talk more about him now than when he was alive. That fellow Garetto who shot him got ten to twelve years hard labor at Windsor, but I don't think he stayed that long. He came back to Barre and went to work. He never made trouble again. I knew Garetto, too. I think he never meant to shoot Corti. He had no reason.

* Fictitious name.

Only thing is—Garetto carried a pistol, he got excited, and he shot. Hot-head stuff. Crazy for a minute and sorry all the times after. A few years ago he and his wife went back to Italy.

My friend Corti was born in a little town near Milan, Italy. He learned the carving trade there. Some say he studied at the *Reale Accademia*, some say no. Anyway, he was a fine carver when he came to America in 1890. He got married and had three children. He became a junior partner in a granite statuary firm.

The trouble was an old feud between the Socialists and Anarchists, that started when the Socialists built a block on Granite Street for their meetings. Garetto was a Socialist. A man named Serrati owned a Socialist newspaper—*Il Proletario*—in New York; he called the Anarchists some bad names. Anyway, one Saturday night in 1903, Serrati was coming to give a speech in this Socialist building. It was advertised for every laboring man to come. He didn't get there at seven o'clock sharp, so some of the men they began to holler and yell. The excitement was at a mad point. Then Garetto pulled out a gun, a .32. The men told him to stop. Corti was standing by the door, not yelling, not even talking, they say. Anyway, Garetto fired two shots. One hit Corti in the stomach. The men threw Garetto down the stairs. He ran to the judge's office for protection. The police got him there.

At half past ten that night they brought Corti to the Montpelier hospital in an ambulance and the police took Garetto in front of Corti. Corti said: "That's the man." He said it twice, and Sam Novelli, Corti's partner, got mad and made a grab for Garetto. Chief Brown had to hold Novelli from taking his own revolver and using it on Garetto.

Three doctors helped with the operation on Corti, but no good. The doctors couldn't find the bullet and Corti died at midnight. Only thirty-four years old.

Corti was buried next day. When he was dying he gave orders for his funeral. He said he wanted to be buried right away, and he didn't want a band at his funeral. The funeral was held from his home. I remember the street outside was filled with Barre people. Not only his friends—Anarchists, Socialists, everybody. The monument they set up over Corti's grave gets more notice today than any other one in Hope Cemetery. It is a statue of Corti, carved by his brother. He looks alive. Everything is perfect—bow tie, the buttons on his shoes, the wrinkles in his suit. Beside him, carved from granite too, are his stoneworking tools. With a stone like that, Corti will not be forgotten! If he could see it he'd be proud of his brother for cutting such a piece.

John Lynch

# THE STRIKE

*Labor troubles were very much on the minds of Barre residents. In the three interviews that follow, the widow of a granite cutter, a rank-and-file union militant, and the grande dame of Barre each spoke of "the big strike" of 1922. During the early months of the strike, quarry owners brought in hundreds of poor French-Canadian farmers as strike-breakers. They were paraded up Main Street to the music of bands and fed free Sunday dinners of chicken and ice cream. Eventually the quarry owners succeeded in breaking the strike and it took the unions\* of Barre years to recover.*

## Mrs. Lachance

I don't know much about the big strike. My husband struck along with the rest of them. I used to hear him talk about it a lot, but you hear so little about it now that I've forgotten. I *do* remember my husband saying that some of the unskilled French who came in to break the strike could be excused. That was quite a statement from my husband; he was as much against them as anybody. One of those strike-breakers was a friend of his. They'd grown up together in Chambly, good friends. He hadn't seen or heard from him for years, then all of a sudden he sees him parading through town with the rest of them. My husband was dazed; he could hardly believe it. This friend, Pete was his name, came up to the house to see my husband the next day. His farm, like so many other French farms that year, wasn't paying. The crops amounted to nothing. He had a wife and three children to feed. He could see no signs of work for him in Chambly. Then this opportunity for work in Barre came to him. Work meant keeping his family together.

Can you blame him for accepting it? I don't. He'd never worked in granite. He'd heard, of course, of Barre and the granite workers. But he knew of them vaguely, just as he knew of miners and steelworkers. I mean, how hard the work was, and dangerous. But he had to be amongst the workers, live with them and do their work, before he could

---

\* The quarriers were represented by the Quarry Workers International Union; the finishers were members of the Granite Cutters International Association.

really appreciate the fact that they needed a strike to better their conditions. I haven't seen much of him since my husband died. But I know he's a union man now, and a good one.

Mari Tomasi

# Manuel Terel

Of the some 150 non-union men in the Barre district, most of them are French. I ought to know. A bunch of squawkers and suckers. They've come up to me and pulled their sob story. "Look," they complain, "my work is as good as So-and-so's. He gets his eight-fifty a day, I get only five dollars. I'm worth as much as he is. I put in just as much time. You've got to help me. What can I do about it?" I should tell them to go to hell. I should say: "You were satisfied to sneak up to some shed boss behind the union's back and beg your miserable five or six dollars a day. You've got no right to bellyache now. Get out." I *should* tell them that. But the union has rules. I have to stick to them. O.K., I tell them, you've been working for five dollars a day for a year, huh? O.K. then, pay up the union dues for that period and you'll get your union wages.

Those French spoiled everything for us back in '22. We'd have a lot more today if it hadn't been for those strike-breaking rats. Farmers, bakers, anyone who had hands to work with. Some of em had never seen granite, I bet.

You know what we should have done? We should have massed together, all of us, down at the Montpelier railroad station, and the Barre station. We should have met them at the train. Warned them to keep out. We'd have kept them out. It wouldn't have come to a good fight. They're too yellow for that. But the union wasn't so strong then, it wasn't what it is today. Today it would be easy.

Mari Tomasi

# Miss Wheaton*

Living quietly here as I do, I know little of labor troubles and less of the granite industry.

I remember little of the strike of '22. I often sit by the window, and I did those days, but I remember no parade and no militia. There was a feeling of oppression in the air, and I felt that plans were being laid in secret. Plans that we outside the granite industry knew nothing of. I saw clusters of men, groups of them hurrying along the street on their way to various halls where they held meetings. Their voices were loud and harsh, raised in anger. They waved their arms and shook their fists. It was all very disturbing. My mother was alive then. Just she, and the housekeeper and myself in the house. The strike made no disorder or confusion in our tenor of living. Not during the day. At night we heard the tramp-tramp of feet on the pavement outside the house. There was much shouting. Cars kept roaring by, going I don't know where. In spite of locked doors and windows, I found it all very disconcerting. I had no inclination to sleep.

I remember vaguely of workers being injured during the strike, and of riots, but I have forgotten the details. I do know that the last granite strike caused a great deal of temporary poverty and need. One Barre charitable organization that I am acquainted with reported thirty new families added to their lists for temporary assistance. Most of the aid was in the form of food; a few families accepted clothing that had been contributed by various ladies of the organization.

It seems to me that if strikes in attaining their end must cause such need and injury, then certainly they are no solution to labor conditions. Perhaps the granite workers were justified in asking for more pay and less hours. It's hard work, and injurious to health. I know that many of these workers have good-sized families. I'm not well acquainted with them. I don't have to be to know that death from stonecutters' tuberculosis has struck members of several of these families. For about fifty years I have read the same pitiful stories repeated in the obituaries in the Barre *Daily Times*:

"Mr. A——, aged fifty, died today after an illness of several months. Since coming to this country he has been employed as stonecutter in the

* Fictitious name.

local sheds. He was a member of the Granite Cutters' Union. Surviving him are his wife, three sons, and a daughter."

Mari Tomasi

# Birnie Bruce

*Birnie Bruce was secretary of the Barre Guild, an association of granite manufacturers, which mediated labor disputes and certified the quality of a Barre monument.*

The workers have had their troubles. I've lived through most of Barre's labor troubles, and I know that although there were agitators and ill-advised stonecutters, they were not the basic causes of the strike. The causes went deeper. We were slowly emerging from the long working day. Men wanted more time with their families. They were no longer content to enjoy the bare necessities of life. But mostly they wanted the elimination of dust. That was always a sore spot. I don't blame them. My father, brother, and three uncles all died from stonecutters' t.b. When I started in this business we had a ten-hour working day. Now it's eight.

The introduction of the pneumatic tool gave rise to the first real attempt to combat silicosis. On fine work the men stooped over a stone; the dust was inhaled in the lungs. The pneumatic tools caused more deaths than the hand ones because they cut stone so fast there was more dust in the air. After discussions and heated arguments it became compulsory to have large dust-removing machines in every shed. And in 1938 it was made compulsory for individual cutters to have smaller suction attachments. There's no reason now why granite cutters shouldn't be as healthy as carpenters.

In the old days we had no such thing as pneumatic tools. Now both quarries and sheds have compressed-air machines. Granite cutters had to be skilled: one twist of the wrist and an entire stone was spoiled. They were so skilled they could take a rough draft and from that chisel a monument with every detail of line perfect. They envisioned the entire monument from some rough sketch.

Now lettering and ornamentation are done by sandblast, and large saws do the surface cutting. I can remember years ago when only one block would be cut at one time in the quarries; now twenty or thirty are cut at the same time. Machinery has displaced many workers. We claim that the granite industry is, if not the oldest, at least one of the oldest in civilization. I know it's a shame to have machinery displace so many men engaged in this ancient industry, but machines work fast and cheap, and we have to fill the demand for stone.

Mari Tomasi

# THREE WIDOWS

*In one Barre neighborhood where silicosis had claimed many there was a street known as la strada delle vedove—the street of widows. The women of Barre gained a measure of autonomy in widowhood although they had to struggle to survive—by taking in boarders, by selling liquor. Federal Writer Roaldus Richmond remembers the granite workers' widows as "some of the nicest women I've ever met. They brought up nice families and somehow a lot of the kids managed to get educated and get good jobs. But if they did sell booze, they were looked down upon by the community."*

## Mrs. Anselmi

Edo never cut stone until we came to this country. He learned it in Barre. We had happy times. I wasn't afraid then. Edo wasn't afraid either. If he was, he never showed it. None of the men do—unless sometime when they're drinking, and then only joking about it. But the women know. We see it coming—the change. It begins to show in a man's face—in his eyes. Sometimes the smell of granite dust on Edo's clothes would make me want to cry—but not when he could see me. Edo was a gay, laughing man, tall and strong. He could sing too, he had a fine voice. And he was handsome, a blond.

His first job was with the Giordi Brothers. Only eight men worked with him. The shed was originally the barn of the Giordi house. Many successful sheds started like that, in a small way. The owners worked, too. They were skilled workers who wanted to be their own bosses. It gave us a good living. We always had that. Edo left me money. I don't know how long it will last—if it doesn't last I can go to work. I'm still young enough. I can cook or even wait on tables. I wouldn't like it, but I'd do it. I'd feel better probably if I had something to do and less time to think.

Now I don't do much. I have a few good friends. They are widows too, some of them. We talk, play cards, sometimes we go out to eat or see a movie, or just to walk when it's nice weather. The ones with children—perhaps they sell a little liquor—but only to people they know, decent people. And they're decent themselves—not like the girls today, always out with a different man every night. I've had a long time now to watch things—to see the change. You're too busy with your own life when you're young to notice others. Everything is yours around you, and your people, the ones you love. Later, your blood slows down and you have time to sit and watch. Sometimes you don't like much what you see. Maybe it's just the difference in age. The people were the same way before, only you didn't notice. I like to just sit here by the window and watch people and cars. I don't feel all by myself—not ever. Some way it seems he is always with me. I guess we had something most folks miss.

His last summer, Edo used to sit on the side porch, in the sun, and watch his friends stop in there for wine or beer after work. They'd call out to him. And sometimes, afterwards, they'd come over full of the news and politics they had talked about over their drinks. If there weren't too many of them I'd make wine or brandy eggnogs—it was the only way Edo would take raw eggs. They never spoke of sickness. I remember the last afternoon he sat in the sun. It was late May. He was looking at the early onion tops that were showing in neighbor Tosi's vegetable garden, and he said, "Remember, Elsa, it was May when we left Brescia. May fifteenth. And over there the potato sprouts were already pushing through the earth. Here the green comes later. . . ."

He was only thirty-two when he died. So very young, and the gray was already in his hair. But his life had been a full one, a hard one. Everything he did was that way. All of himself he put into it, whether it was working or having a good time. He was that kind of a man. I don't mind talking about him. I think he should be in a book. If I could write, I'd put him in a book myself. A whole book about him.

Roaldus Richmond

# Mrs. McCarthy

I was born here in Vermont, but John, my husband, came over from Ireland. He was already owner of the shed when I met and married him. People said he had a fine future; he was a good workman himself and he understood the business thoroughly. He was a hardworking, sober young man in those days. We were happy. He talked granite day and night, but I didn't mind. It was good to see him so interested in the business. It all changed when his uncle died. He and John were very close friends. He had been in Barre only five years when his lungs went bad. His sickness was a blow to John. It seemed to loose some devil in him. He began to drink heavily. Pretty soon it was every day. It wasn't unusual to see a couple of his workmen half-carrying him home after the shed closed for the day.

Of course, business suffered. I tried to talk to him. I told him I understood the friendship between him and his uncle, but nothing could bring him back. He had to think of the living. He had to think of his wife and his three children. He wouldn't listen. When one of his employees, a good friend of his, was forced to leave work, too, because of his lungs, it was more than John could bear. He drank more than ever. I suggested putting a manager in the shed. He wouldn't hear of it. Business became so bad that we had to borrow money on the house to put into the shed. We borrowed twice.

I loved this home. We'd bought it from the people who built it. I liked the privacy of this house. But a seventeen-room house for five people was a burden in those times when little money was coming in. It could be an asset. I saw my duty even though it was a painful one, and I did it. John was so deep in liquor he never even raised a finger to stop me. I went up to the shed one afternoon and talked to every one of the unmarried men. I explained the situation to them, though God knows they must have known it, and told them I would be glad to have any of them as roomers. They were good men, and they were eager to help. By the end of the next week six more were rooming at the house— three Irish, two Scotch, and one Italian. The extra money was a godsend. I went further. I boarded those men. It was hard work even with a maid, but it was worth it.

I had hoped that my willingness to cooperate and my example would straighten John. It didn't. He let go completely. He didn't die of stonecutters' t.b.; it was drinking that killed him. But I can't help feeling that the granite industry which had taken his uncle and his friend was indirectly responsible.

After his death, one of John's best workmen assured me that under his management the shed could again be operated on a paying basis. He was a sober-minded man and trustworthy, but I'd had enough of the granite industry. I felt it had robbed me of a husband, and the children of a father. I was eager to sever all association with it. I sold the shed, and paid back part of the money we'd borrowed on the house.

I kept the roomers. The children were growing, and I wanted to give them a good education. Neither of the boys lives in Vermont now.

One became an electrical engineer, the other a doctor. They have both done well. My daughter married a local merchant.

There are eight of us in this house now. Five grandchildren, my daughter and son-in-law, and myself. The children are grown. The oldest girl graduated from college last year; the youngest boy will finish high school next year. The three grandsons know that their grandfather was in the granite business. They don't seem to be interested in it. I'm glad of that. I seldom speak to them of those past years.

Mari Tomasi

# Mrs. Gerbati

I wasn't afraid until [my husband's] coughing started and kept getting worse. One day I said it was too bad we didn't have a son. My mother said at least the girls wouldn't have to cut stone. And Rodrigo nodded his head after thinking a long way off, and he said: "That is right." Then I knew.

I thought that big strike might save him, you know. That was 1921 or '22. Rodrigo didn't go back to work after that. But it was too late. I think he got hurt too one night when they had a fight. He never told me anything about it, but he came home that night with marks on his face and hands and his clothes torn. After that he seemed worse, the cough was worse, and the life had gone out of him; he wasn't the same man.

The girls were still young when he went, just babies really, not old enough to understand. We had this house all paid for and a little money left, not much. I was still young myself. I could have married again. But I didn't want to. There was no other man for me, I guess. The *Nonna* [grandmother] used to tell me to take another man. She said, "Don't be a fool, you're young and pretty and healthy, you got two girls to bring up. Don't be a fool and waste your life. Your blood is still warm and there is room in a young heart for another man." But I didn't want one. After him there *wasn't* one, that's all. So I never married.

But I had to do something. The money was running out, the girls needed more things as they got older, there was taxes to pay and all that. I had to do something. My mother didn't like it when first I took stonecutters in to room and board. She said it was disgraceful. Then when I started selling liquor she almost died. She said she'd rather die than see that. Now she don't care anymore about anything, she's too old.

At first I just sold to the men who stayed here, you see. Just a few drinks with their meals, you know, maybe a few in the evening. Then they started bringing in a few friends for drinks. It was all quiet and decent. They were good men, some of them had worked with Rodrigo, been his friends. They were good to the girls, to all of us. But naturally more and more kept coming, you know how it is. Their friends brought other friends and I sold more drinks. Pretty quick it got to be quite a business.

They came for Italian food too, parties that order in advance. I am a good cook if I do say it. Everybody knows my cooking. Some say my ravioli and spaghetti is the best in Barre, and they rave about my minestrone and my antipasto. But it's not been too easy; it has made a lot of hard work for me. Anyway it keeps me from thinking too much about—things.

I am not ashamed of it. I have worked hard and always kept a respectable place. It was something I had to do and I'd do it again. I am not ashamed of it one bit. You say I shouldn't be, I should be proud of it? Well, I guess maybe I am, maybe I am proud of it. I didn't like to say it myself but I am proud.

Roaldus Richmond

# Henry Erikson*

*Henry Erikson's farmstead was on the other side of the hill from the great piles of waste granite and deep quarries of Barre.*

They can have their granite. I'll take the good clean dirt for me. I've known a lot of granite workers of course. I used to know all the old-timers and they was good men. I don't know so many now, but the ones I knew I liked. Maybe they lived faster'n a farmer does. They have to, by God, because they don't last so long. I never blamed em for carrying on the way they did. They was good-hearted fellers, good fellers to talk to. They might raise hell but it wasn't out of meanness. The work they

---

* Fictitious name.

do, the life they lead, a man's got to have some way to let go and get away from it.

My life has been spent right here on this farm, put right into these fields. I used to get envious hearin some of them quarriers talkin about the places they'd been, the things they'd done and seen. I was young then. Now I figger it don't make much difference. Most of them fellers are dead and gone. They had a lot I didn't have—and I got a lot they never had, too.

Me—I like the farm and I like farmin. I like to be round the animals and see things growin. To me that's beautiful. It ain't cold like stone. It's warm and fresh and ripe. It's what I raised myself, and it's what I like to look at.

They say granite made this place what it is and prob'ly it did. But where'd they be without the farmers? Where'd anyplace be without farmers? People can get along without tombstones, but they can't get along without food, they can't get along without potatoes, eggs, milk, butter, bread, vegetables. You can't eat granite.

Roaldus Richmond

# RANK
# AND FILE

# Irving Fajans

*Irving Fajans sold merchandise behind the counters of Orbach's, May's, Woolworth's, Grand's, and Macy's. An organizer for the Department Store Employees Union local 1250 in New York, Fajans participated in many strikes, including the famous 1937 Grand sit-down strike. Federal Writer May Swenson met Fajans through the union. Now a poet and playwright, Swenson recalls taking copious notes during interviews in order to make a verbatim record.\**

When you first get a job at Macy's, they start you in the stock room. I was two years out of high school when I got on there and I worked for Macy's five years. Not all the time in stock—I did some selling on the floor too, and I worked in the tube room, where they make change. You're lucky if you get out of stock. Some guys have been there twenty, twenty-five years. They learn one routine job in one department, and then even if they move on to other houses, they'll be placed on the same job because of experience. A few of them get into other departments if the boss figures they got something on the ball—which isn't often.

All Macy's employees have to take intelligence tests before they're hired; the same thing goes for most of the larger houses. Funny thing about those tests, they don't hire you if your average is too high—not to start anyway. If your quotient runs between ninety and one-hundred-ten, you'll get by easier. They figure if a worker's too smart, he's liable to get a notion he doesn't like the way things are done and maybe start the others to getting dissatisfied, too. On the other hand, if he's too dumb, he can't handle the job. So don't be too smart or too dumb.

In Macy's the stock takes up eight floors and they have a warehouse a whole block square. The merchandise comes in on trucks, is unloaded

* Interview with May Swenson, December 1977. Her most recent book is *New and Selected Things Taking Place* (Boston, 1979).

on the receiving platform, and then sent to the stock rooms. Then the checkers look it over, mark down the quantity, and report any damages. After that, it's priced—price tags, pin tickets, gum labels, or string labels put on—then it's sent to the reserve. The reserve room is just long aisles of shelves, where the pickers and distributors classify the stock. When the merchandise is ordered from the selling floor, it's either sent down the chutes or taken down on small floor trucks, or "wheelers." They use mostly women for markers and examiners, that is to examine the stock for flaws and for marking the quantity. The pickers and distributors and truckers are all men. It's one hell of a job sometimes to keep up with the orders from the floor. You've got to run along the shelves, grab the order, and load the trucks or shove it down the chute. Lots of times it'll be a "Customer Waiting" order, and that means hurry it up. They ought to put the guys on roller skates; maybe then they'd get the right kind of speed out of them.

There's a supervisor to each floor, who's generally snooping around hoping to catch you loafing on the job. Mostly the workers call them "supers"; when I was there, we called them "snoopers." One super we had was a tough guy. He had a voice like a dog's bite and he was proud of the way he could lash speed out of the boys picking stock. One Christmas, we all chipped in and bought him a horse whip, one of those old-fashioned ones. He must have caught on to the idea O.K. because he came back after the holidays with a pretty sour face, and gave us tougher treatment than before.

Working conditions are much better in Macy's now than when I used to work there. The place has been fairly well unionized. When I first started there, they were just beginning to try to organize, and everything pertaining to the union had to be on the q.t. If you were caught distributing leaflets or other union literature around the job you were instantly fired. We thought up ways of passing leaflets without the boss being able to pin anybody down. Sometimes we'd insert the leaflets into the sales ledgers after closing time. In the morning every clerk would find a pink sheet saying: "Good morning, how's everything . . . and how about coming to union meeting tonight?" or something like that. We swiped the key to the toilet-paper dispenser in the washroom, took out the paper, and substituted printed slips of just the right size! We got a lot of new members that way—it appealed to their sense of humor. We also used to toss a bunch of leaflets down the store chutes with the merchandise when the super had his back turned. They'd all scatter on the receiving end, and the clerks would pick them up when they handled the stock. The floorwalker might see those pink sheets all over the place and get sore as hell—but what could he do? No way of telling who did it.

The management had refused to negotiate with our committee, and the workers voted for a sit-in to demand shorter hours and better working conditions. The whistles were blown in every Grand store in New York at eleven-thirty a.m. on March 14th. The workers finished their sales and folded their arms, refusing to wait on any more customers. Practically a hundred percent of the workers joined us, and most of the stores immediately closed their doors. We were prepared to stay a month if necessary.

We had cots brought in and blankets, electric burners for coffee, and plenty of eats. There was food and other things we might have used in the store, but none of our people touched any sort of merchandise during the strike. It was pretty cold, being early spring, so we had to huddle together at night. There were some canary cages in the store, and we kept the birds fed; they'd wake us up every morning. We had games like checkers and cards, and we had a radio and danced to the music.

Two engagements were announced during the time we sat in. We even held a marriage ceremony there for a couple who decided to get married during the strike: the girls dressed up the bride; we sent for a priest and he married them. The strike held out over Easter week and since some of our people were Italians and Irish Catholics, we held Easter services for them in the store.

Nobody left the store for eleven days except the committee to contact the management. The girls held out just as well as the fellows, and everyone tried to be gay and have as good a time as possible. Luckily, no one in our store got sick during the strike. The management finally heard our committee and met our demands—largely as a result of the publicity our sit-down had gotten all over the country.

During the Ohrbach's strike a couple of years ago, two salesgirls pulled a neat stunt. Mr. Ohrbach, who is supposed to be a big philanthropist, spoke at a dinner held for him at the Hotel Astor. While he was spouting about some of these public charity funds, two girls who had crashed the dinner in borrowed evening gowns climbed up on the balcony and chained themselves to the railing. Nobody noticed them, and suddenly they began shouting in the middle of Ohrbach's speech: "Charity begins at home! Give your employees shorter hours and better pay!" Of course, there was a big hubbub, and the girls were arrested. But the papers carried a big story, and the boss had to grant our demands to appease public opinion.

May Swenson
New York City
1939

# Evelyn Macon

*In a 1937 organizing drive the United Laundry Workers enrolled nearly fourteen thousand new members, including Evelyn Macon, in its New York City locals. A CIO union affiliated with the Amalgamated Clothing Workers of America, the United Laundry Workers negotiated contracts for a five-day week and a thirty-five-cent minimum wage.*

Conditions in the laundry where I work are a hundred times better than they were two years ago, and they're still far from ideal.

I worked as a press operator before we unionized. *Slavery* is the only word that could describe the conditions under which we worked. At least fifty-four hours a week it was speed up, speed up, eating lunch on the fly, perspiration dropping from every pore, for almost ten hours per day. When I reached home sometimes I was too tired to prepare supper. I would flop across the bed and sleep two or three hours, then get up and cook and then fall back into bed immediately after eating—you know how unhealthy that was.

The toilet at our place wasn't fit for animals, much less people, and there was but the one for men and women. When I complained, the boss said, "There ain't many places paying ten dollars a week now, Evie." That ended my protests, because I didn't want to get fired.

The girls who worked in the starching department used to sing spirituals to enable them to breathe standing ten hours and sticking their hands into almost-boiling starch—it's so hot they have to put camphor ice on their hands before they can put them into the starch.

*Laundry workers on strike in front of their Brooklyn, N.Y., work place.*

They used to sing, "Go Down Moses," and "Down by the Riverside," and God, the feeling they used to put in their singing. As tired as we were, those spirituals lifted up our spirits and we joined in sometimes. The boss said that was too much pleasure to have while working for his money, and the singing was cut out. But that was where the boss made his mistake. While singing we would forget our miserable lot, but after the singing was cut out, it gave us more time for thinking about our problems.

One day a fellow got a job at our place as a sorter. We didn't think he would be there long because he certainly did not speed up like the rest of us. The boss told him he would have to work faster. He laughed at the boss and told him that a man was a damn fool to rush during the first hour when he had seventeen more staring him in the face. I guess the boss felt like firing him but he was a giant of a man and as strong as an ox, so he let him slide. But the boss hit the ceiling when lunch hour came. He came out and yelled, "On the fly," which meant for us not to stop for lunch, but to eat while we worked, as there was a rush.

"Bruiser," the new fellow, picked up his lunch and went out. The boss raved and cussed, almost tearing his hair out, because Bruiser had caused work to slow down. In exactly one hour Bruiser was back. The boss charged up to him demanding, "What the hell do you mean by going out to lunch during a rush?" Bruiser laughed at him and said he always ate his meals on time. We were sorry to see him go, but the boss paid him and fired him.

That night when I got off and reached the outside, Bruiser came up to me smiling. The face seemed familiar but I walked faster thinking he was trying to flirt with me. Then I recognized him. He said his main objective in getting a job in our shop was to see the lousy conditions in our place. He said he was a CIO organizer and he gave me a leaflet stating that he was trying to unionize our shop and that there was to be a meeting the following night. As disgusted as I was with my lot, I don't have to tell you that I was the first one to reach the meeting. Almost everybody was there for the meeting; within six months everybody had joined with the exception of one girl. She wouldn't join, and when we persistently tried to recruit her she told the boss.

The boss was frantic. First he tried to intimidate, then he offered to start his own union "with the same stipulations" in our CIO contract, but we were not to be tricked by promises. We held our ground. He fired some of us and the rest walked out. We threw a picket line round the place. We had the one scab and the boss imported others, protecting them by sending them to and from work in cabs. They messed up so that the boss called us back to work at union hours, union wages, and better conditions.

Vivian Morris
*New York City*
1939

# Eva Hardison

*After Eva Hardison's husband lost his job as a box-car carpenter following a strike, the family moved to Wilmington, North Carolina, where Otis Hardison found work in a mill. He joined the United Textile Workers Union and participated in the national strike of 1934, which ended in a crushing defeat for the union. Although President Roosevelt urged the textile mills to take back strikers, many firms refused and evicted workers like Otis Hardison from company housing.*

I was so happy, watching our house go up. Papa had always said he hoped all of his children would live in homes of their own. We had it all paid for when the union called a strike. Otis was loyal to his union and he wouldn't go back to work until he got orders from the union. When he did go back, the railroad wouldn't have him and he couldn't get anything else to do. Finally we had to mortgage the home to get food. That was the last of our little place for us. It was a whole year before Otis got regular work and it was too late then to start saving money for the mortgage even if he had been making enough so we could.

Otis got work in a cotton mill in Wilmington. In a year or two he had worked up to eighteen dollars a week. The thought of losing our home had got to where it didn't hurt so bad and we were taking great pride in our children. The oldest boy had finished the tenth grade and he said there wasn't anything that could keep him from finishing high school. The next to the oldest one was in the ninth grade and everybody said he had a good chance of being one of the best football players in school. Jim, the oldest one, was always planning ways he could help himself. When school was out we managed to get him in a CCC camp* and I was to save the twenty-five dollars a month he sent home so that he could have things like other boys during his senior year.

Then the strike was called, and Otis, who'd joined the textile union, walked out with the other strikers. The company opened the mill and sent out word for all the help to come back, but it hadn't given the workers any of the things they'd struck tor. The union told its members to hold out and they'd win in the end. Otis waited while, one by one, folks gave in and went back to work. One morning he came to me and said, "I can't hold out no longer. We don't have a place to mortgage this time and I'm not going to stand by and see my family starve." I looked at Otis and said, "No, you're not going back now, Otis. I didn't want you to join this union because I remembered what a strike had cost us. But you joined anyhow, and now you're not going back on the union when it needs you. I'd rather starve than see you turn yellow."

I kept Otis out and when the strike was called off he went to ask for his job back. His boss man looked at him right hard and said, "I'll let you know when we need you." The next day we got our moving orders. We moved to an awful little house in another part of town and there we stayed. School started, but Jim stayed on at the CCC camp. The twenty-five dollars a month he sent home was all me, Otis, and the other three boys had to live on. You couldn't imagine unless you'd been

---

* The Civilian Conservation Corps was a WPA relief program that established work camps for jobless men between 18 and 25.

through something like it yourself how we suffered that winter. We didn't have half enough to eat and no clothes at all. Day after day I had to sit and think of my boy in the CCC camp while his heart was set on finishing high school. And, Claude, the second one, wouldn't go to school because he didn't have decent clothes to wear. I thought I'd go crazy seeing him look so sullen and bitter, and thinking maybe he blamed me because I had persuaded his papa to stick by the union.

Until yet I don't know how we lived through that winter. The year wore on and Jim was still at the CCC camp. We sold our furniture, and with the money came to Durham looking for work. Moving some distance away was the only way a striker could get a job. Durham strikers went to Wilmington and Wilmington strikers came here. They didn't ask us here if we had been in the Wilmington strike, and if they had, we would have lied. Working people can't live without work, you know.

After all I've suffered from the union, I still believe that we've got to organize if we're ever going to get paid a decent wage. The first thing we've got to get is the right to organize. Some people think we have that now but it doesn't always work. Do you know what would happen to my husband at this mill if he so much as talked union amongst the workers? They'd put him on a new job he didn't know how to do and give him three times more work than he could do. In a day or two his boss man would say, "Guess I'll have to let you go since you can't keep up with your work."

Another thing that makes it hard on the union is the feeling folks hold against it who have been hurt by it. My two oldest boys are so bitter toward the union, they don't even like to hear the word mentioned. From what I've been able to understand in the papers, the government is doing all it can to give workers the right to organize, and I hope they'll be successful. I want to know for sure before Otis ever joins again. My life has been made hard by doing what seemed to be right and I don't want a threat hanging over me any longer. Me and Otis will live at the mill as long as we can get work, I guess, and I don't mind it at all. If he could get regular work and a good wage, I'd just as soon be here as anywhere else. But my boys hate it and I pray for the day when they'll be able to find something else to do.

Ida Lou Moore
*Durham, North Carolina*
*n.d.*

# Elmer Robinson

*Until the 1880s the work of assembling a shoe and nailing the leather to the sole was done by skilled hand-lasters like Elmer Robinson. Before his retirement, Robinson worked for many years as an organizer in Lynn, Massachusetts for the Lasters' Protective Union.*

In the early days, the Lasters' Protective Union had the industry sewed up. You just couldn't get work in Lynn unless you had a permit from the Lasters' Union. Lasters used to work in sort of a circle we called a rink. We had a collector in every rink who collected the dues on pay night. And if there was a non-union man working there, or one without a permit from the union, the boys would all knock off until he was let go.

The union held that kind of dictatorial power until the lasting machine came in. And if they hadn't voted to fight the machines they might have kept that power. If they weren't no good, then we wouldn't have lost nothing by voting for em. And if they did turn out to be practical, then we'd be the boys to run em. But the majority of the boys in the union felt we should fight em so I joined in. I always believed in majority rule. The old niggerhead* did prove practical, and because they fought their coming, many of the men lost out on the jobs of running em and scab labor was brought in from outside.

After a while, there was a scramble for them niggerhead jobs. Prices were set by the Labor Relations Board with ten dollars a day the most you could earn. That was good pay but some of the men connived to earn more by working beside a slow fellow who could only get out about forty dollars' worth of lasting a week. The smart fellow would do ten dollars' extra work that week and get the slow fellow to hand it in on his work card. Then he'd pay the fellow for the favor. There was all kinds of tricks to the shoemaking trade same as any other trade.

Anyone that would study the situation could see how the old Lasters' Protective Union was laying the groundwork for the industrial form of union that the CIO has today. The Lasters' was the only strong shoe union of that time, and it just about controlled the workers and manufacturers. We were known as the shock troops because we could tie up a factory with a strike. If all the lasters were out on strike, no one

---

* A shoe nailing machine, so named "because a man from Brazil invented it."

else could work for very long. We got so strong there for a time that anyone who wanted to work at any kind of work used to come to us for a work permit. But after the machines come, it was easy to shove in someone else at the niggerhead, and we gradually lost a lot of power. All the strikes that were called to fight the machine lost out in the end. But all the time, the leaders in the labor movement saw the need for strong unions. Soon after 1900 I set out to organize the girls in the shops, the stitchers. Most everyone said it just couldn't be done. But I did it all right. I called what was probably the first sit-down strike in America. In a large shop in Lynn where they put out between eight and ten thousand pairs of shoes a day, the manufacturer had agreed to raise the girls' wages and to date the raise back a few weeks. Well, he kept putting off paying that back pay part of the raise. I tried to get him to pay it every way I could, except call a strike. I didn't want to antagonize the manufacturer if I could help it, and if I called out all the girls in the shop an awful lot of workers would lose at least a couple of days' pay.

Finally I said to the girls, "When I give a signal in the morning, just stop work, and then I'll disappear." They did this, just sitting still at their machines. When the manufacturer saw this he started hunting around wild for me but I was under cover and couldn't be found. Long about eleven o'clock that morning, just two hours after the girls stopped work, I showed up at the factory. "When will you pay the girls?" I asked the manufacturer. He walked up to one of the bookkeepers and asked how much he owed them. When he was told, he turned to me and said, "I'll pay them now, if they start work." All I did was raise my hand, sort of like a salute to the girls. But they knew what I meant. Right away the machines begun to buzz again. So far as I know, that was the first sit-down strike in America. It never got in the papers. But we organizers used it two or three times on different manufacturers in Lynn. It worked every time.

From my experience in shoe union work, I always thought it took three different kinds of leaders: first the fellow to line up the union and get the members, the second one to whip the organization into shape and maybe call a strike, and the third fellow would be the negotiator to settle the strike. I often tried to work with someone else when we had a strike. There was one fellow in particular—oft times I would go in to see a manufacturer for him in settling a strike, if he didn't stand so well with the manufacturer himself. And he didn't show his face all the time I was carrying out his plans. He often did the same for me. There's absolutely no use trying to get somewhere with a manufacturer if he's turned against you. It's best to work under cover in such a case.

Union work is politics of a high order. You have to be a good diplomat to be a good union agent. Or else you're sure to be in hot water most of the time. The smartest union workers don't want notoriety. They work from behind the scenes.

Jane K. Leary
*Lynn, Massachusetts*
1939

# Mary Sweet

*Mary Sweet, a black presser, was turned away from the International Ladies Garment Workers Union in Boston in 1932, and she then refused to support the general dress-industry strike in 1933. Later on, though, the ILGWU—which was among the more integrated trade unions—hired her specifically to organize black garment workers in Boston.*

All workers, white or colored, are hard to organize. They're afraid for their jobs. With the Negro the fear is much greater; it's much harder for them to find jobs. And the union has been dumb in its attitude towards the Negro garment workers in Boston. You see, the important workers in the shops are the cutters and pressers. If you're going to organize a shop you got to get those two. Now, many of the colored girls are pressers and the union simply wouldn't take them in. They weren't prejudiced against our race. It was just that the men in the ILGWU here wanted to keep the pressing jobs for the men, and they kept the union from taking in women pressers. They'd take in the other colored workers, but they couldn't get them. You see, you couldn't tell the colored girls that it wasn't prejudice. I didn't believe that, but almost all of them did. Besides, it wouldn't do em much good to get the other girls if they wouldn't organize the pressers.

I lost my job because of the union. In 1933 we had a general strike in Boston. The ILGWU called out everybody, the union and non-union shops. My shop had about half union members. When the strikers came up to my shop to get the workers out, you should have seen the way the union members ducked. They hid under the tables and in the toilet.

They expected I'd go out, but I didn't. My foreman, who was a pretty good union member, said, "Mary, I'm surprised at you." And I said, "Well you wouldn't take me in the union so I'm independent and I'll do what I want. You gotta take me in before I'll strike." The boss asked if I was afraid and I said no. We had to sneak in and out through the back way. Near the end of the strike he hired thugs to protect us. They finally settled the strike. Our shop signed a union agreement and the women pressers had to get out. They gave us four months to find other jobs.

I loafed for a while and things were tough, real tough. Meanwhile the ILGWU got around to looking at the women pressers the same way that they did in New York and other places; besides, they felt that it was important to organize the colored garment workers of Boston. One day my old foreman came down to see me. He said, "I want you to come with me to talk to some officials of the ILGWU." We went to an Italian restaurant for dinner and they asked me to go to work for the ILGWU as an organizer. They wanted to organize the colored workers, and experience had shown them that it wouldn't be done by white organizers. They had put one white woman on the job as an organizer and then another, and they couldn't get to first place. We talked about it for a while and I said okay. The union sent me to New York and got me a job in a shop and I learned about the union setup and how it worked. I lived while I was there in the home of Mark Starr, the educational director of the ILGWU. He's a fine man and a fine unionist. Then they sent me to Brookwood Labor College for a six-week course, and when that was over I went to Boston and began to work.

It was very discouraging. I sent out a hundred letters for the first meeting I called of colored girls. Six turned out. They told me that wasn't so bad. I kept calling meetings and only a few turned out for each meeting and never the same few. I also went house to house to talk with the girls. Some refused to let me in; some threatened me with knives or said they'd beat me up. One woman in Somerville said, "I'll let you in only because it's freezing out but I'm telling you now that you can talk from now till next week an it won't do no good, my mind is made up." Some said the boss'd told them they didn't need no union.

I worked a little over a year and then the union gave me one week's pay and laid me off. I told them they were making a big mistake, that the only way to organize the colored girls was to stick to it even if it takes years and I knew it would, though they thought it was something that could be done in a few months.

We've got about a hundred in the union today but we're not organizing anymore. I'm an active union member. I work a union shop, but it's really a sweat shop. I guess I average about twenty-five dollars a week. I've got hopes that we may be able to do a lot to make our people union-minded through a Negro Labor Committee such as they have in New York.* We've set up such a committee here and I'm the secretary.

The most inspiring thing I ever knew was in New York. A manufacturer, a Jew, ran away from the union and opened up a shop in Harlem. He hired experienced colored girls, and paid them the lowest sweat-shop wages, next to nothing. On the front of the building he put up a sign, "Jesus Saves." He needed an experienced man to cut, so he hired a little Jewish cutter. Before very long the ILGWU organized the girls, about thirty of them, and a strike was called. The Jewish cutter joined the union, too. The strike went on for several weeks and the workers were having a real tough time They were new to the union and flat broke after a few days. But they stuck it out and the boss cracked first. The union and the boss sat down to negotiate and the boss gave in to almost every demand, but one thing he wouldn't do. He wouldn't take the Jewish cutter back to work. He felt that the cutter should have stuck by him because they both were Jewish. Well, they called a meeting of the crew, the thirty girls and the Jewish cutter, and the strikers were told what the boss offered and they were to vote on it. Mind you, they were all dead broke, but they voted unanimously to stay on strike until every one of them was taken back. And they won.

David Boynick
*Boston*
1939

---

* The Negro Labor Committee was formed by representatives of over 100 New York City unions in 1935 to fight discrimination in the labor movement.

# TOBACCO
# PEOPLE

Durham, North Carolina
1938 and 1939

John Mason, a tenant farmer, told a Federal Writer that tobacco was a thirteen-month crop: he cut flue wood and prepared a seedbed for next year's crop before he had finished selling last year's. In the late 1930s the hard work of cultivation brought an uncertain return. If he were not ruined by any of a raft of natural hazards ranging from hail to blue mold, the tobacco grower and his family tended the crop through the complicated curing process. They then graded the tobacco and delivered it to a warehouse in town, where a range of market variables affected the sale. The crop was auctioned off for a price that fluctuated according to "last summer's weather in South Georgia, the buying instructions issued by the big three tobacco manufacturers that morning, the farmer's knowledge of grading, the position of his tobacco on the auction floor and whether the buying line happens to approach it from the east or west and the fortunate chance that he took one of the buyers fox hunting last spring."*

Tobacco was a gambler's crop. The uncertainties of prices and crop yields that confronted all tobacco growers were even harsher for tenant farmers and sharecroppers who owned no land. A nonperishable cash crop, tobacco was particularly suited to the tenant system, in which farmers either rented land or worked it in exchange for a share of the crop. Landlords and larger land owners could afford to wait until tobacco prices rose before disposing of their share of the crop. Tenants could not. As the high tobacco prices of the World War I era declined during the 1920s, more and more tobacco farmers saw themselves and their neighbors losing their land, changing from farm owners to tenants and sharecroppers. Prices continued to fall in the early 1930s during the period people called Hoover Times. By the end of the decade three out of four farmers were tenants in the most productive tobacco region of North Carolina. Even by Depression standards, their poverty was extreme: a WPA study found that the average family income for share-

* "People in Tobacco," U.S. Works Progress Administration Collection, Series B, Group 3, U.S. Library of Congress Manuscript Division, Washington, D.C.

croppers was four hundred dollars in 1937, a good year for Southern agriculture.*

These circumstances—together with New Deal agricultural policies†—favoring land owners—combined to drive tenant families from the farms and into cities like Durham, where they might find "public work," or paid non-agricultural employment. Even those farmers who were not forced off the land by poverty frequently made their way into the city. Most of the men in this chapter had abandoned full-time tobacco farming to work in the warehouses of Durham, where the season's crop was graded and auctioned to manufacturers, dealers, and speculators. The move was not made easily. Both Arthur Barnes, a black handyman who slept in a vacant room in an auction warehouse, and Earl Brady, a skilled auctioneer who probably earned as much as ten thousand dollars per season, communicated a longing for the farm, a pride in having mastered the intricate techniques of tobacco cultivation. Jim Wells, who took factory work in Winston-Salem, expressed a common sentiment when he explained that he preferred life on the farm any day, "but on a farm you just work yourself to a frazzle and don't get anything for it."

The low tobacco prices drove marginal farmers off the land and into the cities, so providing the giant tobacco companies (American, Reynolds, Liggett and Meyers) with plenty of labor for their factories. Meager though it was, the average annual wage in the tobacco industry of $925—lower for black workers—looked good compared to the money to be made in farming. The factories employed blacks and whites, men and women, in jobs that were segregated by race and sex. White men usually monopolized the supervisory and skilled jobs of running the cigarette-making machines, while white women assisted male operators and ran the packing machines. Black men and women were generally confined to handling the tobacco leaf before it reached the machines.

Partly because of the large numbers of unorganized black and women workers who went into the factories in the 1920s and '30s, union activity in the industry had been limited. But in 1937 the CIO turned to organizing tobacco workers and paid particular attention to blacks. This had a galvanizing effect on the AFL's Tobacco Workers International Union, which increased its own organizing efforts and

* This figure includes cotton sharecroppers, who were even poorer than tobacco sharecroppers.

† The Agricultural Adjustment Act of 1933 and subsequent New Deal farm relief measures attempted to raise farm prices by crop reduction and government price supports. These policies primarily benefited land owners, especially owners of larger farms.

became more democratic internally in response to competition from the CIO.

Leonard Rapport, director of the FWP tobacco study, interviewed four of the six people presented here. Rapport grew up in Durham, across the street from a tobacco warehouse. During the winter of 1938–39, he gathered life histories by hanging around the tobacco market, making friends, talking, and endlessly playing a card game called setback.

Rapport concedes that his method of returning to see his subjects again and again was "not the most economic way of getting things done, but you did get to know people very well that way."* Although he frequently made notes during conversations, Rapport also sometimes wrote things down as well as he could remember afterwards. "If you're playing cards with somebody it kind of strains the atmosphere to pull out a notebook." Rapport nevertheless insists that his interviews are, as they were intended to be, "told in the words of the subjects . . . almost stenographic accounts."† He recalls that "there was a lot of selectivity, of course, but I never put words in someone's mouth."

Claude Dunnagan, who interviewed the union organizer and the tenant farmer, also recalls that "the stories were pretty accurate. We took the episodes people described to us. The main thing we had to do was organize the sequence of events to make a valid story out of it."‡

# Danny Kelly

*Danny Kelly, operator of the Leaf Warehouse, began share-cropping and renting on his father's place in Granville County, North Carolina, in 1902. As he said to Leonard Rapport, "To tell the truth I just started warehousing because wildfire got in my crop and pocked it up, and I had five children. So I came to town to ask for a job that would give me enough to feed them on."*

---

\* All quotations from Leonard Rapport are from an interview with the author, June 1977.

† "Instructions for Gathering Tobacco Material," 27 November 1939. Papers of Leonard Rapport in possession of the author.

‡ Interview with Claude Dunnagan, May 1978.

Tobacco is something that takes a lifetime study. If I live on sandy land and you live on gravelly land I can't tell you how to cultivate your tobacco. Land on the same plantation sometimes takes entirely different methods of cultivation. The government agriculture people can't tell us much about it; tobacco's something that will fool somebody who thinks he knows all about it. I remember a speculator in our section, Hal Ewart, who went one time to buy some tobacco from an old fellow who lived near us. That was when speculators used to pinhook by buying right in the fields. So he came up to this old man—an old man, not dead old, but pretty old—who was ploughing with an old white ox, and bought his crop from him. The old man made him give him cash right there, and this fellow was so pleased when he left he said, "That old man's going to keep on ploughing with an old white ox if that's all he knows about what tobacco's worth." Well, I ran into Ewart one day and I asked him about that crop. "Dan," he told me, "that old man don't need to be ploughing no ox; I paid him enough over what I got for that tobacco for him to buy a damn good horse to plough with."

Leonard Rapport

# Harry Sloan*

*Harry Sloan's main pleasures were hunting, drinking, and churchgoing. They diverted him from the "careless, mean land-lords" who prevented a tenant farmer from prospering. According to Sloan, low tobacco prices hit tenants especially hard because of the vicious credit system employed by the landlords.*

Pa was a tenant farmer, just like I am now. Ma and the girls tended the house and the garden, while pa and us boys worked the tobacco. We generally had plenty to eat—roasting ears and string beans and Irish potatoes and okra and collards and turnip greens in summer, and grits and cane syrup and fresh hog meat in winter. We bought green coffee in the bulk and roasted it—only ma kept a package of Arbuckle brand for when the preacher come. On Sundays we had fried chicken, especially if there was company.

---

* Fictitious name.

*Farmer and his wife waiting for their tobacco to be auctioned at a warehouse in Durham, North Carolina, 1939. Photograph by Marion Post Wolcott.*

None of us children got no education to speak of. There wasn't no compulsory law then to make us go to school. Sometimes now I wish there had been. I can read printing a little but I can't read writing, and I never was no good at figuring. We went for a couple of seasons to a little one-room school two miles from home. A funny thing happened once. The teacher had just give me a whuppin for talking too much, and I was feeling powerful bad, and mean, too. On the way home a toad-frog came a-hoppin across the road, just as happy and careless. I couldn't stand to see him looking so pert—so I took a big rock and mashed him out flat. "You won't hop no more," I says.

Just then Bud Seegars come up behind me and says, "Good Lord, boy, didn't you know it's bad luck to kill a toad-frog? It'll make the cow dry up every time, or maybe die. You watch."

When I got home I seen my daddy a-runnin out to the barn with a big long-necked bottle in his hand. The old cow was a-lying on the ground, all bloated up, and pa was pouring a dose of castor oil and turpentine down her throat. "She bust into the clover patch and foundered," he says. I didn't say nothin. That night the old cow died. Pa kept complaining about the green clover a-killing her, and I never did tell him no better. He woulda just a-give me another whuppin.

Our church was named Welcome Home Church, and it was set way back in a shady grove. In the cool of the evening we'd load up the mule wagon with straw, and all pile in and drive along the sandy road. Then we'd git out and hitch and talk to our friends a few minutes. At the church door the men and women would separate and set on opposite sides of the house. There was lots of babies, and in one corner at the back a bunch of quilts was put on the floor and the babies laid down to sleep till the meeting was over. There wasn't no light but a couple of kerosene lamps, and it was right hard to pick out the right baby when the meeting broke up. Old Jim Vincent over here has complained all his life about not really being a Vincent—says he was swapped off at a revival meeting when he was a baby.

People know'd how to sing in them days, and the preacher know'd how to preach. He showed us hell on one side and heaven on the other, and there warn't no middle ground. We had to make up our minds, one way or the other.

After the meeting had run about two weeks, there'd be a big baptizing in the creek. The preacher would have on a long black coat and wade out to his waist in the muddy water. He'd poke around with his walking-cane to see there wasn't no roots or stumps for nobody to get hurt on. Then he'd stand there in the water and tell how John the Baptist baptized Jesus, and how there wasn't no other way to salvation. The converts was all lined up on the bank, about forty or fifty of em. The girls was dressed in white and looked kind of scared. Then the crowd would sing, "Shall we gather at the river, the beautiful, the beautiful river," and the line would move down into the water. The girls' dresses would float up around their waists, and the preacher would poke em down with his cane. He'd lay his hands on each one and say, "I baptize thee in the name of the Father and the Son and the Holy Ghost, amen," and then he'd dip em over backward into the water. As they come up, he'd pat each one on the shoulder and say, "Sister, you're saved." The girls would come up on the bank all dripping wet, and the women would throw a cloak around em and take em off somewhere and dress em in dry clothes.

That's the way I happened to marry Sally. We was converted at the same meeting and baptized at the same baptizing. When she come up out of the water, all shivering and blue around the lips, I know'd right then I wanted to marry her. She was sixteen and I was nineteen, and her folks didn't make no objection. We rented a little place back in the Blue Creek district, and I got a job sawmilling. I got fifty cents a day, and it was pretty hard getting along. Sally had a baby that year, and by spring the mill had cut all the timber out and I lost my job. Then I rented another place and went to tobacco farming on the shares.

Tending five acres of tobacco is hard work for one man and a mule, especially when you got a landlord like I had. His name was Harold Kimzey. He advanced credit for fertilizer and stuff and charged me ten percent interest. When it wasn't paid on time, he added twenty percent more. At the end of the year we had a little trouble. We had a record of all our dealings, with the date of everything on it. Sally kept the figures and she's good at it. Come settling time, by the landlord's figures, all the crop was his and we still owed him. Our figures showed he owed us. We got a third party to help us, and we found we had a lot of the crop to our part. Mr. Kimzey had took our peas and all our corn, but when the mistake was found we got our twelve bushels of peas and twenty barrels of corn back. But Kimzey was mad, and he turned us out of the house on January first with no meat or other provisions except the peas and corn. We went from one landlord to another, and each one was worse than the last.

Then I rented a farm from H. K. Fettor, the best man I ever farmed with. His land wasn't much good, but he treated us right. By that time I had six children and seven dogs. Some of the children was big enough to work, and we put in fourteen hours a day in the field. When the tobacco was being barned and graded, we put in eighteen. I worked myself sick and didn't make nothing much. I decided it wasn't no use, and went to hunting with my dogs and getting drunk. Seem like it was all the pleasure I had.

One Saturday night I come home pretty well filled up with liquor, and I was mighty cold. Sally and all the children had gone to bed, and the house was dark. I saw a few coals in the fireplace, and got down on my knees to blow em into a flame. I blowed and blowed, but nothing happened. Then I seen I was just blowin at a patch of moonlight that come through the window and fell on the ashes. I got up and tried to go to bed, but the bed was going round and round, and I couldn't catch up with it. So I just stood by the door and waited for it to come around to me. Every time the bed would come around I'd make a jump for it, and every time I jumped I'd hit the floor, kerplunk. Sally woke up and got me onto the bed and took off my shoes and covered me up. This oughta broke me from drinking, but it didn't.

I reckon we've got along pretty well, considering everything. If it wasn't for careless, mean landlords and low tobacco prices, a tenant farmer could make out. Most of the houses we've lived in have been in bad shape—glass broke out and half the windows boarded up. If the roof leaks the tenant has to fix it himself—no use waiting for the landlord to do it. We've never had electricity, nor any water except a well. I never heard of a telephone in a tenant house—but we wouldn't have no use for one anyway.

The worst trouble is never knowing what you're going to do next. A farmer never knows what his tobacco will bring. There ain't no regular market price like there is for cotton. There's a hundred different kinds of tobacco, and the farmer's always got the wrong kind to fetch a good price. The buyers know what they're doing, and the warehouse-men know, but the farmer don't know nothing. He has to take what he can get and be thankful he ain't starving. I don't believe nobody knows what the auctioneer says. It's just a lot of stuff got up to fool people.

When I first started out I hoped to buy a farm sometime, but I soon saw I couldn't do this, so I give up the idea. My next aim was to have a good pack of hounds and some good guns. I have them. Best of all, I've raised my children to be respectable. I've got ten, which is one short of what my daddy done, but Sally says she don't care if it is. Her health ain't what it once was, and she has to take medicine for female trouble. But we have a happy home, plenty of dogs, stock, and farming tools, and we are satisfied and happy.

T. Pat Matthews and Claude V. Dunnagan

# Arthur Barnes

*Upstairs, over the office of Danny Kelly's Leaf Warehouse, was a room reserved for black farmers to spread their quilts and sleep when they brought their tobacco in to auction. During the off-season it served as handyman Arthur Barnes's bedroom. Barnes lived in the warehouse, but because he was black, he was not included in the ongoing setback game. Leonard Rapport recalls that, "The card players liked him, there was a mutual respect, but the boundaries were familiar to all concerned."*

### PREACHER'S LICENSE

"Go ye into all the world, and preach the Gospel to every Creature."

This certifies that Brother <u>Arthur Barnes</u> is a member of the Mount Pisgah Baptist Church of <u>Creedmoor</u>, State of <u>North Carolina</u>.

Being in good and regular standing, he is held in the highest esteem by us. Believing he has been called of God to the Work of the Gospel Ministry, we do hereby give him our entire and cordial approbation in the improvement of his gifts by preaching the Gospel as Providence may afford him opportunity. We pray the Great Head of the Church will endow him with all needful grace and crown his labors with abundant success.

11 day July, 1936
Rev. Tarlington, Pastor
Miss Eunice Hollowell, Church Clerk

The Mount Pisgah Baptist Church is my home church. All my folks, my sisters and brothers, my daddy, my uncles and their families, belonged to it. That was near where we were raised, on the old McNeir plantation four miles from Creedmoor by the old road.

The first work I ever knew was to work tobacco. I like it better than anything I ever did. My daddy was a tobacco farmer; he never raised any cotton. He was a sharecropper and he always made a good crop. I took the family in charge when he died, July 26, 1911; I was seventeen, there was nine of us, and I was the oldest boy. I've been having a load from them until now. My daddy always tended what we called thirty thousand hills of tobacco, and corn and cane in proportion. There's four thousand hills of tobacco to the acre. It was what we called a two-horse crop; probably with these new ploughs you could work it much nearer than a two-horse crop.

After my daddy died, the landlord sold the place and we had to move. We left that fall, after we housed my father's crop. I wanted more land. I seen where I had a big family and could use more land, and the new owner wouldn't give it to me because I was a boy. When they wouldn't give me a chance like they should of, and then saw I was going, they come and begged me to stay, but I went anyway. I kept on improving until I was experienced and could cure and tend as well as anybody.

We went to Mr. Robert Thompson's plantation, about two miles north of the McNeir place. I worked on shares there. He had about eight hundred acres and could of give me a chance, but he didn't. I had plenty of land but didn't have the horsepower to work it. I used his stock and he fed it; I paid half the fertilizer and we split what the crop brought.

The next year I sharecropped with Mr. Charley Powell. He gimme a good chance; I cleared six hundred dollars on a two-thousand-dollar crop. My next oldest brother worked for wages, and all the rest helped me. The next year I rented a whole plantation for standing rent, a hundred dollars a year, and paid part of that in advance. That was a bad

*Church service in Heard County, Georgia, 1941. Photograph by Jack Delano.*

crop year; the wilt hit me and the crop got drowned out and left me six hundred dollars in the hole. I'd bought two horses the year before and I turned one of them back in and sold the other one. Next year we moved to Mr. Luke Lang's. I was keeping on moving in just about a mile circle right back toward the McNeir plantation where I was raised.

One reason you move around so much is you get land in cultivation and then the man will want the land, and rather than cultivate new land or old land grown up with little pines and broomsedge you move on to another place. In those days I never was interested in buying a place. I could have very easy, but I just never did.

We made a good crop on shares with Mr. Lang, and I got married. My wife was from the edge of Wake and Granville County and I'd met her at church singings. When we was young boys, we'd walk all over the country to see girls. It wasn't nothing to walk five or six miles at night to see a girl, though the places where I was I could use the horses day or night—they knew I'd take care of them. She was a member of the Salt Branch Church and I was carrying a choir at the Mount Pisgah Church and we'd meet and sing against each other.

On April 4, 1917, my wife gave birth to a boy. She never was well no more. She had heart dropsy and there was nothing could be done for her. The baby died on the eighteenth of June and she died on August twelfth.

I finished out my time and then carried my things back to mamma's. The next year we went to Mr. Harvey Martin's. He had about fifteen hundred acres of land and wouldn't rent no way but on shares. I bought me another horse. Mr. Martin would furnish stock or else feed yours. He was a fertilizer dealer too, and he was awful free to furnish his people all through the year, but when fall came he got the big end of the horn; in the windup most of the people on his place owed him all they made.

In those days I was selling mostly in Oxford. When I was on shares I'd take the crop to market and sell it. If the landlord wasn't along we'd meet at the bank or else I'd leave his half there and bring him a stub. We'd have an understanding before I made a crop, but I never had it down in writing. I got good prices for my tobacco; I never had any trouble about it on account of being colored. It seemed like I always had pull with the leading men. If I had a grade of tobacco Colonel Matthews of the Imperial could use, I'd call him; he'd look out for me. On a market generally the average good-thinking man never gets in trouble or robbed. He might get tackled sometimes; I've had em try me. If you'll just keep out of the bootleg joints you're all right.

The next year I moved to Mr. Jackson's. He had a man on his place and they'd had differences and he wanted somebody to finish out. The man who'd left had his wood all cut, his corn planted, and his tobacco plants ready to be set. I used Mr. Jackson's mules and made a splendid crop.

While I was on Mr. Jackson's place I had some trouble with his cousin. His cousin was a dirty man—the only man who ever tried to mess me up. He rented some land from Mr. Jackson the third year I was there. He asked me to go and buy him a horse at a sale and he'd pay me for the horse and for feeding him. I bought him the horse on October fifteenth —and I fed him off my feed from then to March second. He should have gone to the store to make arrangements for feed for the horse but he didn't do it. So I went over and got some in his name. That fall when it come due he tried to jump the account. He finally met up with me in the sorting barn and struck me in the forehead with a mattock—we had a bloody fight. I run him off and he went to Creedmoor and got a warrant and the police. We went to court, and he had to pay the bill for me feeding the horse for three months.

We came to Durham about fifteen years ago. My sisters and all wanted to come to town and I knew if they could make it in town I could. When we first come here I started working for Mr. Kelly in the winter seasons unloading and packing tobacco that farmers brought in to sell, and when I'd get through I'd work in the leaf department. I'd work here by the hour and sometimes get in enough time to make twenty or twenty-five dollars a week.

I got married again about three years ago. My wife's out in service and stays with her mother. I moved up here in the warehouse at Christmas. This room is where colored people stay when they bring in their tobacco. They sleep on the benches and we keep this stove going. All this furniture's mine: the bed, table, frigerator, and bureau. I'll have to move it out again when the season opens. Mr. Kelly lets me stay here just to be on the place. The insurance people has to have somebody here on the place all the time so I stay up here. I cook my meals on the stove and burn old baskets and scrap wood and coal.

Most of the hour hands during the season are from Durham, but some packers come from South Carolina and some follow the markets all the way around. We've been getting right smart white hands in late years; the biggest majority at this house are white. Lots of those fellows are living now on just any kind of work they can pick up in town. Some don't get more than a couple hours a week. The way I get more is I get in more time than the others.

I go out and preach whenever I get an appointment. I was ordained a deacon in 1914. Some of the old members kicked on it, I was so young, but the church pulled it on anyhow. I worked all the way through the church, from sexton on up. I was teaching and leading singing for twenty or twenty-five years; that was one of my reasons for coming to town. I taught one choir here and it won fifty dollars, first prize in a singing contest in the city auditorium. I've got lots of books over at mamma's now; I think I'll organize another choir this summer. A preacher friend wants me to go up to Danville. He says there are twelve or fifteen churches without pastors and I might be able to take up pastoral work there. I'd like to meet the deacons and see what there is to it. After I get in a little better shape I think I'll get out and do some evangelistic work and preaching.

Leonard Rapport

# Clyde Singleton

*Clyde Singleton told Leonard Rapport that he could make more money speculating on tobacco than at his job as a door-man at his cousin's warehouse. He had given it up, though,* because "there's something about it—I just never particularly cared for speculating." A speculator needed to be part tobacco expert, part snake-oil salesman. It was not uncommon for a speculator to buy a basket of tobacco at auction, rework it to look better, and in a half hour make more on it than did the farmer who raised it.

Us Singletons were born, lived, and died in Person County; I'm the first in my branch of the family to leave it. My grandfather owned a thousand acres there and I don't know how many slaves. He raised tobacco and my daddy raised it. My daddy was Smith Singleton; he was in the war and was captured by the Yankees. He went and marched three days and nights on one pone of bread and got so weak he fell out and the Yankees got him. They was just as nice to him as anybody—as his own folks would have been. Course, they was against him and all that but they fed him and doctored him and that saved him. When the war was over, he went back to farming. He bought himself a place joining the old family place, about 350 acres at a dollar an acre. Today that land's worth sixty dollars an acre. He cleared it, built himself a house, and got married.

My daddy died when I was eight years old, and the next year I started hanging up harnesses in a warehouse in Roxboro. I moved to Durham fifteen years ago. I'd worked here before that and my daddy used to bring me here with him when I was a little boy. We'd leave home one morning, spend the night on the road, and get into Durham the next afternoon. We'd take our tobacco to Cap'n Parrish's place; he had a warehouse on what's now Parrish Street—they named the street after him. When we'd get close to town he'd have a pair of big mules waiting to hitch on and haul us in to the warehouse. The mud in the streets sometimes would be knee-deep to a mule. He had stalls for the horses and mules and quarters for farmers, though some would sleep in their wagons. Everybody brought their provisions and cooked their victuals. Now as soon as a farmer gets to town he hits out for a cafe. Every warehouse has to have one to take care of him—we've got one here in Singleton's.

Singleton's warehouse is mostly owned by two of my cousins. My job is to see that tobacco is put on the floor in the right order and that each man has a ticket and that nobody steals any tobacco out of the warehouse. I keep order—watch out for stealing and fighting. There's not many things that come up that I have to call in the Law to help me handle. If I can once get my arms around a man I'm alright.

*The wife of a tenant farmer with harvested tobacco, Granville County, North Carolina, 1939. Photograph by Dorthea Lange.*

I've had seven days of schooling in my life, but my job is meeting men and women, white and colored, and I've learned human nature. If a man will give me a hint I'll know what he means. I've had to learn people; and no college graduate or just anybody can do that. I know every man's face I ever saw and where I saw him. Moving around from market to market has ruined me on names but I never forget a face. A man can leave his tobacco on the floor and when he comes back I'll take him out there and find his pile of tobacco.

I go out and help my sister and her family with their tobacco, especially at curing time—that's the main time I try to be there. They don't understand curing like I do. Why, at one time I was raising more tobacco than any man I knew of in Person County. It was right after the war; I was working in Mebane those days and driving back and forth. My wife and boys were living on the farm and I had four wage hands and four houses full of big families. Had eight mules and two horses and twenty-six or twenty-eight hands living on the place. I used four, five hundred bags of fertilizer. I brought in a load of tobacco on a Model T that year that brought $1.40 a pound. I sold between thirteen and fourteen thousand dollars' worth of tobacco that year. I never raised any cotton; why, I couldn't do a thing in it, I never would be any good in cotton. I've never known nothing but tobacco.

Leonard Rapport

# Earl Brady*

*Auctioneers such as Earl Brady were the aristocrats among tobacco warehouse employees. Leonard Rapport remembers watching Brady sell on the floor. "He was a top auctioneer and had about him an aura of confidence. He knew his business and was in full control as the sale moved down the aisles."*

Herbert Baker was the best auctioneer I ever heard. He had the prettiest, softest voice, clear as a bell, and his lower jaw would be going like a sewing machine. When he came out on the floor his clothes were pressed as if he was going to preach, and he wore a high starched collar with the tie tight at the top. People would come a long way just to hear him; from a voice standpoint he was considered great. He'd get five, six, seven thousand dollars a season. When he died, his brother called me long distance to ask if I wanted to take his place in the burley that season—it paid $2,500—but I couldn't get away.

I got started auctioneering in Wendell in 1910. My dad had stopped me from school one spring and that made me hot, so I went up on the tobacco market at Zebulon. I tried to figure something I could do, but jobs for country boys then were scarce. I'd done a lot of singing—used my voice a lot—and I realized I had voice enough for auctioneering, so I went after it. In August I had a job selling on the Wendell market. The first day I sold I was scared just about to death, scared I couldn't make the grade. Once I got started I was all right. I suppose I sold thirty-five or forty thousand pounds at three hundred piles an hour that day. I was twenty years old.

* Fictitious name.

I had good training in tobacco; I've seen it from seed to cigarette. When I was twelve, fourteen years old my father used to bring me to market with him along about from November through January, with two mules pulling the wagon and sometimes a third carried along to help over the bad places. I did quite a bit of curing under his direction. When I was a boy we'd plant Warren tobacco and White-stem Orinoco and Broad Willow Leaf; my daddy would turn twelve or fifteen of the healthier stalks out to seed and he'd save what he needed and he'd give a lot away. Now the tendency among farmers is to buy improved seed instead of using their own.

It takes about five to eight years for an auctioneer to hit his prime. One of the main things he has to learn is to work with as little outward effort as possible. If a man looks to be in strain it's likely to get tiresome and bothersome to the buyers; he has to have the appearance of going along with ease. It's best to pitch your chant in a medium key, for then it's more easy for you to talk and you can rest by varying up or down. In my selling I use a little bit of everything to keep from getting monotonous. I make the syllable or sound; I don't sound out the whole word. "Seven, seven and a quarter, half, three, eight and make the eight plain." I'm a baritone and at times you can hear me clear across the warehouse —when I'm feeling good or coming in about through.

The spirited bidding will come when you hit smoking type; American, Liggett and Myers, Imperial, and Reynolds can all use that. There was a time when it was different—when American had the tobacco trust and you had to stand around and wait for the American buyer.* If he'd been on a poker party or drunk you had a bad sale; sometimes you had to go to the barroom to get him.

In those days we were in no hurry. We'd stop by the factories going from one warehouse to another and there'd be lots of homespun liquor. There was good apple brandy made by double distilling, strong as alum. I remember old man Sullivan who bought for Imperial saying, "Earl, you know when I get hold of that stuff it makes me wish I had a neck a yard long and a taster all the way down." He was a fine old man, an elegant dresser, but he liked his liquor. He'd come onto the sale and lean over to pull a hand of tobacco and I'd have to grab him or he wouldn't be able to get back up. We all knew he was old, and his job was his job, and our job was to take care of him, and we did.

I've sold in North Carolina on the Lumberton, Chadbourn, Zebulon, Wendell, Fuquey Springs, Henderson, Winston, Durham markets; in

---

* In 1911 the Supreme Court ordered the reorganization of the tobacco trust, and American Tobacco Company broke up into fourteen companies.

South Carolina at Kingstree, Lake City, Lamar, Darlington, Dillon, Mullins, Heminghay, and some I've forgotten. I sold on the first sale ever sold in Baxley, Georgia, and on the opening sale in Valdosta. I've sold in Tifton, Waycross, and Douglas, Georgia. In Virginia I've sold at Abingdon and a little sale at South Hill. I was stopping through South Hill and was invited in to see a few rows—it's customary among auctioneers when a visiting auctioneer drops in to ask him to sell a row or two. It's a funny way of entertaining guests, isn't it? But that's the custom, to have them go down a row and back.

I am supposed to go out in the field today with the Lucky Strike cameramen; we spent two hours yesterday in Sparrow's warehouse taking colored pictures of tobacco sales. I got five hundred dollars for my endorsement and they've been sending a carton of Luckies a week for fourteen months now. They've just given all of us a round trip to the World's Fair; enough for Pullman tickets for two and expense money for the time we're there. I don't know whether I'm going; the warehouse talk is that a lot aren't going to go—going to keep the money for other things.

I've a seven-room house I built twelve years ago out of town here; I've got an acre of land, nice trees, and a deep well. My oldest boy has finished Carolina and is on a newspaper in the eastern part of the state, and my other boy is a sophomore at Carolina. I've been taking the boys to South Carolina, and Ted, the oldest, made almost enough for his last two years of college. The first summer I took Ted to South Carolina I was busy, so he walked around and almost went off his head. He worked around the warehouse but it cost nine dollars a week for his room and board—they always hike the prices in the season and in a small place boarding and rooming houses are scarce. Anyhow, he got pretty discouraged, so I let him speculate on a pile or two occasionally, buy a pile that the house had bought, and pull out the blue leaves and the burnt—put its Sunday clothes on, we call it. He messed around like that and averaged sixty dollars a week. By the end of the season he had $156 left for Chapel Hill, and he was eighteen years old, the youngest man on the floor.

Some people are just more apt than others; Ted's more apt at buying than my younger boy. Ted could learn company grades and get to be a company buyer quicker than I could; a young man's quicker to learn that way. I've tried my younger boy at selling—let him sell a sale a time or two—and I think he might get in it unless he finds something else he wants to do. It's one line of work that if he can get in it when he finishes school he can make more right off than in any other. I myself am about played out. Thirty years at this is a long time.

Leonard Rapport

# Jim Wells*

*In April 1939, not long after Jim Wells was interviewed about
his work as a union organizer, the Tobacco Workers' International Union called a strike against the Liggett and Meyers
factory in Durham, which resulted in wage increases and company acceptance of the union.*

I was born in a house with tobacco fields on one side and curing barns
on the other. Ever since I can remember, my people have worked in
tobacco, mother and sisters, too. When I was five years old my dad made
me go out in the fields when tobacco was ripe and pick tobacco worms.
I was so afraid of those big green worms I just walked up and down the
rows of tobacco, scared to death one of em would crawl on me. I got over
that later, though, I could go out and pinch off their big greasy heads
without batting an eyelash.

We didn't live any too good on the farm. Hailstorms, big rains, and
dry spells would come almost every year, and some years we didn't even
make back fertilizer money. We grew some vegetables and had a cow,
so we didn't starve.

I like the farm better than the factory any day, but on a farm you
just work yourself to a frazzle and don't get anything for it. So I up and
went to the city to get a job in the Prince Albert smoking tobacco department. I worked down on the first floor where they make the tin cans
for the tobacco. Those tin-cutting machines make so much noise you
can't hear a thing, nothing but the factory whistle when it blows at noon
and quitting time. And believe me, when you've stood up on your dogs
all day, shoving big sheets of tin into a slicing machine, and handled tin
cans till your hands ache, you're damn glad to hear that steam whistle.

I got to going around with a girl whose mother ran the boarding-
house where I stayed. She had a brother who was pretty wild, and one
night when I came home he'd skipped out and carried off two of my
best suits and a bunch of my shirts. I was pretty mad about it but didn't
say anything because I didn't want to hurt the girl's feelings. She was a
nice kid, and I thought more of her than I did my clothes. Her folks
was awful broken-up about it and wanted to make it good, but I wouldn't
let em.

* Fictitious name.

The girl worked on another floor in the Prince Albert plant and I saw her most every day. Well, the day after her brother ran off with my clothes, I was passing by her machine and I saw she was crying. I went over to her and asked her why. She said because her brother had disgraced her family and that I wouldn't like her anymore. I tried to comfort her and told her not to worry about it and that I liked her just as much as ever.

While I was talking to her, the foreman on that floor came over and told me to get the hell back to my machine and quit running around making his girls cry. I told him I hadn't made her cry.

"You're a damn liar!" he said, just loud enough for her to hear. Well, I lost my temper and slapped that foreman twenty feet across the floor. Right then, I was sorry I did it. Not on account of my job, but because he was an old man. I went over and helped him up and said, "Sorry, old fellow, I didn't mean to slap you so hard. I just lost my temper, but you're too old to be calling people liars when you ain't sure." I lost my job all right, but it was worth it. I wasn't aiming for my girl to think I was afraid of any foreman, job or no job.

I went back to the country and farmed a crop of tobacco with my dad that next year. For all the work I put in I didn't make half as much as I'd been making at the factory, so, after market closed, I wandered back to town and started looking for another job. That was just after the Reynolds company opened up their new employment office.

Well, I went in and found they needed a cigarette packing-machine operator. I had a pretty good record on my machine in the smoking tobacco factory, so they put me on and got one of the older workers to show me how to operate the machine.

One day I was walking down the street beside Camel Plant Number Twelve and I saw a sign hanging in front of a door between two Negro cafes. It said "Tobacco Workers' International Union." I was kind of interested so I went in and talked to the man at the desk. He was a nice fellow and it turned out he was head organizer. After he told me what the union stood for and how it aimed to help the workers, I was convinced, so I joined the tobacco workers' union.

From then on, I had trouble. First, my machine got to working bad and would mess up a lot of cigarettes. The boss would come around and act like he was going to fire me if I didn't quit ruining so many cigarettes. I asked him to send the mechanic around and work on it. Well, he did, and when the fixer had gone over the machine it worked all right for about three hours and then it was worse than before.

One day, while they were working on my machine, I was helping paint the big pillars that support the floors. While I was bent over a can of paint, one of the Negro workers I knew came over to me and said in a low voice, "Mr. Jim, how is the union coming on?"

I knew the chief operator was around somewhere. I said, "Mose, I can't talk to you now on factory time, but I'll see you at dinner or after work today."

Well, the next thing I knew, the floor boss had collared him over in a corner and was talking to him. In a minute he came back and said for me to come to the office. I went and the boss said, "Jim, I hear you've been stirring up trouble among the Negro workers with your union talk. Is that right?"

"No," I said. "One of em asked me about the union and I told him I couldn't talk on factory time. That's all."

"Well, don't let me hear of you talking union around here to these Negroes anymore," he said. "Now get back to work and stay at your machine. It's fixed now."

And it stayed fixed about three hours. When I got home that night, I made up my mind that I was going to get that machine fixed. The next morning, I went up to the chief operator and said, "Look here, Mr. Smith." I said, 'If you can't get somebody to fix my machine so it'll run right, I'm going to see some higher authorities about it, and maybe they can get it fixed."

Well, sir, he just blowed up.

"Jim," he said, "when you talk about going to higher authorities, you're getting just a little bit too big for your pants. You're fired!"

While I was in the tin plant the second time I had got married and my wife had been working at the factory all along. After I got fired she stayed on and she's still there. Well, Mr. Allen, the head organizer for the tobacco workers' union, cottoned to me and put me on as part-time organizer, and I've been there since. I don't get a salary, just expenses, and that's just enough to get around over town and see the workers and talk to em. You have to keep dressed nice, have a haircut now and then, and keep your shoes shined, so the people will respect you. Getting the respect of the workers in this business is mighty important if you're going to do anything for them.

You run into all kinds of people in this work. Some of em are in sympathy with unionism and a lot of em are just plain scared for their jobs and won't join because they're afraid they'll get fired. Every now and then you run across some poor sucker who thinks the company is a fairy godmother, and wouldn't think of joining a union.

One evening I went to see a white family over in East Winston. They lived in a four-room shack that a self-respecting pig wouldn't inhabit. The chairs were all broken down, and the three beds in one room were on the floor where the mice and cockroaches could run over em, and the stove was tied together with baling wire. They had about six kids, the oldest one working in the leaf house. When the old man found out what my business was he got up and said, "You get the hell out of my house. My company's treated me good, and here you come wanting me to turn against em and lose my job!"

I'm a church man, but I don't attend regularly. I'm so busy helping organize the workers I don't have much time to be with my family. What we need now is a workers' religion that won't talk so much about getting pie in the sky when you die by-and-by, and teach something about how they can better their condition here on earth and enjoy the fruits of their labor while they've got a chance.

We'd have a whole lot better world to live in if some of our preachers and teachers would help the people understand how to live together better and help one another, instead of talking all the time about rich rewards in heaven for those that suffer here on earth. Why don't they get out and suffer a little, so they can get some of that reward. The higher-ups that preach that stuff don't seem to be suffering any.

Claude V. Dunnagan

# WOMEN
## ON WORK

# Alice Caudle

*It was a source of pride to Alice Caudle that the spinning room of Cannon Mills, where she worked, employed only women "because of the patience and skill required for such work." Caudle worked on the morning shift from 7 a.m. to 3 p.m., with a half hour for lunch; for two full five-day weeks she was paid thirty-one dollars. She lived with her daughter and grandchildren in a company house in a mill town near Concord, North Carolina.*

Law, I reckon I was born to work in a mill. I started when I was ten years old and I aim to keep right on just as long as I'm able. I'd a-heap rather do it than housework. When I started down here in plant Number One, I was so little I had to stand on a box to reach my work. I was a spinner at first, then I learned to spool. When they put in them new winding machines, I asked them to learn me how to work em and they did. If I'd been a man no telling how far I'd a-gone. It was mighty convenient for em having a hand that could do all three, but I got mad and quit. In them days there was an agreement here that if a hand was to quit one mill, then the other mills in town wouldn't hire him, so I went over to Albemarle and I got me a job in the knitting mills.

*After the death of her husband, Alice Caudle moved back to Concord and again went to work for the Cannon Mills.*

I've worked for the Cannon Mills now for over thirty years. I have one of them pins they gave at that big supper last spring. One day someone come around asking all the hands how long they had worked for the Cannon Mills. Course nobody knew why such a question was being asked and some of the hands was afeared to tell how long they had worked. Well, I wasn't. When they asked me I said thirty years and was proud of it. Several days after that they sent for me to go to the office. I said to myself, "They're going to fire me now." When I went in the office

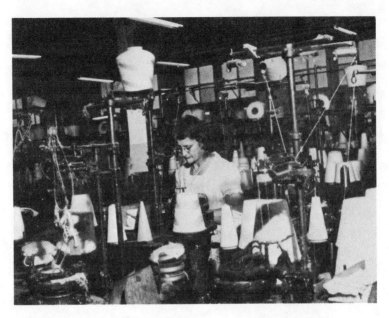

*A textile mill at Union Point, Georgia, 1941. Photograph by Jack Delano.*

Mr. Smith says, "Miss Caudle, you've worked for the Cannon Company for thirty years, ain't you?" and I said "Yes sir, that's right." Then he said, "We're having a big supper up at Kannapolis on Friday night for them that's worked twenty-five year or more for the company and here's your ticket."

"Well, sir," I said to him, "in all these here thirty years, this is the first time the Cannon Mill ever offered me anything. . . . Are you right sure they're not going to take it off my pay?"

The supper was held in the Mary Ella Hall in Kannapolis. You went into a great big room, furnished just as nice as you'd want, and they had a man there who didn't do nothing but take your hat and coat when you come in and hang em up for you. I thought we would kill ourselves laughing and Rose kept a-wondering if we'd get the right coat and hat back. The room where we was to eat looked as pretty as anything you ever saw. Such a sight of tables—and every one was covered all over and down at the sides with some of that white cloth that was finished down at the bleachery; and there was flower pots set about them. I didn't think they'd have much to eat for such a crowd, but the tables was covered. They had turkey and everything; it was real good.

Charles Cannon made a fine speech and give out the pins to us.

He told about the way young'uns used to stand on boxes to work—the way I done.

Muriel L. Wolff
Concord, North Carolina
1938


# Elizabeth Miller

*Elizabeth Miller, a native of Vermont, was ninety at the time of her interview.*

I was the oldest of six children. Mother was never very well, and when I was about ten she was taken real sick and had to be abed most of the time. We had help sometimes but I took over and did the work as soon as I could. I learned to wash by scrubbing at the wash tub while the woman who helped was at the table with the family. I've always said I was born to work because I came at one o'clock of a Monday morning ready for the wash tub. I have been at it steady for eighty years, ever since I was ten.

Mother would sit in the wheelchair when she was better and give me advice while I worked. When I scrubbed the floor, she would say, "Now, Lizzie, scrub it hard and then wipe it good and dry with clean water." I learned to do things well and it has stayed with me all my life.

I didn't have no education, but I had the chance of one. I might have been a woman of letters and used my head instead of my hands, but I had to do what was before me to do. My uncle lived down the road on the next farm and they were real well off. One day when I was calling there, I remember just as plain, I sat there and uncle said he would pay for my schooling if I would come and live with them. I looked at him and said, "Uncle, I can't. I've got to stay with mother. She needs me." That was all that was ever said about it.

When I went out to work, no one ever found fault with what I did. I helped the minister's folks clean house one spring, and we did up the curtains. They said they had never been done better. What did I know about doing up curtains? We had never had anything like them at home. It was my mother's training. If you learn to do small things well, you can do all things well.

A farm kitchen in the vicinity of Bristol, Vermont, 1940. Photograph
by Louise Rosskam.

My father's farm was just off the road to Jefferson Hill, on the
branch that goes to Limekiln. We used to go to church in South Ryegate
three miles away. We would take our shoes and stockings in our hands
and walk to church barefoot. Then we went into the house next door to
put them on and again to take them off after church. We had to save
shoeleather, and bare feet don't wear out. With six children and an
invalid to take care of, my father had to scratch some. I took mother's
eggs to the store in South Ryegate in a pail every week, and tugged back
a load of groceries. Father had just the one horse, and he had to be
saved for farm work. He couldn't go gallivanting unless it was necessary.

I never went much to dances. Mother didn't hold with it for girls
but didn't seem to feel the same about the boys. My brother George
went. He didn't want to take his older sister; he had some other girl on
the string, and I had to stay at home unless someone chanced to come
for me. I went sometimes, though. Brother George could kick it up—

he never went to dancing school, either. All the girls liked to dance with George. One time I was at a dance and someone asked George if I could dance, and he said, "Her dance? Why, she couldn't dance no more'n a cow." Quite like the thing from a brother!

I did like to go to singing school. They were held about twice a month down in the Town House. I could sing out, too, in those days and all the girls would come and sit around me because I could hold them to it. I had a lot of push then. It was two and a half miles to the Town House from our farm and many a night I walked there and back. I was young and strong and I never had time to be sick.

Mother and I knit all the long stockings for the women and girls, and mittens from yarn I had spun. After I was married I was never without a pair of needles in my hands. When I went out to a sociable or a farmer's meeting in the evening, I always took my knitting. I knit uphill and down when we went out in the carryall [a one-horse wagon]. My knitting went everywhere but to church.

One time I had company and they wanted to know how many skeins I had spun that day. I sent my little Clarence in to get all the skeins. He was just a small one then and he was loaded with the ten skeins. Granny Miller lived with us then and she thought Clarence was the only child ever was. She would call him "Ma bonnie prince, ma wee king," and was in a fair way to spoil him.

We had the spinning wheel here until the old house burned down in 1926. So many things went then that meant so much to me. But I never let myself think about it. There's no use and it was hard enough for the boys without my complaining.

Those were good times, but they are gone now. Life is nothing but changes.

We never used to can things the way we do now. We salted pork down, froze the beef and packed it in oats, and had the root crops in the cellar. One fall we had a 550-pound dressed hog hanging in the yard. The men went off to Wells River to take up another hog they had dressed at the same time and left it hanging there and the caldron kettle half full of water. They aimed to get back and take the hog down cellar before it froze. It would never do to let pork that was going to be salted freeze. I was all alone with the children and I waited until almost twelve. My husband didn't come, and so I took a lantern and a saw and knife and went out to fetch in that hog. I emptied out the water from the caldron kettle so it wouldn't freeze and burst. Then I cut up that hog and loaded it piecemeal onto the sled. The worst part was getting it through the front door, but I managed. I had it all done before my husband got home. He asked who had brought the hog in. I said, "I did." He asked who helped. I said, "Alone." I wasn't wasting many words on him. He was struck dumb.

Rebecca M. Halley
*West Newbury, Vermont*
1938

# Izzelly Haines

*Izzelly Haines, a midwife, lived in the small Conch fishing village of Riviera, Florida. The Conchs—named after the conch shellfish, which was an important item in their diet— came to Florida from the Bahamas in the early twentieth century. Of mixed English and Bahamian Negro descent, they were isolated from their white neighbors and many, like Izzelly Haines, retained British citizenship.*

*Accurately recording the Conch dialect, which combined elements of Cockney and Bahamian Negro speech, presented a challenge to FWP interviewers. In a report on the dialect, Federal Writer Stetson Kennedy wrote, "The peculiar Conch inflections cannot be set down. Sentences frequently begin with a drawl, the body of the sentence is spoken with a rush, and the sentence concludes with another drawl."*

I was born in the Bahamas and I'm still belonging to that country. We never got papers ere, cause we hain't never needed them. I was back ome to visit this spring. It's changed a lot, but folks still as a ard time there and I sure don't want to live there no more.

When I was little I live most of my life with me aunt. She was sure a smart woman, and a real English lady. She worked as a midwife mostly and she ad books that told er ow to tend sick folks. That's ow come me to know what little I do about this work.

I been a midwife ever since I was seventeen. I uster tend all the women around where I lived in the Bahamas. I've tended me own girls as well as meself. I still go when I'm called ere in Riviera, but if it gits beyond me I always calls a doctor. Most of what I know I owe to me aunt, for it was er what ad the books although she kept them under lock and key, cause she didn't want us childrens to read them. I uster steal the key and then open the case what she kept the books in, and sneak them out and ide until I could read them. As I growed up, I got more and more interested, so after reading them books I decided I'd be a midwife too, and sure enough that's what I did.

I was seventeen when I took my first case. This case was sure pitiful, that's ow come me to take it. If I adn't the little mother woulda died. In them days folks was ignorant about sech things, and in the Bahamas there warn't no doctors at all. There ain't many now, and midwife does most everything, but it's better than it was in them days. All I knowed about this work was what I read in them books and what I'd already seen.

This woman ad given birth at about six o'clock in the morning and by four o'clock that afternoon the afterbirth adn't come and she was dying from the poison that sets in. There warn't a soul around that could do nothing about it, so remembering what I could, I took two pounds of onions and pulverized them; then soaked it in a pint of gin. Then I took it all and put it in two cloth bags. One bag I put to the lower part of the woman's stomach and the other to er back. Inside of a alf our it ad come and she was gitting along fine.

I learned a lot of things down there in the Bahamas and I tended a lot of cases. One ome remedy what can be used for the same case I jest mentioned is to boil mud-dauber nests that still have the worms in them and give the woman the tea. It always works. Another remedy is tea made from the wild peanut; it grows to ome in the Bahamas, and it will start labor pains again if they have stopped and shouldn't. I never practiced under no doctor's orders, and I don't yet unless the situation gets beyond me.

As for pay, I takes whatever they give me. I can't expect much for folks ere is most as poor as they was in the Bahamas, so I'm willing to tend the women for whatever they can afford and as glad to do it. What little I does git out of it elps though, cause there hain't much in fishing now days. Prices hain't so good, but they never is, so that hain't nothing neither. That's another reason how come I'm always glad to make whatever money I can as a midwife or by weaving.*

My girl's usband is out fishing today. The blues is running eavy. These ere windy days what's chilly brings them down fast from the north, and I'm oping the catch will be a good one. The men been out ever since

---

* Conch women wove palm fronds into hats, baskets, rugs, and purses, which were sold to tourists.

early this morning. They gotta work and work ard while they can. They work nights, too, every time they git a chance.

I worry so about the men folks when they're out. To catch them blues they ave to come in close to shore, for the fish play about in the breakers. Sometimes when the boats come in too close, they git caught in them same breakers and is washed ashore. When this appens the boat is torn to shreds on the coral, and sometimes the men don't make it neither.

So far, all of mine as come ome safe, but there hain't no telling. One time last year I seen their boat smash plumb to pieces on the rocks and wash all away in jest a few minutes. All that was left was the engine. After cleaning the salt water outten it they built a new boat and they's still using the same engine. It's dangerous though and I worries so, so much about them when they're gone. But I reckon that's ow it's meant to be.

Veronica E. Huss
*Riviera, Florida*
1939

# Marie Haggerty

*Marie Haggerty left the New Brunswick farm where her Irish family had settled to move to Boston. She didn't want to be a housemaid, so she took a job in a dressmaking shop, "but for two years all the mistress allowed me to do was baste, and I got tired of that. I could never raise my head up, look at anyone, or talk without getting scolded." She then entered domestic service. Seventy-two when she was interviewed, and still cleaning others' houses by the day, Marie Haggerty loved to sit and think of the time when she had worked for "quality." Federal Writer Emily Moore described her "longing for the soft beds and beautiful candleholders in her room, for the fine horses and carriages she used to ride in, and 'right in the same seat with the children.' "*

It wasn't housework I did. I was a nursemaid or a second girl—never just an ordinary girl out to service. My aunts and uncle were very glad to have me working for such nice people, real high-class people. I had a good home and I was treated good. Now if I had gone into a factory to work, the folks would have been worried. The girls in the shops never made over six or seven dollars, and them that dressed so well on that, and paid their board, too, made people lift their eyebrows. I was lots better off. I got seven or eight dollars a week, my room, and it was always a nice one, and the best of food. I was really next thing to a lady's maid, for when the children went to bed, often the mistress would let me hook her dress, or brush her hair, and all the time she'd be talking to me, just like I was her equal.

I always had good jobs, and we usually worked by twos, another girl and myself. A body didn't have to show references for jobs like they do now, but that wasn't the half of it. You got hired by your looks, and even if you looked honest, they would test you out. Once I was making up a bed, and right beside it was a five-dollar bill. I knowed nobody dropped that for nothing, so I didn't know if I should pick it up and tell them, or what, but my face burned like fire, for I knowed I was getting tested. I left it there all the time I worked in the room, and when I got done I put it on the bureau and put a vase over the end to make sure it didn't blow off. I was just going out of the room when the madam came in. I often think what would've happened if she'd come in while I was smoothing the bill out—would she believe I was going to put it on the bureau. I don't think so, for I was so new there. They often left food and fancy cakes around, just to test us, but I learned my lesson early on that. Once I just had my hand on a fancy cake in the parlor, and I got such a crack on my hand from the cook. She pulled me back to the kitchen and made me sit down and eat my fill of fancy cakes and told me never to take anything that was outside the kitchen, for it was always a trick to see how honest we was.

My specialty was as a nurse girl. I took care of two lovely children. Do you know when the boy was married, he invited me to his wedding just like I was rich folks. They was an awful nice family, so refined and kind. We went to the beach every summer, and what a place it was. They had two saddle horses, two horses for carriage and garden work, and four cows for their own use. There was three men to work around the grounds, and two coachmen. They had a playground for the children and it was kept up swell, better than most public playgrounds. We had lots of good times, especially when the mistress went away. She'd be gone to Europe for months at a time and the mister would let us ride all over Cape Cod with the coachman and the children.

I was living with those folks when I met Pa. He was the grocery salesman and come for orders three times a week. I can hear him even now, for he was a great whistler, and very jolly. I could hear him a mile off, and I usually went out near the back, never letting him know, of course, but I always managed to make him see me, and he'd come and talk. He rode a horse and buggy, and they didn't deliver mail them days, so I would usually be on my way to the post office and he would drive me there and back. After a while, we got to keeping company, and we used to drive around the Cape Sundays.

I knowed Pa for three summers before we got engaged, and I well remember that day. It was Sunday afternoon, and he come by with his horse and buggy. It was a hot day, so he tied up the horse, and we went walking. We walked down by the water, and he was very quiet, and there was people all around, so he said, "Kitten"—he always called me Kitten —"let's walk through this little woods, tain't very thick." Well, I felt something was about to come, and I didn't know what. We walked for an hour or more, and then we set down on a tree stump, and while I was just picking grass and chewing on it, he outs with it, and asks me to get married. Mind you, first I was glad and said I would, but next I got mad. Tweren't like any proposal I'd ever heard of. I always thought when I was asked to be married, he'd do it kind of grand like—get down on his knees maybe. Wasn't I the fool? Well, I gave him one look and I ran away from him right down to the water where all the people was. He came after me, and then I got to feeling how silly I was, so I told him I wanted to go home and I went right into the house without even saying good-bye.

After he left I got to thinking about it, and I got sick to my stomach, for I had just about made up my mind never to get married but to learn to be a real nurse. When I got to my room and quieted down I decided definitely I wouldn't marry him at all. But the next time I saw him, he started to tease me about acting so and I couldn't help but feeling sorry for him, so I told him I didn't mean to act so. So that was the end of it. I married him.

We went to Boston to be married, for we was only summer people at the Cape. The lady I worked for let us have the coachman and the best carriage to go in, and when we got back to the Cape that night, they had a big party. It wasn't exactly like the rich people, but nearly. She had the gardeners and coachmen clear the barn for dancing, and the cook made up all the refreshments, and she gave us all the punch we could drink. Then before Mr. and Mrs. went to bed, they came out and drank to our health, and wished us their blessings and happiness. The only difference in my wedding and the rich people was that our party was in the barn; but it was nice there, and we had an accordion and a fiddler for music. All night long, as long as the party lasted, people come from all over with tins and pans and beat a serenade, and yelled for the bride and groom.

When Pa and I got married, his uncle set him up in the grocery business in Cambridge and we got along swell. But he had a nervous breakdown from working too hard and the doctor said he had to change his business and go out in the country to live. We moved to Whitinsville and Pa went to work at the machine shop on the trucks and teams. I didn't like it there. Most of them people were just mill people. Pa knew I didn't like living with them so he got a job with the Electric Light Company, and we moved to Worcester. Then he got to be a foreman and we bought a house down in Millbury. We were happy there until Pa died. He didn't leave much money—it wasn't his fault, though. We always tried to give the children the best and that took money.

Pa and I used to talk about what we hoped our children would be when they grew up. We always thought they were the best children—I guess all fathers and mothers think that. We made them all finish high school. Pa and I didn't have much education but we wanted our children to so they could have a chance to become high-class people. We sent Kitty, my youngest daughter, to Normal School, because Pa always wanted one of his daughters to be a schoolteacher. I don't know why things never turn out the way you want them.

I didn't mind that there wasn't much left for me because I knew Pa meant well, but it left me depending on the children and they got their own troubles. The children are good but they're too busy to bother with me much. Pa never denied me a solitary thing when he was living, but now, if I didn't watch out for myself, nobody'd care what I had. Pa would turn over in his grave if he knew I went out washing and cleaning, but I have to. Of course, I don't go out working for just anybody. After all, I wasn't used to working for cheap people and I don't do it now. I have my special customers—all real nice people. I don't mind going out to work—I'm independent and that's something. But I won't be bowing to anybody.

I like things nice, but there's no use pretending; I can't have them that way now. The boys don't like me to fix things up much. I tried just once after Pa died. I was having company at the house, and I kind of put things on a little fancy, like rich people do, but the boys made so much fun of me, I vowed I'd never do it again. If Pa had been living, they'd have known better than to laugh at me. Pa would have socked them.

I never thought I'd have to work after I was married, and wouldn't have to, if Pa'd lived. Pa knowed I was used to better things, and he always tried hard to get them for me. Once he came home with a diamond ring for me. I knew he couldn't afford it, and I was afraid to wear it, thinking as how he might not have come by it honestly. I didn't want to question him, though. He might feel bad. I never wore the ring and not long ago, my daughter Marie had it set over for herself. Two or three years after Pa died, I found where the poor man had paid for it bit by bit. Poor Pa, he was a good man.

I never worked at a place before I was married that they didn't treat me as good as anyone in the family. When I worked for Mrs. French, I was second girl; and even if I did have to wait on table, I was served just like the rich folks when it came time for me to eat. Maybe the difference was that I never said "marm" or never had no brogue. The only thing I didn't like about working for people was that we did have to wear uniforms, usually dark blue, and stiff white collars, depending on what kind of work you had to do. Being next to a nurse, I wore about the same as she did, and if there wasn't any nurse in the family, I wore about the same as a parlor maid. We could frizz our hair, or wear it like we wanted to, just so it was neat. I guess I never minded being a maid, and to tell the truth, I'd rather my Marie was in some nice family, looking after babies, or the like, than working as a waitress. She'd be better off. Kitty would never have made a maid—she's too fly-by-night and independent, but she's a good girl. I think Marie takes after me, in a way. She's contented with her job. Oh, well, the poor girl—I suppose she could have a worse one.

Emily Moore
*Worcester, Massachusetts*
1939

# Babe Parmalee

*Babe Parmalee was interviewed in Barre, Vermont—"the sticks"*
*—where she had spent the winter. Reared on a farm near*
*Calais, Vermont, she considered Barre "a pretty good town for*
*a small town, but my God it's dead after you've been around*
*like I have."*

I've been in the racket a long while now; I've done about everything in the show business. Night clubs, cabarets, burlesque, vaudeville—and carnivals too. Lots of the big shots started in a carnival tent, went up to burlesque, and then hit the big time. Plenty of girls that are stars now were nothing but kootch dancers [strippers, also known as shimmy dancers] in road shows when they started.

*The "girlie" show at the Vermont State Fair, Rutland, 1941. Photograph by Jack Delano.*

That's the way I started myself. My girl friend and I were still in high school and one summer this carnival comes along. We were both kind of wild and crazy, we wanted to get away from home and see the world. We were sick of school and getting hell when we stayed out late at night, and we were sick of the silly boys around town. So we went out with these fellows from the carnival. We thought they were swell, the real McCoy. They dressed snappy and talked big city stuff, and we ate it up. They spent money on us—we weren't used to that—and they told us a couple of good-looking girls like us could go places. They made a lot of promises and put a lot of wild ideas in our heads. They did kind of fall for us—for a while. We were different from the hard-boiled babes they were used to playing round with. We were young then, and innocent—kind of innocent—and we *were* pretty.

They had a couple of girls with the show, a couple of kootch dancers, and their girls got burned up because they fooled around with us. They had a hell of a fight one night and both girls quit the show and scrammed. So the guys put us in the show. God! but I was scared the first time I went on, and so was Kitty. We were both natural dancers

—you don't have to do much dancing in a kootch tent anyway—but we were scared. Of course there were men and boys who knew us and that made it worse. But we said to hell with them. It was our chance to get a start and we were going to take it, so we went out there and stripped down and shook it for them. The other girls showed us how to shake it good enough to get by. In that kind of show all they want you to do is strip and squirm around. It's not dancing. But we thought we were on our way to Broadway sure.

We traveled all over the state with that bunch. One day at a fair our fathers showed up with a sheriff, but we ducked out back of the tent and hid in a truck until they went away. We thought it was a great life. All that money to spend on clothes and things, nobody to tell us what to do or when to go to bed, and all kinds of men after us. But the show broke up in the fall, and our two guys took a powder, beat it without a word. And the rats took our last week's pay besides. I guess that was our first real lesson.

But we'd been in it long enough so it was in our blood then; besides, we didn't dare to go home. We had some money saved, a lot of clothes, and we were still young and pretty. We had learned plenty about the racket, so we went to Boston.

Kitty picked up a guy in Boston who said he'd take us to New York and get us a real spot. He knew all the big names and places, and he had a good line. Kitty thought he was going to make us famous, and even marry her, but I wasn't believing things so easy anymore. He borrowed money from us and we started for the Big Town. The sonofabitch ditched us in a restaurant in New Haven when we went to the ladies' room. We were almost broke and all our bags and things were in his car. Kitty was brokenhearted about it. I told her we were lucky to get away from that guy with the clothes on our backs.

We got hold of a couple of college boys, nice kids too, and we gave them the old hard luck story. This time it was true. They bought us a couple of suitcases, filled them up with some kind of junk, and took us to a hotel. We stayed three or four days. The boys had money; they liked to drink and wanted a good time, so we had one. But their money ran out before time to pay up the hotel bill, so there we were stranded in that room with two empty suitcases, a flock of empty bottles, and no dough. We threw the suitcases out the window into an alley and sneaked out of the hotel. We started hitchhiking and we rode into New York in a truck, the first time for both of us.

It was pretty tough for a while, I'm telling you. We couldn't get a job, we had no clothes, nothing. There was just one thing for us to do, and we did it. One of the customers kind of went for me, and he got us a job as entertainers in a little cabaret. It wasn't much, but it was better than what we'd been doing. It's plenty hard to break into anything good in that town. All the show people who aren't in Hollywood are in New York. Kitty finally got into a better nightclub, and I went with a burlesque company. I lost track of Kitty after that, but a couple of years ago I heard she was hitting the dope and she had committed suicide. I don't know if it's true or not. She was a good kid, but an awful sucker for any guy with a line. She was always handing money over to some no-good stooge. She was too big-hearted, that kid.

Well, it was up and down for me. I was doing okay for a while there, but I got in with a bad bunch. I started smoking marijuana and that queered me. When I came to I was out in the sticks kootch-dancing in another carnival. And the next thing I knew I was back home here, flat on my fanny. I've been down to New York quite a few times since, and every summer I've traveled with road shows, but I can't seem to hit anything good. I'm not so young anymore and I've put on too much weight.

I used to be a lot slimmer than I am now. I had a real swell shape and natural blond hair. Sometimes I'm sorry I dyed it black, but at that time they told me there were too many blonds and a brunette would go over better. I had it red once, too, before I dyed it black. My eyes were nice, they still are, but that's about all I got left. I had a good voice once, but something happened to it. Probably I smoked and drank too much. Anyway, it got too coarse for singing, and it had to be dancing for me.

Roaldus Richmond
*Barre, Vermont*
1940

# Ellen O'Connor

*Ellen O'Connor had fallen on hard times when she was inter-viewed by Nelson Algren, but there was a snappy bravado to her observations about living "like I done." Algren later used a similar milieu in* A Walk on the Wild Side, *his novel about prostitutes and those who profited from their work. He echoed*

*O'Connor's complaints when he wrote about those who "charged the girls double for joint-togs and drinks, rent, fines, towel service, and such."* \*

W̲hen you live like I done people give you a line all the time, all day long, wherever you're at. All day long, everybody's givin everybody else a line, and after a while without thinkin much about it one way or another, just tryin to get along you know, there you are givin somebody a line just like everyone else is doin—only what you're really doin is just givin yourself a line I guess, cause nobody is listenin to anybody else these days anyhow. Like my boyfriend used to comment, whenever you think you're screwin somebody, take a look around and you'll see it's just you gettin screwed as usual, same as always. So you got to be real careful. You got to lie to *everybody*, you can't believe *nobody*—but still sometimes you got to believe *something* that *somebody* says, but most of all you got to lie to yourself. That's the main thing. Sometimes you can take a chance and talk straight to somebody else—but when you live like I done you can't ever stop kidding yourself a second or you're through. It'd just take all the heart out of you, you'd get blind drunk and blow your top. So you got to be more careful what you say to yourself even more than what you say to cops and doctors.

I went into a house on Eighteenth and Indiana, that was in Prohibition years. Then over into the big one on Twenty-second and Wabash—that used to be Four Deuces, then over to Nineteenth and Dearborn. After that I got transferred to the Paris Hotel on South State, and then around the corner to the Best. I was in the Best when I got sick. I been on the bum ever since; I got no money to go to a real hospital, and I know what they do to you in the County. They give you the black bottle [a sedative].

All at once I owed everybody and I couldn't figure out why. They charge you four times over for everything. You got to pay for the towels, for the music, for the Lifebuoy, for the guys who stay overtime, for guys who lose money somewhere else and think they lost it in your outfit, for the high-school kids who come up with two dollars even and carfare and then forget and put a nickel in the slot machine. Then you got to give them carfare, you got to pay off the doc who finds out you're sick, a sawbuck just to let you off, a fin to the bondsman when the house is pinched—and still you aren't really sure you want to get out. Even

---

\* Nelson Algren, *A Walk on the Wild Side* (New York, 1956), p. 109.

when some duke tells you about some job in a big office, you don't try for it. You got no heart for it.

We all know what kinds of jobs girls like us get anyhow. Twelve hours a day for six dollars a week at Goldblatt's [a Chicago department store] maybe. I can make that in six minutes, sick as I am, and I don't feel I'm making a fool of myself any more one way than another. I'll have a house of my own someday, managing one that is, keeping an eye on things, seeing that the girls stay sober and the drunks don't cause trouble, being able to think faster than cops and doctors and such.

And the dame who went to work for eight or twelve bucks a week, all she's getting now is fifteen, if she's still got a job at all, and I'll bet she looks like a wreck besides, worried all the time and more than likely got a couple of kids and a drunken bum in a room somewhere to take care of. I bet she expects every day to get fired—and who cares if she does or not? She knows that too. But take me now. I know the city and every night-sergeant in it and all the ins and outs. I've got friends, people I've gotten out of jail, people I've loaned money to, women whose bills I paid, guys that I perjured myself for—I could go to any one of them tonight, they wouldn't ask no questions, just give me how much I asked for. But I don't figure I'm down that far yet. I figure I got myself into this, I can get myself out. That's how I always figure.

It ain't women like me ends up on the street, no siree. It's the department store dames who put in twenty years and then get the gate that end up that way, not us girls who been outsmartin doctors and coppers since we was maybe fourteen, fifteen years old. My kind got a little business of her own somewhere, raisin chickens maybe, going to church regular as clockwork, and raisin her sister's kids or maybe one or two of her own and raisin em right, so nobody don't make suckers of them.

I don't mean it's no bed of roses. It's bad alright, but it ain't no worse, take it all in all, nor no better neither, than the next racket that girls without folks or schoolin can get into. When a girl got nobody who cares and she got to quit school like I done, it don't matter much what line she goes into, she ends up pretty much the same way every time. Whether she hires out to cook some college-dame's meals and scrub her toilet or run a twenty-six game [a dice game] in a bar or tap tacks in a shoe factory, she's bound to take a beating in the end. The smartest just take it lying down. You last longer that way.

This Nineteenth and Dearborn territory has been my territory for years, even before I got on the bum. I know every window, every alley, every bust-out lamp, every car-line, every newsboy, every cigar store, every cop, every Chinaman. I even notice where somebody tossed out a cigarette against a wall and the next day the wind has blew the snips into the middle of the street. I've walked this corner at four a.m. and four p.m., summer and winter, sick and well, blind drunk and stone sober, sometimes so hungry I'd have to walk slow so as not to fold up the pavement and get pulled in, and once with a month's rent paid in advance and thirty dollars in a purse under my arm.

There's only one kind of man I ever met and that's the bad kind. I wouldn't even mention my man, but I got to have him whether I want him or not, being on the bum temporarily like I am. Men won't pay no unprotected woman, out of a house I mean, unless they're scared not to. I'd get beat up three times a night if Abe wasn't around somewheres. He used to be a wrestler up at Rainbo fronton* once in a while and they called him Chief Eagle-Feather then and he had to wear moccasins every Wednesday night. He's good to me though. So long as there's enough for hamburgers and beer, Abe don't care for nothin.

You'd think fellas would be the one to remember a girl, wouldn't you? I mean the fellas being the ones who's having all the fun, and her just seein one right after another all night long, it seems like he'd remember what she looked like better than she'd remember him. It ain't that way though, it's the other way around. You think I forget one single fella? Say, I could recognize them from six years back and the guy who was up here last night wouldn't know me from Hedy Lamarr right now, I bet. I'll tell you why that is; I figured it out. You can't forget one of them because you have to get the best of him as soon as he come in the room and takes off his cap. And nobody don't forget anybody that they got to get the best of.

Nelson Algren
*Chicago*
1939

---

* A building in which jai alai is played.

# TROUPERS
# AND
# PITCHMEN

Vaudeville palaces and carnival jammers. Doc Porter's Kickapoo Indian Medicine Show. The Mighty Yankee Robinson Circus. "Hey Rubes" and "cat-in-the-bags."

The world recalled by troupers and pitchmen was fading or had already vanished by the late 1930s. Many of the stories that follow reflect back to the turn of the century and earlier when touring companies of performers criss-crossed the countryside playing for city and small-town audiences. Entertaining and selling often merged into one; as a retired patent medicine pitchman put it, carnival ethics required that you amuse the suckers as you parted them from their money. Medicine shows usually traveled with a full complement of performers—singers, dancers, jugglers, comics, clowns, whose task it was to draw the crowd and warm it up for the pitch. A single entertainer's experience might span circuses, honky-tonks, medicine shows, and vaudeville.

Some thrived on the rough apprenticeship of the carnival entertainer. They dreamed of rising from seedy boardinghouses and one-night stands to the plush life of the big-time vaudeville headliner, earning as much as two or three thousand dollars a week. This opportunity for individual enterprise made the trouper a symbol of the American dream, an example of what might be achieved with talent, luck, and determination. He became a kind of American hero, an itinerant adventurer who lived by his wits.

The entertainers who reminisce in this chapter—purveyors of patent medicine, a rodeo clown, a circus hand, vaudeville comedians—celebrate their freedom from the humdrum of conventional life. A few of the troupers and pitchmen were still performing when these interviews were collected, but show business was no longer the freewheeling enterprise it had been earlier in the century. Radio and movies were already attracting a national audience. The Depression extinguished many of the tent shows and circuses. Stricter FDA regulations dampened the gaudy, hustling patent-medicine shows. Five-and-ten-cent stores stocked many of the pitchmen's wares. And by the end of the Thirties all of the elaborate vaudeville palaces had become movie houses.

Vaudeville grew out of medicine shows, Wild West shows, and touring circuses, and many of vaudeville's moguls had circus backgrounds. Entrepreneurs B. F. Keith and Edward Albee, who began by scalping circus tickets and hawking merchandise on the side, went on to build a chain of theaters that dominated vaudeville. Variety was the hallmark of the vaudeville stage. The ethnic jokes, horse acts, and dance numbers described here shared the billing with slapstick and mime, with Will Roger's political satire and Harry Houdini's baffling escapes. During the years vaudeville flourished, from the 1880s to the 1920s, it produced some of America's greatest performers: George Burns, Mae West, Eddie Cantor. But by the late 1920s vaudeville was dying. Many blamed Albee. He had busted an actor's union, set up a company union and the United Booking Office to better control the performers. He established a long history of underpaying and overworking them and blacklisted those who rebelled. Groucho Marx is said to have remarked that Albee had much in common with the owner of a cotton plantation. Albee's tactics drove vaudeville's best performers into more lucrative fields of entertainment such as movies and radio. But many couldn't make the transition.

Throughout the Thirties there were halfhearted attempts to revive vaudeville—with few results. Vaudeville was dead, and the men and women who depended on it for their livelihood were stranded, left with their memories of stars they had known and palaces they had played. If they were lucky they could get an occasional part in a Federal Theater Project* production. Despite hard times, however, there was a sense— for circus troupers, vaudevillians, and medicine-show entertainers alike— that it had been worth it, that show business was the best possible calling. As a circus hand put it, "If I had it all to do over again, I would still want you to give me the same route."

# J. C. Julian

*J. C. Julian (nickname: High-John-the-Conquerer) worked in the oil fields near Seminole, Oklahoma, and sold his lucky toby charms on the side. In a pool hall on Main Street, Daniel M. Garrison heard Julian's sales pitch, recorded it for the Federal Writers' Project, and parted with a dollar to buy*

---

* Like the Federal Writers' Project, the Federal Theater Project offered employment to artists under the auspices of the WPA.

himself a toby. "Son," Julian assured him, "you'll never regret buying one of my tobies."

Daniel Garrison joined the Oklahoma Writers' Project after having farmed tobacco in Maryland, worked as a deckboy on a freighter, and as roustabout for Standard Oil.* He also interviewed the rodeo clown on page 199.

If I tell you about tobies, I don't want you to be talking about them to nobody else. If you do, don't tell nobody I was the one who told you. It's against the laws of the state of Oklahoma, and lots of other states, to sell tobies. They claim us toby-sellers are running a racket, deceiving the people, that there ain't nothing to tobies. But I know better, and you ought to know better.

You believe in luck, don't you? Sure you do! Everybody believes there's such a thing as luck. You know yourself, things don't just happen. Some people are lucky and some people ain't so lucky, and all people sometime or other have luck. A toby helps people to be lucky. If you want something real bad, you don't get what you want without some help. That's where my tobies come in. I sell them for just one dollar, but they're worth fifty times that amount. And I guarantee my tobies. But don't never let nobody else touch your toby. If you do, the toby will lose its charm.

A toby is a lucky charm. It's what you put in them that does the trick. It ain't just everybody that knows how to make them. It took me a long time to learn. I put eight things in my tobies. The most important thing is high-john-the-conqueror. It's a kind of lucky root. Then I put in a four-leaf clover, five-finger grass, a white powder, a black powder, and a pink powder. That white powder costs plenty, over twenty dollars an ounce. I don't put in much, just a smidgen. I don't recollect the name of them powders, but you can get them at any lucky shop. I put two more things in my tobies; they've slipped my mind for the present.

You put all these things in a little fancy colored bag, known as a lucky bag. Then I usually wrap the lucky bag in cellophane, and tie it up with pretty ribbon. The cellophane keeps the lucky bag clean, and helps to keep it from wearing out. I'd show you my toby, but it would take all the luck out of it, showing it to someone else. One quick peek wouldn't hurt very much, but like a fool when I changed my pants this morning, I forgot and left my toby in the right-hand pocket. It's a wonder I ain't been run down by a car.

* *Economy of Scarcity: Some Human Footnotes* (Norman, Okla., 1939).

The last time I got careless and left my toby home, I damn near got myself killed. I ought to of had better sense than to go to a dance sober and without my toby. I knew I didn't have it with me when I reached for my change to get into the dance. If I hadn't of been sober, I couldn't of got drunk. And if I had had my toby with me, I wouldn't of got in that fight. And even if I couldn't of kept out of the fight, I wouldn't of been the one to get all cut up.

I sold a toby to a woman in Walters, down in Cotten County. She had been full of religion when she was a young gal, but when she married, God left her. Her husband was a poor cotton farmer and had to make whiskey on the side to make a living. This old gal got a liking for whiskey and she could drink ten men under the table. All this drinking led to looseness, and she started trifling on her old man. Then she did get herself in a fix. One day it come to her that she was going to have a baby. She knew her old man was suspicious of her conduct, and if the kid didn't look something like him, he'd break her neck, or run her off. It scared her so bad that she gave up drinking and trifling and started going to church, but it didn't do no good. She couldn't get salvation. It just wouldn't come to her.

The woman was just about dead with worry when I hit town. She heard through one of my customers that I sold tobies that never failed, and she looked me up. I sold her one for five dollars, but it was worth five hundred to her. When her baby was born, it looked like her. That toby sure enough saved that woman from shame and a good beating, maybe death itself. But my tobies never fail—never fail! Of course, if you don't put no faith in a toby, a toby won't help you none. It's like everything else: you've got to put faith in it or you won't get no results.

Here's my sales talk:

"Put up and built by the Seven Sisters at the Crackerjack Drug Store at New Orleans, Louisiana. My toby will bring you Honor, Riches, and Happiness. It will help you Win in all Games. It will bring you Health and Wealth. It will Protect you against Evil Spirits and Witchcraft. Thieves nor Enemies cannot bother you. Now listen, everything you turn your hand to Prospers you and makes you Money. You succeed in your Trade, Job, or Business. You got Seven Wishes to make with each Lucky Bag. Hold the Bag in your Left hand, blow your hot breath on it Three times, and Make your Wish, and see if it don't come to Pass before the Seventh day is gone.

"To hold your True Loved one. To get anyone you love. To Protect yourself against all Law. To Kill all Voodoo and Witchcraft. Buy a toby. Just One Dollar. And if you ain't satisfied with my Toby, I give you your

Money Back. Don't be Foolhardy. Don't run no Risk. Keep a Toby on your person all the Time. Just One Dollar. But it's worth Fifty." I've sold tobies to all kinds of folk. I've sold them to politicians and big businessmen, to gamblers, and to thieves. I've sold lots of them to folks wanting to get married, and to folks who don't want to get married but want to live like married folks. But the poor whites and the poor Negroes are my best customers. It ain't because they're dumber than rich folks. Some of them ain't as dumb. And young man, let me tell you right now, it's the dumb folks that don't buy tobies to help them. Understand that right off! Poor folks need more luck than rich folks. That's the reason they buy more tobies.

D. M. Garrison
*Seminole, Oklahoma*
1939

# Josiah Roberts*

*Josiah Roberts was peddling cake flavoring door-to-door in Durham, North Carolina, when he was interviewed. Roberts's protestations that he was too honest and too full of brotherly love to make a successful pitchman alternate with descriptions of elaborate cons he witnessed or pulled off himself, stories of fake diamond rings, lucky charms made from grassnut roots, medicine-show spiels, and bogus unions. Leonard Rapport, who talked to Roberts several times in the winter of 1939, believes that he was honest. "Regardless of how he may appear, he was really a gentle, thoughtful man and I doubt he ever really made much as a pitchman."†*

Medicine is the biggest thing that's pitched. But the doctors and druggists got down so strong on it I think you now have to have a special license to pitch it. You should go to Winston-Salem about two weeks after the market opens—if there was ever a medicine racket it's operated

---

* Fictitious name.
† Interview with Leonard Rapport, June 1978. For other narratives collected by Rapport, see Tobacco People.

*A patent medicine salesman, Port Gibson, Mississippi, 1940.*
*Photograph by Marion Post Wolcott.*

there. You can learn more about rackets and pitching on Trade Street in two days than you can in two months in Durham. The people have money and are in a carnival mood, buying and spending. All a man has to do to get started is to shake a cowbell and ballyhoo. They're pulling games twenty-five years old. They even sell them "cat-in-the-bag"—a box with something in it. They'll say, "Go ahead, boys, open the box; if it's not worth fifty cents, here's a dollar."

Chief Running Fox, a full-blooded Indian, works there. He's got seven or eight people in his crew. I've seen him with as high as fifteen entertainers, including musicians. When the show's over, the entertainers go through the crowd selling the medicine. And there's Doc Cheshire who sits around all summer getting fat on what he makes in the market season. The thing about pitching medicine is to make a fuss and in any bunch of men you draw, half are going to have aches and pains due to over- or under-eating—malnutrition, I believe they call it. And the less education they have, the more they'll believe in the power of a bottle to cure them. People believe what they want to believe.

The jam-man is the best pitchman of all; he's a smoother talker and he can get and hold a crowd more than any other pitchman in the field. He always has a helper, either his wife or another man. I've seen women jamming in Texas, Oklahoma, Missouri, and Illinois, but only once in North Carolina; they rely more on their feminine attraction than on their sales ability. If a jammer has a pretty wife helping him, lots of times it allays suspicion.

A good jammer is somebody to watch work—and all forty-four states, the four commonwealths, and the District of Columbia fall for him. It used to be that every circus and carnival carried jammers, but now a first-class circus or carnival won't permit them. Lots of the states won't either. North Carolina is open, and though it costs plenty to jam here, they can pay.

You can tell a jammer the minute he starts and a block away. They're usually working from the back end of an automobile. A good kind of car for them is a one-seater where the back lifts up. Sometimes they'll have a little platform back there. They all use the same system and the same sort of speech. Usually when they start they'll hold up a catalog and say, "I'm representing a large company—second to Sears and Roebuck," some say. "My company wants to advertise and they've sent me here to give away several presents." Then he takes out wrist watches, fountain pens, knives, silverware sets, carving sets, rings, cameras, razor blades, and all kinds of things, and holds them up and says they're the things his company wants to advertise.

A jammer worked here thirty minutes this fall and took $160, of which $130 was net profit. He was from Oklahoma; I used to know him. I talked to him before he pitched and asked him how much he was going to take them for. "I can't afford to pitch for less than a hundred dollars," he said. "Go ahead," I told him. "I hope you get a couple hundred." He drove into Deevers' warehouse before the sale quit for dinner at twelve-thirty. It took him thirty minutes to throw his jam.

This fellow got a crowd of farmers and some of the boys working in the warehouse by throwing out cheap razor blades and key rings. He said, "Yes, my company wants to advertise—get em." Then he threw out two or three pocket knives—they cost him fifty cents a dozen. By that time he had the crowd grabbing and in the mood to believe.

He started with pocketbooks—cost eighty cents a dozen. He picked up some; and as he did, everybody jumped. Then he says, "My company wants to put these pocketbooks in reliable hands. They want them to go to reliable people who after I'm gone will visit the drugstores and shops that handle our stuff and call for our products. Now I want to get rid of the chiselers and children. I want a man to give me a dollar for this pocketbook and I promise I will make him say, 'Thank you.' "

Somebody will take him up; he doesn't need a plant in the audience. There's always enough who believe in the American theory of something for nothing. When the man gives him his dollar he'll ask him, "Are you satisfied to pay a dollar for this?" The man says, "Yes." Then he gives him the pocketbook and says, "To show you the kind of company I represent, here's your dollar back." I've never seen it fail yet, and I reckon I've seen twenty-five jammers. All based on the same theory— the crowd thinks he's trying to get rid of the sorry ones, and they pay, expecting to get their money back.

He sold thirty-six pocketbooks and marked each box with a number. He laid a bill on each pocketbook and made a motion like he was going to pass out the pocketbooks and the bills—and then he stopped and held a pen-and-pencil set and asked who wanted one for five dollars. Somebody gave him five dollars. Then he said, "I've got a few more responsible gifts for responsible people. Anybody who hasn't got five dollars isn't responsible." There were nine of the sets sold.

Then he sold four or five carving sets at five dollars and one or two watches at five dollars. Then he brought out silverware sets that could be bought downtown for $2.98 and still give the merchant a forty percent profit, and sold three or four of them for ten dollars a set. He got ten dollars for one manicure set that could be bought anywhere for two or three dollars.

Then he started handing out the presents, the large ones first. He'd ask each one as he gave his present to him, "What do you say?" Each one would say, "Thank you." Then he'd ask, "Are you satisfied with what you paid?" And each one said yes, fully expecting, of course, to get his money back.

After all purchases were handed out, he stepped back, holding the money, making them think he was getting ready to hand it out, and said, "If anybody is not satisfied, say so now before we proceed." One man gave his pocketbook back and somebody else stepped up and bought it. Then he asked them, "Are you as satisfied as if you bought what you got from a merchant up the street?" and they all said yes.

His assistant had the car motor running. Now, at this point, some jammers throw out cheap samples to get the crowd to back away from the front and sides of the car, but he didn't have to do that. As soon as he got every man to agree he said, "Well, if you're satisfied, so am I," and got in the car and drove across the floor and on out the warehouse. It took the crowd a minute to realize what happened, and some of them chased the car. They were so mad at themselves they could have torn him to pieces. Yet he could probably have come back and worked again the next day. I've seen people who knew what it was try to stop their friend, but people get intoxicated with the idea of somebody giving away something for nothing. Old Doc Epsom Salts, who peddles an epsom-salts tonic around here, fell for eleven dollars on this jam-man. I asked him if he'd never seen a jam-man and he said he never had but he'd know the next one he saw. He was originally from a small town and he just never seen anything like that before. He said, "I thought sure he was going to give me my money back." I asked him, "If you'd been in his place would you have given it back?" He studied a minute and then he said, "I'd a been a fool if I had, wouldn't I?"

If they hadn't tried to make a minister of me when I was a boy I guess I could do good as a pitchman or a jammer, but I've got a little too much religion. Those early teachings about brotherly love caused me to pass up plenty. My mother wanted to make an Episcopal minister out of me but she didn't have enough money to educate me. I went to work when I was twelve. I worked in feed stores, grocery stores, cotton mills. I helped raise tobacco and one summer I tended five curing barns. When I was sixteen I worked a season on a warehouse floor in Kingston unloading and packing tobacco at twenty-five cents an hour. When I was twenty my mother went to live with her cousins. She told me then, "I'm going to turn you loose; I won't need your money anymore. You haven't had the opportunities I'd like you to have had; but whatever you do, don't let me hear about you being in jail."

After that I began to roam; there's a lot of nomad in my blood— gypsy, you might call it. I went from one town to another. I wandered through twenty-eight of the United States, selling or following my trade, which was baking. I followed baking for nine years and then I quit it due to long hours. That, and the fact that when a man gets to be thirty years old and a little gray comes in his hair he's too old for the job. I'm gray now and I'm only thirty-seven. Now I'm selling flavoring, cake coloring, and herb tea. There are ten or twelve regular peddlers like myself in Durham and then there's six or seven extras who come in during the tobacco season.

Some pitchmen work here who follow the tobacco markets right on up, starting in Georgia in the summer. I never have followed the markets; I never did have a racket to work on farmers. You have to have something you can make about three hundred to four hundred percent on, though it doesn't necessarily have to be crooked. Pitching is gradually going out, especially due to five-and-ten-cent stores carrying so many of the things pitchmen used to sell, but there's still money in it. Most of the pitch business now is based on some novelty trick or other. A good pitchman will do two thousand to five thousand dollars a year with seventy-five percent of the take as profit.

I've never pitched but two or three times in my life. I once made hotel expenses and meals from Wilmington, Delaware, to Norfolk by selling Mexican diamond rings along the way. I bought three dozen of them at ten cents apiece in a five-and-ten-cent store in Pocomoke City, Maryland, and sold some of them for from two to four dollars each. I was catching rides down. I'd get into a town and find a boy about twenty years old and looked like he might have a girl. I'd tell him my girl had kicked me, I was broke, and I had a ring I'd paid seventy-five dollars for. How much will you give me? It was better to find several of them together because one by himself was afraid. When there were more, they'd sometimes bid for it—they'd think they had me with my pants down. I sold one ring for seven dollars. They could beat me down to two dollars; I wouldn't go below that.

People don't know diamonds; that's what lets you get away with it. After being worn two or three days the ring starts to stain the girl's finger and the boy will take it to a jeweler. You couldn't work that in a place you had to come back to anytime soon. But if you wait five years, the chances are the boys you sold to are married and working and not on the streets, and you can work the very same thing again. Though it doesn't go as well now as it used to, I know the trick to be worked in North Carolina last year.

I have done good around here selling Adam and Eves; they really are grassnut roots, about the size of the tip of your little finger. I usually dig up several hundred when I visit my mother in the winter and I string them and let them dry. Negroes buy them for luck. I fasten two together with a piece of thread and say, "How about an Adam and Eve?" and then I'll show in a glass of water how one floats and the other sinks. I tell them, "The one on top is Adam and the other is Eve, trying to pull Adam under." The idea is the old Adam and Eve story with Eve, the mother of sin, pulling Adam, the man, down. I get anywhere from twenty-five cents to a dollar a pair. I suppose the roots that sink are the fertile ones—the roots that germinate—and the floaters are the sterile ones.

All sorts of things are sold around the warehouses; watches that can be ordered for $4.75 and sell for nine or ten dollars, rattlesnake oil that never gets nearer a rattlesnake than oil of mustard, and blood purifiers that are sodium sulphate, which is Glauber's salts and can be bought at fifteen cents a pound and is commonly used as a horse medicine. However, a good physic corrects many ills. If it wasn't for constipation, medical doctors wouldn't have a leg to stand on. It's the only thing they can really treat except for something like broken bones.

To show you how simple people are, I take this flavoring that I sell in Durham for thirty cents and go to Hillsboro, come to a door, knock, and tell the lady of the house I want to introduce a new product. I show her a pot cleaner that can be bought for seventy-five cents a dozen, and sell the flavoring to her for sixty cents and throw in the cleaner free. They fall for it; they fall for the gab of getting something for nothing. It's an American habit.

I've got several good propositions in mind. I've got some formulas I am certain would be money-makers if I could get the money to manufacture and distribute them. Anything new can be sold. That's one reason I'm not interested in selling Bibles: every house has one. Also, I think a Bible salesman should be conscientious in his belief. But a good salesman can sell anything legitimate and lots of things that aren't.

I'm handicapped myself by lack of capital. A man can start out selling with from three dollars up, but the chances are that with three hundred dollars he will prosper a hundred times as fast. When you peddle small items from house to house all day, your feet get to hurting, your nerves wear, you slow down, and there's not much money in it. Now, I'm too honest to make a pitchman, and peddling doesn't allow me to work as fast as I'd like to. A peddler will always be a peddler unless he gets out or starts his own line like the big men have done. Take Frank Fitch, who started out house-to-house with his hair tonic, or Emerson, who was from this state and started out making Bromo-Seltzer in the back of his drug store and hired men to peddle it from door to door. Right here in Durham we have the men who discovered BC [a headache powder], and they're making millions from it. Now here in the *Specialty Salesman's Magazine* is the story of a truck driver who gave up a forty-five-dollar-a-week job to work house-to-house, though all his friends were against it. Now he's a success; here's his picture on the cover. He says it's all in your attitude; he believes in smiling.

Leonard Rapport
*Durham, North Carolina*
1939

# William D. Naylor

*William D. Naylor trouped with Doc Porter's Kickapoo Indian Medicine Show in the late 1880s, when such entertainments were a familiar pleasure. Touring medicine shows had much in common with touring revival meetings: one dispensed Kickapoo remedies while the other offered spiritual balm. Naylor's description of the cooperation between Doc Porter and an evangelist he chanced across recalls Huckleberry Finn's encounters with con artists on the banks of the Mississippi.*

I was born in New York City on the West Side, but when I was just a baby my people moved up to the Bronx. Our chief diversion on Sundays was to go to Coney Island and ride our bicycles out there. I suppose I always had a flair for the kind of entertainment Coney Island offered. There was a kind of fascination to me in the excitement and glamour of the carnival spirit.

Eventually, when I was about nineteen years old, I joined DOC PORTER'S KICKAPOO INDIAN MEDICINE SHOW. The show was then playing in the Bronx and every night I'd go over and listen, envying the performers who entertained the crowd before Doc Porter came out to give his lecture and sell his medicines.

I stayed with Doc Porter for six years, singing "Poor Mourner, You Shall Be Free," "Kansas," and some of the popular songs like "Two Little Girls in Blue," "Down Went M'Ginty," and "After the Ball." All my work was black-face, and I imagined I was just as good as most vaudeville performers on stages in theaters. We traveled in covered hacks or spring wagons and all our shows were given out of doors. Our lights were gasoline flares on each side of the stage, which was a platform at the back end of the wagon. We traveled all over the small circuits of upper New York, part of Pennsylvania, New Jersey, and as far south as Virginia. In the days of the medicine show there were not so many laws regulating the practice of medicine or the sale of drugs and not so many licenses and restrictions as now. This was especially true in the backwoods towns we'd usually show in—often towns without railroads and where other shows didn't come.

So Doc Porter didn't have to do anything but drive into a town, pick out a vacant spot somewhere, and set up our pitch there. Everybody would know as soon as we got into a town, but Doc usually hunted up the newspaper office if there was a paper and gave the editor an ad

*Outside a tobacco auction warehouse in Durham, North Carolina, 1939.*
*Photograph by Marion Post Wolcott.*

telling where our show was located. That got him on the good side of the editor, and the editor in those backwoods places was an important person. He would call on the marshall, and if there was a mayor he would visit him too.

With his "dignity," Prince Albert coat, silk hat, and double-breasted watch chain with a buck-eye set in gold bands—Doc believed the buck-eye kept him from having rheumatism—he looked and could act like a combination Bishop, Senator, and Supreme Court Judge all rolled into one. The natives in those small backwoods towns never had a chance with him.

Once we hit a place back in the hill country of Virginia called Rocky Comfort. It wasn't really a town. There was a water-power grist mill, a store, a blacksmith shop, and about a quarter of a mile up the little valley there was a meeting house, where traveling preachers would sometimes hold revivals, which were called camp meetings.

Doc Porter stopped there to have the horses shod, and it happened there was a camp meeting going on. It looked like a pretty busy place. The natives from miles around had come, brought their families, their hound dogs, and their rifles and were camped out in the grove around the meeting house. Doc got the idea that our Medicine Show would add to the general entertainment and we could give shows between religious services. It worked. Doc was diplomatic and didn't try to compete with the preaching but sort of helped it out and never gave a show while preaching was going on. Instead we'd all attend the services. That put us in solid with the brethren and we sold a lot of medicine.

Doc Porter's medicines were all made up by himself, and he was jealous of the "ancient Kickapoo formulas" he used. They were all made "from roots and barks and the tender succulent foliage of healing, life-giving herbs the Great Manitou of Nature planted in the forests, on the hills, and in the valleys to give his children, the noble tribe of Kickapoos, those priceless secrets of Life and Health and Happiness; they were handed down from father to son and from generation to generation— cherished and guarded with the very lives of their possessors! Then when my great-great grandfather saved the life of the Chief Medicine Man of the Kickapoo Tribe, the 'Bounding Cougar,' that great Chief showed his gratitude by giving my noble pioneer ancestor their marvelous formulas and he bade him go forth and give his White Brethren the blessings the Great Manitou had bestowed upon his Red Children."

Doc Porter sure had a great string of palaver, and though I heard it a thousand times I never got tired of listening to his lecture.

One of the tricks Doc Porter used to stimulate sales of his Kickapoo Indian remedies was the psychology of suggestion. Doc had it down fine. He would always wind up his lecture with a detailed description of the symptoms of all the diseases the Kickapoo Indian medicines were supposed to cure. The way he described those diseases—how anybody would feel when they were getting them, or had them or were about to have them—was enough to make anybody shiver. By the time Doc got through describing symptoms, practically everybody in the neighborhood would be imagining they felt at least some of them. Why, I used to sit and listen to Doc's horror stories of diseases till I'd get to feeling the symptoms myself! Doc was a foxy old bird and I guess he wasn't far off base when he'd say, "Most diseases people get are just imagination, anyhow!"

We ran across one queer get-whatever-they-imagine disease cases down in the backwoods hill country of Virginia. The people in that section were pretty poor and on most of the farms they used water from shallow open wells, natural springs, or creeks. Naturally the springs and creeks and even the open wells were often infested with frogs, water skimmers, beetles, and things like that. One night at one of our shows a young fellow asked Doc if his Indian Medicines would cure an "inside frog." "My Uncle Zeb Hurst took a drink of water down at our spring one night a couple of weeks ago and he swallowed a frog by mistake, at least he says he did. He also says it's still in him and still alive and he can feel it kicking and twitching around in his stomach. He's getting mighty peaked and thin from worrying about it. He's afraid it will grow and get so big it will kill him."

The young fellow took Doc and me out to see Uncle Zeb and we found the old fellow in pretty bad shape, just barely able to hobble around. He kept holding his hands over his stomach and swearing that every once in a while he could feel the cussed frog kicking and jerking inside of him! Doc put his hand on the old fellow's stomach and kind of pressed down on it for a minute. "There, he kicked!" the old man said. "Didn't you feel him?"

"Yeah, I sure as hell felt something jerking inside of you, but are you sure it's a frog you swallowed?" Doc said.

"Course I am sure," the old man replied. "I went down to the spring to tote a pail of water up to the cabin and I thought I'd take me a fresh drink while I was there. It was sort of dark and I didn't notice much, and before I knowed it I'd sucked the danged frog in my mouth and felt him slip down my throat."

Doc said he'd go down to the spring and look around a bit; it might be something else Uncle Zeb had swallowed. Anyhow, he'd want to see what sort of frogs there were in the spring so he could tell better which variety of Indian medicine would be best to use to make the frog come out.

When Doc came back from the spring he was grinning with that grin he used to have when he'd get a big idea and felt confident of what he was about to do. He told Uncle Zeb he'd found out the kind of frog he'd probably swallowed and that he had to work to get him out of Uncle Zeb's stomach. He had Uncle Zeb lie down on the ground under a tree out in the yard, close his eyes, and open his mouth. Then Doc squatted down by him, put his silk hat over Uncle Zeb's face, and told the rest of us to stand back, he had to have plenty of room. Then he said: "Now, Uncle Zeb, keep your eyes shut tight and I'll stick this medicine under the hat, slush a little of it in your mouth and when the frog smells it he'll come out of your stomach in a hurry. He'll come up so damn quick you won't hardly feel him until he hits your mouth, then I'll grab him and pull him on out. Now hold still, I'm going to do it."

Doc run his hand under the hat and Uncle Zeb sort of grunted and gagged. Doc jerked his hand out and damned if he didn't pull out a little green-back bull frog about an inch and a half or two inches long! "Now you can open your eyes," Doc told Uncle Zeb, "here's your cussed frog. I knowed my Kickapoo Medicine would bring him up!"

Uncle Zeb opened his eyes and heaved a sigh of relief. "You sure got him, Doc. I feel relieved already! I'll never take another drink of water out of that damn spring in the dark, you can depend on that!" He bought three bottles of Doc's Kickapoo Rheumatism Rubbing Oil— which smelled like hell—so he'd have it on hand just in case he did accidentally get another "inside frog."

Doc Porter was versatile alright, and nothing ever seemed to stump him. He used to say: "It ain't what anybody knows for certain, but what they *think* they know for certain that counts, and if people buy Kickapoo Indian Medicine and think it'll cure them, it's darn near sure to cure them. And so they haven't been cheated!"

Which shows that Doc was sincere in believing that the stuff he mixed up out of wild cherry bark, senna leaves, slippery elm bark, sassafrass roots, and other "Indian herbs"—all of which he fortified with about sixty percent of good raw whiskey—were genuinely beneficial medicines and that he was a human benefactor. One thing I'm sure of is that our old Medicine Show gave a lot of people who otherwise didn't have very much entertainment a chance to see and hear something different and be amused.

That's the way a carnival man is. He don't give them anything, yet he gives them *something*—entertainment, experience, or amusement for the chicken feed he takes away from them at his rack or wheel or ring-board. And if he has a run of "mud-luck," he always finds a way to get out somehow, raise a stake, and climb back into the game. You don't see any genuine old-time carnival birds working the street for a dime, or picking up crumbs from a kitchen back door. They're independent; and even if they're down to the last two bits, you'd never know it by looking at them, or hear it from their own lips. They might do a lot of cussing in private, but never a hard-luck story to outsiders. They've always got some kind of idea tucked back in their head that they can pull out and turn into ham-and-egg money somehow. Even if the show goes flat, they'll raise tickets to the next burg someway. And they'll raise it on the square, according to the ethics of the profession: "Give the suckers *nothing* for their money—but when you give them nothing, you give them *something!*"

Earl Bowman
*New York City*
1938

# William Moody

*Away from the rodeo, clown William Moody dressed in conservative businessman's fashion, according to Federal Writer Daniel M. Garrison. "No cowboy boots. He looks more like a traveling salesman than a colorful cowhand. He has never lived on a ranch. His rodeo clowning is strictly commercial." According to what he told Garrison, Moody earned an average of thirty-five dollars a performance.*

The idea of a rodeo clown is not only to make folks laugh, but to attract the attention of the steer after the rider has been thrown. If this is not done, the steer will turn and stomp the rider to death. All clowns wear red shirts.

The first steer I ever rode was in Burkburnett, Texas, in 1921. I was a yard clerk for the M. K. & T. railroad, and got to know all the cattlemen in those parts. They would be in the yards when their steers were loaded in the cattlecars.

Two of those cattlemen, Colonel Whit Phillips and T. Guy Willis, promoted a rodeo. This rodeo, like many others throughout the West, was a local affair, with only cowhands on nearby ranches taking part. They were held once a month except during the winter months. It was not an invitation contest, like the professional championship contests held at Fort Worth, Cheyenne, and Madison Square Garden.

A bunch of cowhands would get together at these local rodeos and bet that some other cowhand couldn't ride a certain horse or steer. Each ranch had a string of steers and horses that couldn't be rode, so the owners boasted. These steers and horses were plenty wild. They didn't have to use a hot-shot [an electric cattle prod] on those babies. As a matter of fact, hot shots were unknown in those days.

At one of these rodeos, I was sitting on the rail watching the steer-riding, when everybody north of Tulsa was asked to ride a steer. The other rail-setters egged me on, knowing I was from Missouri. The cowhands in the Southwest thought themselves better riders than the cowhands in the Northwest, and the same goes the other way around.

Well, the boys bulldozed me into riding a steer. And let it be known that the only difference between riding a steer and a hanging is you've got the noose in your hand—that's all! It's the first jump the steer makes when the gate is open that pops your neck. A man never really knows

A rodeo clown in Quemado, New Mexico, 1940. Photograph by Russell Lee.

just how long his neck is till he rides a steer. Your neck stretches like an elastic band. With a pair of binoculars you can look down and see if a giraffe parts his hair in the middle or on the side. After the second jump, you don't know whether you're riding the steer or the steer is riding you. More than likely, the steer is riding you. Six out of ten "good" cowhands stay with their steers. The second jump always brings me and the steer to a quick parting. We put air between us.

My first steer-riding took less than five seconds, but it took me more than five days to get over it. I was so stiff from that ride I had to turn my whole body to look sideways. But a fool never knows when he's well off. So I tried my luck again and again—the steers winning each and every time. The folks got such a kick out of me riding steers—being tossed in the air and getting all tangled up in my own arms and legs— that Colonel Phillips said that from now on I'd be the clown for the shows: a job that paid whether you won first prize or not. And that's how come I'm a rodeo clown. And that's how come I'm all busted up and ain't worth a damn for nothing.

Don't let no one tell you different—a steer knows how to use his horns. He knows just how long his horns are, and he knows just how each horn is twisted. His mammy teaches him how to use his horns, and he puts in a little horning practice every day. This might sound like a lie, but it's the God's truth—a steer can scrape the ground so close that he can scratch up a cigarette paper.

When a cowhand is thrown, the clown whoops and hollers and waves his arms to attract the steer. The steer soon forgets all about the rider who has gouged his sides with spurs, and becomes double mad at the clown. Then the fun begins—for the spectators. Can the clown get to safety before the steer impales him? The clown often wonders. So far, I've been on the winning end. But I've had many close calls—too many.

Sometimes steel drums are used. The clown runs and dives into a steel drum, braces himself, and waits for the steer to knock the drum for a loop. It jars the hell out of you. But you live to tell the tale! If the steer is coming after you and you can't get away, don't try to sidestep or dodge. Fall flat on the ground and the steer will jump over you. After he jumps, get up, and get for cover before he turns around. Never let a steer get set so he can use his horns. He'll tear you to pieces, and they'll have to wire you together for the burial.

The most dangerous contest at a rodeo is steer-rassling, known as "bull-dogging." Two cowboys participate. Your partner rides along one side of the steer, keeping him close to your horse. You leave your horse, grab the steer by the horns, and throw him—maybe! The average time for a cowboy to throw a steer is twelve seconds.

Now the clown, to get a laugh, grabs the steer by the tail when he's down. Then when the steer gets up and streaks off, the clown, holding on to the steer's tail, turns a flip. The clown sometimes sits on the downed steer and lets the steer throw him when the steer leaps angrily to its feet. I quit that foolishness. The last steer I jumped on, leaped to his feet, bucked, threw me high into the air, and then bucked again and met me coming down. I landed first on the steer, then on the ground, and then in the hospital. Anything for a laugh.

D. M. Garrison
*Seminole, Oklahoma*
1939

# "Doc" Van Alstine

*Doc Van Alstine's fifty years of circus trouping included the "Golden Age" of the American circus during the last quarter of the nineteenth century. The Mighty Yankee Robinson*

Circus, which Van Alstine joined in his teens, was one of the first "big show" circuses; it combined in 1884 with Ringling Brothers to form the Yankee Robinson & Ringling Brothers great Double Shows, Circus and Caravan.

At an early age I had a yearning for the show business. School didn't interest me a bit. I hated books. I wasn't a danged bit interested in reading about what somebody else did, or where they went, or what they saw. I wanted to go, do, and see things for myself, and I couldn't think of any better way to satisfy my ambition than to join up with a circus.

Come a day, once, when I was a young gaffer in my early teens, I had a chance to run away with the Mighty Yankee Robinson Circus. The lure of sawdust and spangles was much stronger than family ties or the red schoolhouse, so off I went.

I was hired as a block boy to help set up and tear down the blues [seats]. There wasn't no commoner job, but I remember how proud and thrilled I was merely to touch anything that was a part of the circus.

I was only there four days when I was dragged home to the family fireside and my place at the table, but not without a trip to the barn first, where my father strapped me around the legs and across the back with a tie-strap until I weren't hardly able to navigate. As tough a lickin as the old man gave me, I soon forgot it—but I didn't forget my first four days with the circus.

I remember how I gazed in awe at the performers, and to think I was so close to them. I seen a lot of beautiful women in my day, but I don't believe I ever seen a woman in my later life that looked so beautiful to me as them circus women did. I had the feeling that they was queens, or goddesses, or something too beautiful to belong to the world. And I recall the thrill of thrills when a clown—circus folks call the funny men Joeys—said, "Hey, lad, run out to a butcher shop and get me a pound of lard." The Joeys used lard for taking off their makeup. I was so excited at having a performer actually speak to me that I couldn't say yes or no. But with the ten-cent piece he give me clutched in my fist, I run like lightning to the nearest butcher shop. Boy, oh boy, was I happy.

When I went back to school after my four days with the circus, I cut quite a figure among my schoolmates. Being with a circus made me a hero, and did I glory in it. I knew that when I got a little bit older I was going to join up with a circus and be a showman for always and always.

*Smithland, Kentucky, 1935. Photograph by Ben Shahn.*

My family was determined that I was going to be a doctor, like my old man. In them days, anybody that thought they was cut out for it could be a doctor if they wanted to. All you needed was a little schooling and be handy around sick folks and not be afraid of the sight of blood. All medicine was bitter if it was any good, and if they didn't know what ailed a person they drew some blood. Then he either got better or worse, as God willed. I might have made a good doctor at that, if I only could have got show business off my mind.

When I got a few years older, I was able to out-talk the old folks and get my own way. I give up all thought of pill-rolling and left home to join a circus. I stuck with circuses for nearly sixty years of my life and I worked on all the big shows one time or another. Studying for a doctor, though, give me the nickname, "Doc," and that's the name I'm knowed by wherever on this globe a "big top" is being raised.

There just ain't no comparison between the circus of today and the circus of the past. The circus in this day and age seems really to be the stupendous, gigantic, colossal exhibition the advance billing and the "barkers," "spielers," and "grinders" claim for it. The circus your grandfather went to see as a boy was nothing more than a variety, or vaudeville, show under canvas. Pretty near all the acts they done in the circus could have been put on in even the ordinary theaters of that time, but the kids of today ain't so wide-eyed and amazed at what they see at a circus as they was a quarter of a century ago. So many marvelous things goes on all the time in this day and age that kids probably expect more from a circus now than it's humanly possible to give.

The people who works for the circuses today is all trained specialists. Everybody has only one job, and he's supposed to do that one thing well. The old-time trouper was a Jack-of-all-trades. He could shoe a horse, if he had to, he could clown, drive a ten-horse team, lay out canvas, and fill in at anything around the lot except perhaps aerial acrobatics, and believe it or not, many of the old-timers could even double in acrobatics.

Circus people in the old days was considered social outcasts. "Decent" people wouldn't have nothing to do with troupers. This brought the show folks closer together; made em clannish. Circus people was just like one big family, and was always a good lot, always willing to help each other over the bumps. People don't look at it the way they used to, anymore, but circus people is still clannish just the same.

A "Hey Rube" is practically unknown today. A Hey Rube was a fight between the circus folks and the town yokels. Those ruckuses used to come regularly every so often in the old days. Many of the Hey Rubes was started by folks figgering they wasn't getting all the circus advertised; if the stupendous wasn't stupendous enough, the gigantic wasn't gigantic enough, the colossal wasn't colossal enough, or the "largest in captivity" wasn't large enough, the town folks felt like they had grounds for a fight. Another common cause of a Hey Rube was because petty thieves, purse-snatchers, and pickpockets followed circuses from town to town. The circus got blamed for what them slickers did, but there was nothing they could do about it. When the crooks hit a crowd too hard, and too many people got plucked, the town folk got together and tried to take it out on the circus people. Pretty near every Hey Rube I ever seen ended with the town folks coming out second best physically, although the circus usually lost out financially. Lawsuits always followed a Hey Rube, usually by some innocent bystanders who got hurt in the scramble, and circus people had no chance for a square deal in a prejudiced small-town court.

The circus had always been one of the world's most progressive enterprises. New inventions, if they was something the circus could use, was grabbed up by the circus as soon as they come out. The circus was always away ahead of anybody else in lighting equipment. Modern methods and high specialization has made it a lot easier for the circus man. Transportation is improved, and accommodations is a lot better than they was. You don't have to be tough inside and out to troupe with a circus nowadays. In the old days any handler of circus stock knowed how to mix up a batch of kerosene or paregoric liniment to dope an ailing animal. Nowadays the big show troupes a staff of veterinarians, and each valuable animal is watched as close and its diet figured out as carefully as for the Dionne quints.

I got a lot of respect for Clyde Beattie and other of today's animal trainers, but I don't think there is any comparison between the temper and ferocity of jungle-born cats that the old-time trainer faced twice a day, and the animals born in captivity that the present-day trainers work with. You don't hardly ever hear of a trainer getting killed in an exhibition cage today; but in the old days I have seen trainers torn to ribbons in the twinkling of an eye.

The circus reached its greatest size in 1908 when Ringling Brothers introduced the first "spec," or spectacle. Since that year the spec was a feature with all circuses. The first spec was called "King Solomon" and later "Arabian Nights," and others. I was boss canvasman for many years with a number of different circuses. Boss canvasman is a good job on a big show and pays from seventy-five to a hundred dollars a week. I made quite a lot of money in my day, but I haven't got anything to show for it now.

The show business may be a hard life, but if I had it all to do over again I would still want you to give me the same route.

A. C. Sherbert
*Portland, Oregon*
1939

# Ernie Van

*Ernie and Joe Van started out as medicine-show entertainers, developing the song and comedy routine they later took to the vaudeville stage.*

My brother and I started in show business in 1894. I was sixteen then and we were a couple of stage-struck kids. We shipped out of San Francisco—that's my home town—with the Pawnee Indian Medicine Show. Eight of us traveled by wagon up through California, mostly places with no railroads, around Chinese camps. I being the youngest and cleanest shaved, I done all the girls' parts.

I remember we hit a gold-rush town in Columbia that had once had a population of twenty-five thousand and it had dwindled down to eighteen hundred, and I got up early and went panning. I really did find a piece of gold worth eighty cents under the hotel, so you see there's still gold in them thar hills. According to our arrangement my brother got ten dollars for playing comedy and I got five dollars for doing what I could. We went months without pay, so when the show broke up, the boss owed my brother a hundred dollars and me sixty dollars, and even with the gold strike I was a loser.

We traveled to Chicago and stopped at the Old Keller House at Washington and Franklin, with a twenty-dollar gold piece between us, which we put down for two weeks' board. A nickel-and-dime agent got us a three-day run with no money. The next one we played we got closed. By this time the two of us had worked up a routine with comedy and music and this led to $120 vaudeville. When this gave out we went with Beach and Bowers Minstrels and next to Vogel and Deming Minstrels, during which time we would improve our act until we would arrive in New York. We closed the show and came on east, playing Proctors' Fifth Avenue Theatre. Then we toured the sticks, playing at high schools in the evening. We would pull into town and go right to the school, but we couldn't get in because school wasn't let out yet, so we'd hang around until the janitor would clear out the place. We'd fill a bucket with water backstage and when we wanted to wash we'd have to break the ice. I remember in Michigan it was very cold and the place we put up in turned off the heat at night. We almost froze. So we worked up a routine for the audience:

Boy, to his father: "Pa, I'm cold."

Father: "What you think I'm having, a sunstroke?"

They used to laugh like the devil at that. The audience wasn't as sophisticated as it is today. Anything got a laugh if the situation was right. In those days, when we got into town we used to parade in Jockey makeup, worsted tights, leggings, and a coat and cap made of goods like plush, that furniture material. It was nothing to parade in twenty below.

When we finished a stand, usually in one day, we'd go down to the car and wake up next morning in the next town. I remember somewhere in Illinois a barber who joined the show as an acrobat would shave us for three cents, five cents with Bay Rum. He collected all our old underwear and socks, which were all full of holes and sent them to his wife in Aurora. She would patch and wash them and send them back to him and he would sell us reconditioned underwear for fifteen cents and two pairs of socks for a nickel. We couldn't afford to buy new ones.

My brother and I thought we ought to get back to big time again, and after a little burlesque we hit the one-a-day, one matinee a week, around 1904. We became very good friends with Will Rogers, Eddie Cantor, and went to Europe with W. C. Fields. I guess my brother and I played together for thirty years. We were one of the first to play two saxophones, but already the jazz acts were moving in and they put a damper on all musical acts like ours. My brother Joe was about the only one that ever really made a success at playing a zither on the vaudeville stage, playing as high as eight encores at a performance. We couldn't hold on together any longer, so I went with a horse act. Since then I've been a steward on the S.S. Virginia between New York and California; also had charge of the incubators at Coney Island, which I'm taking to the World's Fair, and I wind up my season being Santa Claus.

I don't think the old-timers expect much of this new vaudeville revival. You can't get that kind of comedy over a mike. The situations are the important part of the act, and it was really a continuous show. By that I mean although each act was separate, one built the other up. It had a pattern: first acrobatics or some such act, then a little comedy with some music, next the after pieces, like a skit, "Who Died First?" or "Razor Jim," followed by two or three vaudeville acts and a finale in which everybody joined in. One thing I will say, it's all over and I'm glad I was part of it. Some of the boys were smart enough to lay something aside; some have pensions and others have WPA, which is a wonderful thing.

Terry Roth
*New York City*
1939

# Ed Renard

*The Lower East Side of New York was thick with dance halls when Ed Renard was growing up; in 1907, there was one for every two and a half blocks. Renard describes working as an instructor at one of these dancing schools with comedian George Burns. In his autobiography, Burns tells of a stint as an instructor at a dancing school at Second Street and Avenue B: "New York was full of newly arrived Poles, Lithuanians,*

*Hungarians, and others who wanted to learn to dance and couldn't speak English. . . . Admission was ten cents for men, and five cents for ladies. If business was good I was able to make about fifteen dollars a week."** 

You couldn't exactly call my first stage appearance a success. I was fifteen and I got into an amateur night on the Bowery. They gave me the hook before I could open up my mouth, but that didn't discourage me. I was born on Second Avenue and Sixth Street and the only recreation we had was going to dance halls. We went to seven dances a week and one matinee Saturday. Naturally, we were all good ballroom dancers. So the first venture we had was a ballroom-dancing act with a girl from school—then I had a dancing school with George Burns. We had mostly foreigners that wanted to learn how to dance; the girls would sit on one side of the hall and the boys on the other side. We used to go and give exhibitions for dancers for a cup. Burns would be the judge, so I won the cup. Then I would be the judge, so Burns won the cup.

Then I had an act with Burns. My name at that time was Fields. We went to Brooklyn for the matinee and the manager takes one look at us and closes us. About five months later I decide to do a single so I book myself into the same house under a different name. In the morning, the manager is watching the rehearsal from the back and he comes down the aisle. "Weren't you here six months ago?" "No, not me." "Wasn't your name Fields?" "No, Renard." He looks blank for a minute but goes back, and I start singing my number. All of a sudden he rushes down the aisle. "Get out, Fields." That was that.

After a while I had an act with a fellow, Joseph Regan. He was a waiter. I met him singing in a saloon in Coney Island and I asked him to go in vaudeville. We used to rehearse on the beach and when the weather got too cold, we moved over to the park on the East Side at night. The cop on the beat used to stand around and watch and keep the kids moving. We didn't have a dime between us and the act required scenery, so I borrowed fifty bucks from the policeman to buy scenery. Then we got a booking for ten dollars. But we had to have a trunk made for the scenery and the trunk cost twelve dollars, so we had to borrow the two bucks from another cop. Well, we worked on the road for a couple of weeks for small change and finally got back to New York. In those days we lived in a Turkish Bath when we were in

* George Burns, *I Love Her, That's Why* (New York, 1955), p. 51.

town, and when we got up the next morning we didn't even have money for breakfast. You know how it is at the baths; when you come in you check your valuables in a large envelope, and when you leave you get it. As we went out, we saw a hundred-dollar bill in the basket where people threw away the envelopes. What do you think we did with the hundred dollars? We bought a hundred-dollar trunk. All we carried in it was a bellhop suit, which was my costume, a cane for Regan, a little makeup, and the drop, but we sure made an impression in every hotel with that trunk. Regan's home was in Boston. He was Irish Catholic and I was a Jewish kid from the East Side. We got very popular in town with the girls. An Irish from Boston and a Jew from the East Side—we were a novelty.

Terry Roth
*New York City*
1939

# Andy Miller*

*As a manager, Andy Miller came in contact with some of vaudeville's biggest names. James Duffy and Frederick Sweeney were a legendary comic team, the most talked of "two-man act" in vaudeville. The story about them repeated here was widely told and perhaps apocryphal.*

Did you ever hear of Duffy and Sweeney? They were a wonderful comedy act. Duffy was a real loveable guy with a tremendous talent, but he was always drunk. They were playing the show in the Midwest one night and just couldn't get a laugh out of that house. Duffy was very aggravated and intolerant of the stupidity of the audience. He tried every gag and trick to wake them up, but nothing doing. So after the act was over he walked out on the stage and in a very serious manner he stated: "Ladies and Gentlemen. My partner and I have been playing here four days now and we haven't seemed to be able to do something you would appreciate. Now we have something we have never done in this town. My partner, Mr. Sweeney, will pass among you with a baseball bat and

* Fictitious name.

beat the bejeezes out of you." Duffy and Sweeney never played that town again.

Then there was Johnny Stanley. One night, drunk as usual, he came into a restaurant where we all hung out. "Give me a hunk of apple pie," he said to the waiter. "We haven't any apple pie." That got Stanley. "What kind of a joint is this? Can't you fake it?" He was always in trouble about his salary being attached and he never could get his salary because the sheriff would be there first. So he met Francis X. Bushman, who was as smart as they come and always in trouble with sheriffs too, and Bushman puts him wise to his own way of getting his salary. Bushman would go up to the Manager's house early in the morning on pay day. When the manager opened the door, Bushman would hand him a receipt for his salary all made out. "Sign this please," and with the other hand he'd hand him a package. "Have some breakfast. I brought it for you." That always broke them down and he'd beat the sheriff to his pay that way.

Once I was manager of a theater up in the Bronx. It was the only one with reserved seats in the borough, and I had a doorman who started to dress a little swell. I met him in a barroom one night cracking around tens and twenties, the best in the house for the boys. We were selling out every night and naturally I start looking for a leak. So I asked him, "Willie, what the hell's going on here. You're not getting eighteen dollars a week and spending tens and twenties a night just like that. In fact, a little explanation is coming to me." "Well, boss," he says, "as a matter of fact the time's coming when I need your aid." So we sit down and here's the story. He's going home one night about twelve o'clock, well after the night performance. A woman waiting for him in the alley around the corner calls to him and says, "Willie, have you got a program?" "No, but I can get you one," so he goes back and gets a program. She slipped him a dollar. She had been out cheating on her husband and she needed an alibi. So when he asks her, "Dearie, where have you been all night?" all she has to do is throw him the program, give him the works about the show, and he's satisfied. She's so satisfied with the deal that she tells her friends about this service and pretty soon it gets around the Bronx and finally it wound up this became an industry for Willie. I see that it needs a little system, so I went in with Willie and organized it. I went around to the speaks and I tipped the bartenders off to our little sideline. They would call us up: "Willie, send me up twenty-five pairs of tickets and programs." We built up a regular route all over the Bronx.

Right now, I'm getting together a bunch of refugees and putting on an act with nine genuine refugees, mostly from Germany, Austria, Czechoslovakia, and one concert singer from Spain. All of them were stars in their own country. One of the fellows composes; he's written about a hundred things but only on the other side. The little Spanish girl left on account of the tumult of war, but she doesn't speak much about it. Her family is still over there. They have a lot of confidence in me. Most of them can't speak our language but a performer is a performer in any language if he's good. I got them through ads in the German papers and through clubs. And believe me, they're very well educated. They sing in all languages, and I have a commentator with them. We open Friday at the RKO theaters around town.

Terry Roth
*New York City*
1939

# Thomas Graham*

*Out-of-work vaudeville actors like Thomas Graham looked to the Federal Theater Project for employment. They became "the core of a new people's theater," in the words of Theater Project director Hallie Flanagan. Along with Thomas Graham, half of the cast of the FTP's Living Newspaper unit† had played vaudeville in other days. Even though the Living Newspaper used dramatic techniques drawn from vaudeville, the transition was not always easy.*

I started with a comedy act with my wife who passed away three years ago. Then I was a singer in an act called "Dr. Joyce's Sanitorium," which played all over Keith's Orpheum circuit. I guess I've been in all

---

* Fictitious name.
† The Living Newspaper addressed the social issues of the day using a combination of dramatic and documentary forms.

parts of the theater, dramatic parts and vaudeville. In my day they had variety acts, each individual specialties. In the later years all they had to know was a minute or two of a specialty and they were a star. Why, they couldn't entertain the audience for twenty minutes and hold them that long. The producers knew that, so they switched to short revues instead of vaudeville acts.

The flavor has gone out for the audience, too, I think. Years ago an act kept the same routine for years. Maybe once in a while they put in a new joke, but the act was basically the same. When the audience came they knew what to expect from the last time, and they felt like we were all old friends. They'd say, "Oh yes, I remember that from the last time: it's still funny." And the managers of the theaters knew whether the acts were popular and kept calling the successful ones back. You can't have a new act in comedy and still have the finesse that comes with repeating it. The radio acts have to be crude to put it over. There's no finesse in canned comedy, so the old variety actors haven't much of a chance there because the technique is different. I imagine there's still about twenty weeks of vaudeville around the country, like Paramount and Loew's State and places like that, but you notice it's the old-time variety stars that can still go out and entertain them. It took the old-timer ten years of experience before he could hold an audience for fifteen minutes by himself.

As for myself, I'm on WPA now. I took the part of the landlord in "One Third of a Nation." At first I thought the WPA theater was the answer for a lot of us. I don't know now. A lot of the actors just got cut. I didn't and they tell me I'm going touring with a Medicine Show, but you can't tell about firings. When we started in rehearsal of "One Third of a Nation" I didn't think it was going to go over. It was a little too new for me, I guess. Anyway, we all worked damn hard on it, but there was always something to worry about. The directors were fine and did a good job, but every day after rehearsal, some guy from the office would come down and tell us we were rotten, we'd have them laughing at us, we didn't put enough into it. This is discouraging to an actor who has to feel that he's good before that curtain goes up, and particularly at the Living Newspaper which was so different from anything we'd ever done before that we weren't too sure of ourselves. So for weeks these guys, I don't know who they were, would come down there and raise a rumpus about us playing like wooden sticks. We were the most surprised people when we read in the papers after opening night that we had a hit. And even then, when everybody was raving about how we put it over, these guys would come down and say it was an accident, that it wasn't because we were so good. I guess they had been seeing too many movies where the actor says, "I'll show him. I'll go out there and prove to him that I've got what it takes." Well, let me tell you, that's no way to handle troupers. You got to make them feel sure that they're good.

I really think that the cause of the fall of vaudeville isn't because of vaudeville itself, but because the picture industry bought up all the picture houses. When talkies came in, Wall Street became interested in show business and the big picture industries went out and raised the money to buy up all the show houses they could. And the minute they got the theaters then out went variety. There will never be vaudeville as long as the picture industry owns the houses.

And who suffers but the variety artists? They were getting five, six, seven hundred dollars a week and didn't know what it was all about. A businessman knows how to protect himself for later on, but that's why the other fellow is an artist, because he isn't a businessman. Those guys would have laughed at you if you'd have said vaudeville was going out. They were sitting pretty, spending it as fast as it was coming in, talking about how they wowed them, complimenting themselves all the time. They never thought of the future; they thought it would go on and on forever. A few of them invested some of their money in phony real estate like that land-under-water deal down in Florida. Those who were shrewder bought legitimate stock on the market, but what happened to all that in 1929 is an old story. I could do a swell wallpaper job with the stuff I got stuck with in that crash.

Now a lot of them are on WPA and I don't know what would have happened to them without it. After all, what can a man of fifty do? He can't be a salesman—too many good salesmen can't make a living. And with all this tough going, many of them sit around and talk about vaudeville coming back. But even if it did come back, few have anything to offer, because a lot of people have been inactive for the last ten, even fifteen years. Well, it was great while it lasted.

Terry Roth
*New York City*
1939

# THE JAZZ
# LANGUAGE

Chicago
1939

*Photograph by Gordon Parks.*

*People used to ask Bix to play a chorus just as he had recorded it. He couldn't do it. "It's impossible," he told me once. "I don't feel the same way twice. That's one of the things I like about jazz, kid, I don't know what's going to happen next."*

—Jimmy McPartland*

*Most of the guys wanted to play the way they felt and they hated the idea of playing notes given to them.*

—Bud Jacobson

In the Chicago style of jazz, where inspired borrowing was considered the first step toward genius, no one was imitated more than Bix Beiderbecke. The white musicians who developed the Chicago style learned from the great black New Orleans jazzmen—"King" Joe Oliver, Louis Armstrong—and then from the white cornetist from Davenport, Iowa. By 1939, when Sam Ross visited Chicago clubs to interview jazz musicians for the Federal Writers' Project, Bix had been eight years dead, but his legend touched each of the musicians included in this chapter. Bix's genius was to use his musical imagination in a heroic effort to surpass himself; the mastery and spontaneity of his playing astonished his fellow musicians. As guitarist George Barnes told Ross, "I didn't know what swing really was until I heard Bix Beiderbecke on records. He has been my big influence."

The special pleasure of Chicago jazz musicians was hearing each other play, building on each other's work. Muggsy Spanier described learning to play the cornet from listening to Joe Oliver at the Dreamland Cafe: "Joe would play with that little mute and get some wonderful effects and I decided I'd do that too, which I'm still trying to perfect." In the following pages, Richard Voynow, Muggsy Spanier, Bud Jacobson, and George Barnes mention more than fifty jazzmen who could be heard in Chicago in the Twenties and Thirties. Since collective im-

* *Hear Me Talkin' to Ya*, edited by Nat Shapiro and Nat Hentoff (New York, 1955; reprinted 1966), pp. 157–58.

provisation was intrinsic to the Chicago style of jazz, the litany of names is central to the stories. The musicians stressed the importance of cooperation; their competitive feelings were tempered with delight.

The white musicians Sam Ross interviewed were known as the Chicagoans. Although they were admired for their ability to play "in the Negro style," the jazz bands of the 1930s were segregated. Black musicians were excluded from the better-paying jobs. Despite the prevailing racism, the best of the Chicagoans aspired to make the black musical idiom their own. When Bix Beiderbecke and Muggsy Spanier heard Louis Armstrong play in the Chicago nightclubs, "they understood immediately that this was the real hot style. They soon had courage enough to begin to play in Negro style; I say 'they had courage enough,' because American prejudice against the black race made such a step very unusual."*

Muggsy Spanier and Bud Jacobson emphasized the superior musical ability of the black players; they recalled with pride being asked to sit in with black bands. Though generally prohibited from recording jointly, black and white musicians jammed together at places like Mama Couch's on the South Side, where "you could drink and smoke tea,"† according to Jacobson.

The musicians who told their stories to Sam Ross in 1939 were for the most part reminiscing about a plusher time, a time when Bix was at his peak and the South Side clubs were still at the center of the jazz world. The hey-day of the Chicago style of jazz was from 1925 to 1929, an era when Chicago nightlife was sustained by the rackets. Gangsters often owned or controlled the nightclubs and dance halls that employed musicians. Even when they didn't own the clubs, their free spending—of profits from bootlegging and prostitution—supported the jazz scene. Big-name gangsters were a familiar sight in the speakeasies; Al Capone was known for his hundred-dollar tips and his requests for sentimental numbers.

By the mid-1930s the combined effects of the Depression and the repeal of Prohibition had dimmed Chicago nightlife and the city was no longer *the* place to hear American jazz. Many of the important jazzmen left for New York, returning to Chicago only for occasional engagements.

The idea to document the development of Chicago jazz came from Benjamin Botkin, director of the Federal Writers' Project Folklore

---

* Hugues Panassie, *Hot Jazz* (New York, 1936), p. 28.
† Marijuana; also known as "muggles."

Unit. While Botkin was in Chicago on a field visit, Sam Ross took him around to the South Side to listen to music. Recognizing Ross's enthusiasm for jazz, Botkin suggested that the Chicago office of the Writers' Project assign him to conduct interviews on the subject. "I'd listen to the musicians play and then I'd sit around and talk to them," says Ross, "just what I was doing anyway."*

Like many who worked on the Writers' Project, Ross's career was shaped by the experience of collecting life-history narratives. Forty years later Ross says, "That attempt to faithfully represent language, rhythm, and character heavily influenced my writing." Ross has used material gathered then as the basis for subsequent fiction. His fifteenth novel, *Windy City*,† is set in Chicago during the Depression years and the main character spends a night or two listening to Muggsy Spanier play cornet at the College Inn.

# Richard Voynow

*As manager of the Wolverines, pianist Richard Voynow presided over one of the earliest white groups to play Dixieland. The Wolverines were an offshoot of a Chicago-Michigan City excursion boat band. After Bix left the Wolverines in 1924, the band took on Jimmy McPartland and other members of the Austin High School Gang, a group of young musicians who first played together after school and who became major figures in Chicago jazz. Voynow mentions another member of the Austin High School Gang, clarinetist Frank Teschemacher.*

Jazz was played long before this craze about it came into being. Nobody made too big a fuss about it. There is nothing that is being done today that wasn't done by the boys in my band or by the New Orleans Rhythm Kings. That outfit was the real influence on Chicago style. In fact, the bands today aren't even playing as good as my band was playing back in 1923, because we had Beiderbecke in our band and nobody has been able

---

* Quotations from Sam Ross are from an interview with the author, February 1978.
† Sam Ross, *Windy City* (New York, 1979). Ross's best-known novel, *He Ran All the Way*, was made into a movie starring John Garfield.

*The Wolverines at the Cinderella Ballroom, New York City, 1925.*
*Richard Voynow (far left) and Bix Beiderbecke (far right). Courtesy*
*Institute of Jazz Studies.*

to touch him since. The other day I was down at Nick's in the Village
and Bobby Hackett—he plays just like Bix, almost a perfect imitator—
came up to me and said, "Listen to me, will you, Dick, and tell me if I
do anything that Bix didn't do." I listened to him for some time and he
did almost everything Bix did, but he wasn't as good, nor did he have
Bix's originality.

Bix was really a genius. He was the kind of guy who would never
send his clothes to a laundry. Never thought of it. He would throw his
stuff into a closet and leave it there and rummage through for a clothes
change, and finally some guy in the band would get disgusted and send
his clothes to the laundry. But he was a true artist. Sometimes we would
go down to the Art Institute and although he knew nothing about paint-
ing from books, he would always stop in front of the best paintings and
point them out and admire them. Bix had a fine feel for color tone on his
horn, too. He was doing things musically, along with some of the other
boys in the band, without even being conscious of it. The men in the

Wolverines were all fine musicians who didn't play notes but created them.

I was the worst musician in the band but was the business head. All the boys knew that I was the worst musician but they also felt they needed me to keep them together and to discipline them. We would have to make a train at nine-thirty, say, and I'd be waiting at the station for them, and they'd get off on a drinking spree or a love-fest or something, and come running half dressed to the station just when the train was pulling out. Things like that were enough to drive a guy crazy. But I had a better musical training than all of them. I'd do the skeleton arrangements during rehearsals. But you never had to tell them what to do, even though most of the fellows couldn't read a note. They'd pick up a tune from the melodies I'd knock out on the piano and then in their solos they'd create around that melody so that the music came out like a work of art. In the ensembles they never got lost but stayed in and played in perfect harmony.

Although Bix *felt* more when he played, there was a man called Teschemacher who played clarinet, who was also a genius but who had a calculated manner of playing. He was an intellectual compared to the others—he knew the value of each note he hit, and knew why he played them. He had a marvelous musical background, which most of the others didn't have, and it didn't hamper him any.

Because of Bix we couldn't stand anything but a cornet in our band. When Bix left the band, we were almost driven to distraction trying to get someone who could really fit in. We tried out a few but they didn't do. We even brought up Sharkey Bonano from New Orleans. He walked in with a trumpet and all the fellows shook their heads. Sharkey played fine trumpet, but we had got so used to the cornet because of Bix we just couldn't see a trumpet. Finally one of the boys in the band said that he had heard a kid from Chicago play who sounded pretty good. We sent for the kid and he turned out to be Jimmy McPartland. We were very happy to get him because he filled Bix's place pretty well and he was so influenced by Bix he worked in fine right off the bat. But he could never excel Bix.*

Sam Ross

---

* In *Hear Me Talkin to Ya* McPartland tells his version of the story. "I received a wire one fateful day from Dick Voynow, pianist and manager of the Wolverines. It read: CAN YOU JOIN WOLVERINES IN NEW YORK REPLACING BIX BEIDERBECKE AT A SALARY OF EIGHTY-SEVEN DOLLARS FIFTY PER WEEK QUERYMARK STOP ANSWER IMMEDIATELY STOP. . . . Taking Bix's place was the biggest thing that had happened to me. The Wolverines were *the* jazz band in the country so far as we were concerned. And Bix . . . I remember him saying, 'I like you, kid, because you sound like I do but you don't copy me. You play your own stuff; you're a good guy.' "

# Muggsy Spanier

*Like many of the Chicago jazz musicians, Francis "Muggsy"
Spanier started young, playing his first professional job on drums
at fourteen. He was especially influenced by the Creole Jazz
Band of New Orleans trumpeter Joe "King" Oliver. Spanier
tried to emulate Oliver's style with a mute, and to good effect.
When Spanier visited England in 1930 with Ted Lewis's band,
he was "the special favorite of the Prince of Wales, who particularly liked the way Muggsy played with a plunger mute,"
according to Sam Ross's background notes.*

At first I started out as a drummer. Those days I used to go down to
hear Joe Oliver at the Dreamland Cafe on Thirty-fifth and State.
Before that, Joe played at the Pekin Cafe. I was too young to go inside
and they didn't start playing till twelve o'clock at night, but I used to
stand outside and listen. They used to have matinee dances at the
Dreamland and I'd ditch school and go out there. I'd put on my
brother's long pants and go there and listen to them and get up early
and go to school in the morning. I must have been about thirteen years
old at the time and I was still playing drums. But finally I went to my
mother and I told her I wanted to play a cornet and she bought me
one on time. She paid $125 for it. I'll never forget it. It was a real
pretty thing.

When the Dixieland band began to make records I bought all I
could get and played them on my victrola and played my cornet with
the recording. After that Joe'd let me sit in with his band. That was
unheard of in those days up North here, a white person playing with
Negroes. There were few white guys they'd let sit in with them, but
they let some because some couldn't play that way with any other band.
Then I met the fellows from the New Orleans Rhythm Kings and I
hung around with them. The Rhythm Kings was the best band put
together at the time. Their style affected me. It was a different style;
at the time the rage was sweet music and laughing cornets.

I learned how to play from listening to Joe Oliver a lot. Joe would
play with that little mute and get some wonderful effects and I decided
I'd do that too, which I'm still trying to perfect. When Louie
[Armstrong] joined the band he didn't do much because he was the
second trumpet man, but I liked to listen to him play those pretty parts
against what Joe was doing.

*Muggsy Spanier. Courtesy Institute of Jazz Studies.*

I met Bix when we both came down to the Friar's Inn where the New Orleans Rhythm Kings were. We'd sit around and listen to the boys, and then one day Bix said, "I'm a cornet player." And I said, "I'm one, too." We always met at Friar's Inn and then we'd knock around together. There was one place we dropped in where there was a piano and a drum and we sat in with our two horns. We played together so well we decided we'd be a cornet team.

All this time, while I was going to school and on a day job, I couldn't make up my mind what to do. You see, I was crazy about playing ball. I pitched for the old Chicago Firemen every Sunday. That was a semi-pro team. I wanted to be a pitcher till I got interested in music.

The only jobs I got around town were in back rooms. Those were the only places where they'd allow my kind of music. The other bands had a lot of violins and that stuff, and they didn't go for my stuff. Sig Meyers gave me my first chance. He had the only swing band in Chicago outside of the New Orleans Rhythm Kings. I was with Sig for four years and he taught me plenty. We were at the Columbia Hall for two years and at White City for two years. I went to the Midway Gardens from White City to join Art Kassel, and you might not believe it but he played good clarinet then. I got Teschemacher a job there and Stacy on piano. The crowd followed the band. They liked our swing.

We used to make our own arrangements. We'd go to one of the fellows' houses and have our own fun, singing the blues and playing them. Tesch and I had a favorite place we liked to go to on Tenth and Wabash, a wine place. We'd drink our wine, then we'd go out and listen to guys like Jimmy Noone and all that. Tesch was about nineteen then. He was a quiet guy, a wonderful guy, never talked much unless he got a couple of drinks in him. Tesch really had an original style. He was a funny guy though. If that band didn't play exactly right, he couldn't play. The band had to be perfect.

From the Midway I went to the Merry Gardens. Jess Stacy was with Joe Kayser and I tried to get Tesch in there, but they wouldn't have him and I was pretty sore. After that I went with Ray Miller at the College Inn and then I went with Ted Lewis. Ted Lewis was a fine guy to work for. He liked hot music even if he couldn't play it. He used to get guys like [Jack] Teagarden and Fats Waller and [Jimmy] Dorsey and [Dick] McDonough to make records with him. Boy, I used to get scared in the spotlight. I never could stand having to get up there in the spot and play a solo. I never went for that stuff.

I gave Lewis plenty of headaches. I'll never forget the time I was in the hospital and Lewis came in, and without saying hello or nothing, the first thing he said was, "I told you that stuff [drink] 'd put you there."

Sam Ross

# Bud Jacobson

*Bud Jacobson liked to "knock the crowd out" with his stunts. He could play the clarinet and the saxophone at the same time and he once inserted modified kazoo heads into his clarinet, an experiment that succeeded in producing "a ludicrous tone," according to one follower of Chicago jazz.*

You might say I was born in a trunk. My mother and dad were on the stage. I guess my mother was the first lady sax player in the world, and I can remember there were always horns around the house. The fellow that taught them the act brought us up to his house once. I was about eight then. There were a lot of instruments around and the slide trombone kind of got me. Then my mother bought me one. I can remember the first tenor sax I had; it seemed as big as I was. I played around a bit after I learned the scale, but I took no real lessons, and as an incentive my father used to offer me one dollar for any new piece I'd learn. Then he stopped that—he thought if I had it in me I'd learn without the bribe. I gave up music for a time until I was in high school. The kids liked music a lot and we used to get together and I'd say I could play. And they said: "Can you play sax?" Because the sax was getting very popular then. And I said: "Sure I can play sax." And that got me interested again.

In high school I worked with Bert McDowell at the school dances. We took a summer job at Channel Lake and Bert had to leave because he got another job. So we needed another piano. I remembered that Dave North played piano real nice and I came into town and found Dave. I told him I remembered some of his piano playing and that we wanted him to work with us. He said, "I can't play a job professionally because I only know four pieces." "That's all right," I said. "You'll work in all right."

Back in town we used to rehearse at Dave North's house when our band was called Russ Wilkin's Melody Boys. The band name was changed to the Wolverines, which later had Bix in it and McPartland. I was a little older than the rest of the guys and had been playing on some pretty big jobs. When the guys who became known as the Chicagoans joined the union as a group who couldn't read they asked me to play with them in order to make the band more legitimate.* I joined them at White City after Teschemacher left the band to go to the Rainbow Room and finished the season with them. Then Art Kassel took over and he called us the biggest bunch of radicals he ever saw. "Boy," he said, "you guys play like a bunch of communists. What a radical band!"

He took the band to Detroit to play at the Graystone Hotel, where

---

* The union had adopted a sight-reading test as an admission requirement in an attempt to protect jobs from New Orleans bands. Many of the early jazz musicians couldn't read music at all and didn't consider it important, as a story going around Chicago in the 1920s illustrates: when the manager of a cafe tried unsuccessfully to get the New Orleans Rhythm Kings to read orchestrations and play less improvised jazz, the joke among the members of the band was, "What would we do if the lights went out?"

*Bud Jacobson. Courtesy Institute of Jazz Studies.*

we had to play opposite Fletcher Henderson's band. They had just come in from the east and we thought even if they are colored they are just another eastern band. We looked them over and we thought we'd knock them off. We thought they could only play that eastern style. But Henderson had Coleman Hawkins, Don Redman, Buster Bailey, Joe Smith, Rex Stewart, and they knocked us off our feet on that first number. We played the next dance and we knew we couldn't do nearly as good, but I guess we gave them a wonderful thrill too.

The combination then was Dave North, piano; Dave Tough, drums; Jimmy McPartland, cornet; Jim Lannigan, bass; Rich McPartland, banjo; Floyd O'Brien, trombone; Bud Freeman, sax; Art Kassel, and another trumpet player he stuck in to fill up the brass section. There was a tavern across the way and we'd go there during intermissions and drink ale. The Graystone was the same place where Goldkette's band was playing before us. They had a radio broadcast—which we didn't have—and just before the end of the broadcast Bix would holler through the mike, "Set up four!" And the tavern would get that over the radio and have the drinks ready for the boys during the intermission.

We used to go with Henderson's band to the Radio Club, a sort of a dive, and we'd get together with McKinney's Cotton Pickers, and we'd play for ourselves. Joe Smith would play his trumpet and Don Redman would knock himself out with an English horn, but Coleman Hawkins was the guy. None of us ever heard a sax like he played. Up till then nobody knew what to do with the sax in the orchestra. At White City, Bud Freeman kept apologizing all the time for his playing and about how he couldn't do anything. "Pardon me for playing collegiate, that Northwestern style," he'd say, "but what can you do on a tenor sax?" Bud played very ordinary sax until he heard Hawkins. And from then on, Bud's rise was perpendicular. He'd play those Hawkins things and then let that develop out of himself until he played about the best sax in the business.

Our bunch was the first whites to go to Negro places like the Sunset and the Apex Club. Freeman'd always sit in with them every time he got the chance. Sometimes the colored boys'd come over and ask us to sit in with them. After we worked single jobs, we used to go to the old Dreamland Cafe. There they had Louie's wife [pianist Lillian Hardin] and Baby Dodds and Louie. That was just after Louie had come back from the East, where he was playing with Henderson's band, because he was lonesome for his wife. He used to get so lonesome away from her he couldn't stand it.

I used to knock the crowd out there when I sat in by playing alto sax and clarinet together, a sort of stunt. Teddy Weatherford was one of the greatest piano players in the business and he used to come in but he wouldn't ever sit in with the band. He was so good he didn't want to endanger the jobs of the others. I'd say, "Why don't you sit in, Teddy?" And he'd say, "I sit in, I'd play so much piano it'd sound like an eighteen-piece band." And he wasn't conceited or bragging. He was that good! I remember the first race dance they had in town at the Coliseum. There was an overflowing crowd and a few of the best colored bands in the country. Floyd and I went there and we were the only two whites in the place. Teddy and Louie Armstrong shared honors as king.

At that time Floyd and Jim and myself thought it'd be a wonderful idea to make some recordings with some of these colored artists with our two styles mixed up and coming out like one and like real jazz. We went up to the Okeh company and they thought it'd be a good idea if we could get the union okay. But [James C.] Petrillo [president of the

American Federation of Musicians] wouldn't let us do it. He said it was a national ruling that whites and colored couldn't play together on jobs. The union knocked the idea out. But if it had gone through, those records would have been some terrific things. It would have been an awful big thing for us, them playing with us.

I knew Teschemacher long before I ever began to play with him. When I was a kid, I used to vacation with my folks at Paw Paw Lake and the Teschemachers were our next door neighbors. I was about ten then and Tesch was about eight. The nearest approach I had to music then was a record called "Sweet Emaline." Me and Tesch'd listen to it and we'd drum to it. A couple years later I got my horn and I brought it over to Tesch's and taught him how to play it. He picked it up real easy. He had had a few violin lessons by then I think. His mother always blamed me for making him a jazz musician. She hated the idea with all her heart. I was the ruin of Tesch, she always said. But he'd have played jazz whether he knew me then or not. He had it in him.

I had a lot of trouble playing when a guy like Tesch'd come into the place. I'd be playing nice with power and I'd see him and I'd fold up and go into the melody background. Mezz Mezzrow got talking to me once and he said, "Listen, don't worry about repeating notes someone else played. Play the way you want." But I'd want to be original and every time I found myself playing notes I'd heard somebody else do at one time I'd fold up. And Tesch was the kind of player you sometimes liked to play like and sometimes didn't. Mezzrow's talk snapped me out of it.

In all our jobs the fellows played the way they wanted. The reason we played so good together was because we had so much confidence in each other. For instance, we'd have a rehearsal and it'd come out so good we wouldn't bother rehearsing anymore. Take the recording of "Crazeology." Bud Freeman had the melody and Dave North harmonized it and we learned it orally. Then we rehearsed it once and Bud said, "Gee, that came so good why bother doing it over again. We'll do it again just like that."

Most of the guys wanted to play the way they felt and they hated the idea of playing notes given to them. They wanted to make their own music and that's what we did on our instruments. So when one of the guys'd line up a job and tell the others, we'd say, "You can't take that job, why they're corny, you'll go nuts." And usually they wouldn't take the job. Bud Freeman, for instance, would rather starve than play commercial. He quit a $165-a-week job once because he didn't like the band and what he had to do in it.

I remember when our daughter was born. Freeman got mad at us because we didn't name her Melody. He kept harping on us to call her that. "You get a child," he said, "and you got to call it Melody." [Gene] Krupa'd lullaby her to sleep a lot of times, tapping the floor like a drum and lullabying her. Sometimes the guys'd go goofy and get around the kid and beat out melodies *wa dada wata dadee da.* They thought if they did enough of that they'd instill the jazz beat into her and she'd grow up into a fine musician.

At our house we used to have jam sessions. When the guys weren't working they'd start by laying around the floor and listening to recordings, then they'd play their own instruments. Sometimes they'd start as early as nine o'clock and finish up ten the next morning. They'd play away and when they hit something good, then Bud, say, would call me up wherever I was playing and make me listen to the song over the phone. "I got something wonderful," Bud'd say. "I want you to hear and you quit the job and come on over and arrange it and we'll make a lot of money." Then they'd play for me but they weren't hitting right and Bud'd say, "That sounds terrible. It sounds like Goodman. I'll get it some other time." The guys didn't think much of Goodman. He didn't play our style.

In those days we'd go out to Mama Couch's on the South Side where you could drink and smoke tea. Mama Couch's was a beer flat where both whites and colored people went. Bud and Baby Dodds and Dave Tough and Zutty Singleton would get together with a few others and jam around. Once Tough was pretty high and he went out for a walk. He met a couple of fellows on the street and he was feeling so good he invited them up for a drink. "Come on up," he said. "Lots of drink there and tea to smoke and all that. Plenty." The two fellows said, "Sure, gladly," and wound up to be two plainclothesmen and they took the gang of them to jail. Murph Poldowski went to bail them out and Tough got mad about that. "You went and spoiled everything," he said. "Just when I was getting ready to gather material for a story you had to come." Tough had ambitions of being a writer.

There was a lot of drinking in those days, the Prohibition stuff. You know there are two schools of jazz players: one that drinks and one that abstains. Jelly Roll Morton comes from the last school. He is absolutely down on that stuff. I never drank much—the others in our gang didn't either to speak of—but you remember a lot of the drinking, perhaps because it was a Prohibition era we lived in and in which our music grew.

Lots of speakeasies helped to serve the jazz art. Palmer Cady's Cascades was one of the best spots where the musicians used to go to a lot, one of the original jam session spots. Hell, you should have seen the young kids there with flasks on their hips, drinking to be cute. In 1927 the place to go to was Kelly's Stables. Respectable girls had to go there on the q.t. There was also the Lakeview Pleasure Club and the Moulin Rouge. That's where Teddy Weatherford played. Al Tierney's on Wabash was another spot. That's where Joe Sullivan played. We'd always be stopped by the cops and searched for machine guns. Many times the gangsters would hold them in sax cases and every time a cop saw me or some of the others with sax cases they'd figure: here's a big catch. But all they'd find'd be a saxophone.

                                                                Sam Ross

# George Barnes

*When George Barnes was interviewed he was playing at the Three Deuces, which had been a famous hang-out for Chicago's hot men. According to Mezz Mezzrow its name parodied the name of the Four Deuces, one of the biggest syndicate whorehouses in town; after Prohibition was repealed, the name was adopted officially.*

*George Barnes was just seventeen when he talked to Sam Ross, but already he was featured guitarist at the Three Deuces and "a sensation" according to Ross's background notes. "He is forced to play three or four encores every time," Ross wrote. "He improvises on various jazz tunes until he feels he has exploited the thing. Then he bows awkwardly as though he wished there wasn't as much applause so he wouldn't have to play again."*

When I was five years old I first started to play an instrument. It was a piano. My brother played the piano. My father played a guitar. I used to pick out tunes like "Dixie" and "Yankee Doodle." When I was ten my dad lost everything, his home and all that, and we had to move. After that we didn't have a piano. So I got an accordion about two years later and then I got a banjo and after that a guitar which I've been playing up until now. I never took any formal lessons. Those lessons I did get were from the guys I used to play with. My brother taught me everything I know on harmony and a little bit about counterpoint.

I don't know enough about counterpoint though and I'm going to study it someday soon. My brother had a fine musical training. But in jazz it's very easy to feel counterpoint. You feel your way into it.

I played in my first orchestra a year and a half ago. It was an eight-piece combination called the Rhythm-Aires. I did all the arranging for the band. We did mostly jobbing dates around Chicago Heights. The guys worked during the day and they played around at night to make some extra cash and because they like to play. The emcee at the Club Casanova heard me one night and he asked me to get a couple of guys together to play there. We had a four-piece outfit: trumpet, piano, drums, and guitar. I worked there twelve weeks. I remember that job better than anything. It was the first time for everything for me.

Then I jobbed with Jimmy Reynolds, a ten-piece combination. In the summer we went to Cedar Lake to work in a taxi dance hall. The boys in the band'd call me Junior, but I don't mind being kidded. That was the hardest job I ever worked. There was only one intermission a night of four minutes and then we'd split the band up. That job was so hard we always played our library from one end to the other. And that place was crowded until the doors closed. After the job we could hardly stand up. Even if we wanted to we couldn't drink because we didn't have time. But I don't drink anyhow, and most of the other guys didn't care for it because they had to be all there to perform, and you can't drink and get places too.

I liked swing. I always liked it even when I didn't know what it was. I knew Guy Lombardo was bad. But I didn't know what swing really was until I heard Bix Beiderbecke on records. He has been my big influence. I don't think anybody playing today has not been influenced by Bix. I understand he was a great guy; everybody who ever worked with him thought he was great. Even though I don't approve of a lot of things he done, like smoking weed and doing goofy things, he was still great. Guys like Goodman and Dorsey and Coleman Hawkins never change. They were good when I first heard them and they are just as good now. Their kind of music sort of lasts.

The best jam sessions are in Chicago Heights. I've been around plenty of sessions in Chicago but they are nothing like those in Chicago Heights. In Chicago Heights they really played. There was a trumpet there who inspired us all but now he is definitely commercial in a sweet band. Boy, we used to groove real holes out there. We'd start about two-thirty Sunday afternoon at one joint, and at five-thirty everybody'd go to a hideout joint in order to avoid union complications and play indefinitely.

The trouble with the sessions in Chicago is the musicians like to

show off, they want to show the others what they got. They take as
many choruses as they can get away with; they sort of hog the show,
and then they are not making music and feeling it but are just being
clever. I just can't get in the groove with them. Hell, up in Chicago
Heights we'd sit down and play blues for an hour and a half and we'd
have to stop from mental and physical exhaustion although the ideas
we'd be getting were absolutely inexhaustible. You know you're in the
groove the more you get yourself worked up. You can walk in on a
session and even if they're on the eighth or ninth chorus, if they are
right and in the groove you can tell immediately, even when you walk
in cold—you can tell from the flexibility of tone from the instruments
how long they've been playing and how long they've been in the groove.
When you're in a groove you are lost in what you're doing. You can
talk to somebody, you can be distracted, but the groove stays and you
pick it up right away. You have to relax and let it get you.

Jazz isn't like classical music where you get a chance to describe
things. The images we get are very disconnected, more like a dream.
For instance, just before you came up I dreamed that Jimmy McPartland
was leading our orchestra. And you know what a fine trumpet player he
is. Now if I hadn't mentioned it to you and hadn't talked about it,
tonight he may have had a certain influence on my notes, the way I'd
get them out.

You see, our images are really definite. For instance I wrote a piece
recently called "Howard Street Express." You know how that express
ride can drive a guy nutty and I tried to get it, the thoughts, the sounds,
the feelings of that ride. Now that's definite and I can describe the
meaning of every note; but in jazz it is all that experience of the ride
and more, but you can't put your finger on it exactly.

Here's how I happened to write that piece. That night I took that
ride I had a fight with my girl earlier because I didn't like her to smoke
cigarettes, which I guess was a pretty foolish thing. I was in a terrific
groove. I couldn't eat and I couldn't sleep and I rode that El all night
long. About a month later we made up but that ride and its feeling was
still on my mind and I thought I'd better get it off and write the song.
Writing it got it off my mind. That is the only thing I ever play where
I never change a note. Usually there are certain passages I improvise
when I play even though it is arranged and rehearsed, which might be
variations of those thoughts and others, but that "Howard Street
Express" I play the same way all the time.

I wrote another tune called "Scatter Brain Rag." It sort of
expresses my first time at the Deuces. I played with Jimmy McPartland
for the first time and with guys who really played Dixieland music,

which was always tops with me. And I liked Jimmy a lot, the way he could play that trumpet. Well, we played three, four Dixieland tunes that sounded like marches. That set me in a groove and I got to thinking how close Dixieland music resembles marches and how nice marches sounded even though I never liked them before. I got to thinking about the different licks and I put it together about three months ago one night when we didn't have anything special to rehearse. I wrote the thing almost exactly like a march. Benny Goodman's manager liked it when he heard it.

Most swing musicians aren't well educated and they don't do anything but play their instruments and sleep late in the day, and that's bad. I'm going to get away from that and broaden myself and get a background. I think it'll help my music.

I think American jazz is a part of American folk music. The classical music is a thing of the past; it is European and outdone. In the long run I think jazz will develop into a real music, a finished product, different from the classical stuff and just as great if not greater.

Sam Ross

# TESTIFYING

# Clyde "Kingfish" Smith

*After New York City peddler Kingfish Smith sang his fish songs for the Federal Writers' Project, he composed an extemporaneous "Song About the Recording" at the end of the session. Federal Writer Herbert Halpert, now a folklorist, recalls that Smith was one of a group of New York City street vendors he interviewed.*\*

These songs are not written down. I sing them different: I put the words to the tune, to fit the occasion, to fit the neighborhood. If I go to a Jewish neighborhood, I sing songs like "Bei Mir Bist Du Shon." In a colored neighborhood they like something swingy. I might sing the same song but I put it in a swing tune. I go into a Spanish neighborhood, I speak to them in Spanish.

I started singing when I started peddling; that was in 1932. "Heigho fish man, bring down your dishpan," that's what started it. "Fish ain't but five cents a pound." It was hard times then—the Depression and people can hardly believe fish is five cents a pound, so they started buying. There were quite a few peddlers and somebody has to have something extra to attract attention. So when I came around, started making a rhyme, it was a hit right away. One of the first things I learned about peddling was to be any success at all, you had to have an original cry. I know several peddlers that started out and they hollered, "Old Fish Man," but it doesn't work.

I've gone blocks where several fish men have gone already and sold fish like nobody had been there. When I sing, a certain amount of people will be standing around, looking and listening, and that attracts more people. Whenever people see a crowd they think it's a bargain so they want to get in on it. When I sing it will be so loud that the people come to the windows and look out. They come down with bedroom

* Interview with Herbert Halpert, February 1979.

*Street peddler weighing string beans, Harlem, New York City, 1943.*
*Photograph by Gordon Parks.*

shoes on, with bathrobes, and some have pans or newspapers to put the fish in.

When I first come to a block nobody pays any attention. Then I start singing, get them to laughing and looking and soon they start buying. A lot of them just hang around to hear the song. I always try to give the best fish I can for the money and that makes repeated customers. A lot of people wait for my individual cry. The average day I cover about eight blocks and spend about an hour in each block, sometimes longer.

When I have crabs the kids like to see the crabs jump and bite, so they stand around in big crowds. Sometimes, when I sing, the kids be dancing the Lindy Hop and Trucking. Women buy most of the fish. I find Home Relief and WPA people the best customers. They buy more. They have to budget more near than the average family.

In white and Jewish neighborhoods I feature the words but in the colored neighborhoods I feature the tune. In the Jewish neighborhood they appreciate the rhyming and the words, while in the colored neighborhood they appreciate the swinging and the tune, as well as the words. I put in a sort of jumping rhythm for the colored folks. That swing music comes right from old colored folks spirituals.

On the street whatever comes to my mind I say it, if I think it will be good. The main idea is when I got something I want to put over I just find something to rhyme with it. And the main requirement for that is mood. You gotta be in the mood. You got to put yourself in it. You've got to feel it. It's got to be more an expression than a routine. Of course sometimes a drink of King Kong helps.

### FISH AND VEGETABLES

I got vegetables today,
So don't go away.
Stick around
And you'll hear me say,
Buy em by the pound,
Put em in a sack
Hurry up and get em
Cause I'm not coming back.
I got apples, onions, and collard greens.
I got the best string beans,
That I ever seen
I got oranges, tomatoes, nice southern sweet potatoes.
I got yellow yams
From Birmingham.
And if you want some,
Here I come
And if you don't want none
I don't give a
Yam, yam, yam.
I got green greens
From New Orleans.
I got the greenest greens
I ever seen,
And I sure seen
A whole lot of greens.
I got cauliflower
And mustard greens.
The best cauliflower

I ever seen.
So buy some,
Try some,
Take em home and fry some.

A song like this I'd just look on the wagon and rhyme up something to match it. When I sang this song, this morning, I was just thinking of something to rhyme then.

### DON'T YOU FEEL MY LEG

Don't you feel my hand,
Cause I'm that old fish man.
And if you feel my hand,
I'll fill up your pan.
So don't you feel my hand.
Now, don't you feel my thigh,
I'll tell you why,
And if you feel my thigh,
You'll come down and buy.
You'll come down and buy.
You'll go home and fry.
So don't you feel my thigh.

### BEI MIR BIST DU SHON

Bei Mir bist du shon,
I got big brudder fish again.
Bei mir bist du shon,
I think they're grand.
I could say bello bello,
And even voom de vah.
That would only tell you,
How grand they are.
Bei mir bist du shon,
I got flounders again.
Bei mir bist du shon,
I know they're grand.

This goes over good in either Jewish or colored neighborhoods, but I have to swing it up a bit in the colored neighborhoods.

### FISH CRY

Yo, ho, ho, fish man!
Bring down your dishpan!
Fish ain't but five cents a pound.
So come on down,
And gather around,
I got the best fish
That's in this town.
I got porgies,
Crockers too.
I ain't got but a few,
So you know what to do.
Come on down,
And gather round,
Cause my fish ain't
But five cents a pound.
I've got em large
And I've got em small;
I got em long and I got em tall;
I've got em fried,
I got em broiled;
And I can't go home till I sell em all!
So yo, ho, ho, fish man!
Bring down your dishpan!
Cause fish ain't but five cents a pound!

This was the first fish song in my own tune. So after the people begin to get too familiar with the tune, I grasped the idea of changing my tune to get the tune of the most popular song hit of that time.

### JUMPIN' JIVE

Jim, jam, jump, jumpin jive
Make you buy yo fish on the East Side,
Oh, boy,
What you gonna say there cats?
Jim, jam, jump, jumpin jive.
When you eat my fish,
You'll eat four or five.
Pal of mine, pal of mine, Swanee shore

Oh, boy, oh boy,
Jim, jam, jump, jumpin jive.
Make you dig your fish on the mellow side.
Oh boy, what you gonna say there cats?
Don't you hear them hep cats call?
Come on, boys, and let's buy em all.
Oh boy, what you gonna say there cats?

Jump joints: that means where they dance and drink and smoke the marijuana weed. The marijuana weed is a jumping jive. When you have the jumping jive on, you're supposed to do all these things and buy the fish.

### ONCE UPON A TIME

Once upon a time I fell in love,
With an angel from up above.
Yes, I fell in love,
With a heavenly dove,
Once upon a time.

With fish anything goes, but with this I want to be working a little careful. That's why I only have one verse on it so far.

### SONG TO KID THE ICE MAN

Say, ice man,
I want some today.
So hurry up and bring it,
Before I go away.
Bring fifty pound,
And hurry right down,
Cause you got
The best ice in this town.
You can chop it up
And make it small,
Better bring it quick
Or not at all.
I want to put it on my fish

Because it's nice and hot,
And I better do something
Before they rot.

SONG ABOUT THE RECORDING

Now I sing all these songs,
For Mr. Halpert and Hatch.
I bin singin an hour,
I guess I've sung a batch.
They seem quite appreciative
And I enjoyed it, too.
If nobody else don't like em
They know what they can do.
Mr. Hatch asked me to sing em,
For the WPA.
So when you hear em
Just swing and sway.
Don't fuss,
And don't fight,
Cause the jive is right
And if you wanna,
You can jump all night.

Marion Charles Hatch and Herbert Halpert
*New York City*
1939

# Leo Gurley

*According to Ralph Ellison, the simple prospect of earning "something of a living" by setting words on paper liberated him to explore his creative talent. He particularly enjoyed collecting folklore in Harlem because "I'd always liked the stories and I couldn't get enough of them."\* Leo Gurley told*

\* Interview with Ralph Ellison, December 1977.

*Ellison about a legendary hero who never failed to outwit the crackers.*

I hope to God to kill me if this ain't the truth. All you got to do is go down to Florence, South Carolina, and ask most anybody you meet and they'll tell you it's the truth.

Florence is one of those hard towns on colored folks. You have to stay out of the white folks' way. All but Sweet. That the fellow I'm fixing to tell you about. His name was Sweet-the-Monkey. I done forgot his real name, I cain't remember it. But that was what everybody called him. He wasn't no big guy. He was just bad. My mother and grandmother used to say he was wicked. He was bad alright. He was one sucker who didn't give a damn bout the crackers. Fact is, they got so they stayed out of *his* way. I cain't never remember hear tell of any them crackers bothering *that* guy. He used to give em trouble all over the place and all they could do about it was to give the rest of us hell.

It was this way: Sweet could make hisself invisible. You don't believe it? Well here's how he done it. Sweet-the-monkey cut open a black cat and took out its heart. Climbed up a tree backwards and cursed God. After that he could do anything. The white folks would wake up in the morning and find their stuff gone. He cleaned out the stores. He cleaned out the houses. Hell, he even cleaned out the damn bank! He was the boldest black sonofabitch ever been down that way. And couldn't nobody do nothing to him. Because they couldn't never see im when he done it. He didn't need the money. Fact is, most of the time he broke into places he wouldn't take nothing. Lotsa times he just did it to show em he could. Hell, he had everybody in that lil old town scaird as hell, black folks and white folks.

The white folks started trying to catch Sweet. Well, they didn't have no luck. They'd catch im standing in front of the eating joints and put the handcuffs on im and take im down to the jail. You know what that sucker would do? The police would come up and say, "Come on, Sweet," and he'd say, "You all want me?" and they'd put the handcuffs on im and start leading im away. He'd go with em a little piece. Sho, just like he was going. Then all of a sudden he would turn hisself invisible and disappear. The police wouldn't have nothing but the handcuffs. They couldn't do a thing with that Sweet-the-Monkey. Just before I come up this way they was all trying to trap im. They didn't have much luck. Once they found a place he'd looted with footprints leading away from it and they decided to try and trap im. This was bout sunup and they followed his footprints all that day. They followed them till sundown when he came partly visible. It was red and the sun was shining on the trees and they waited till they saw his shadow. That was the last of Sweet-the-Monkey. They never did find his body, and right after that I come up here. That was bout five years ago. My brother was down there last year and they said they think Sweet done come back. But they cain't be sho because he won't let hisself be seen.

Ralph Ellison
*New York City*
1939

# Norberto Diaz

*Norberto Diaz, formerly a skilled cigar maker, was employed in the Key West Naval Station when he talked to Federal Writer Stetson Kennedy. His story about a Ku Klux Klan murder helped inspire Kennedy to infiltrate the Klan as an undercover agent and gather evidence that sent a number of its members to jail.\* Kennedy has since published a number of books about race relations, including an account of his experiences, I Rode with the Ku Klux Klan, and an indictment of segregationist laws, Jim Crow Guide to the U.S.A.†*

Every time I pass in front of the Cuban Club I think of Isleno. The other day I was down to the beach and seen the palm tree where he was hung. It's funny, but that was the first coconut palm to die from the disease that's killing most all the palm trees on the island. I believe Isleno's *brujo* [ghost] is killing the palm trees, too. People say the whole island's cursed and that's why there is so much bad luck and people do not have enough to eat.

Isleno's curse has already killed five of the Ku Klux Klan who beat and hung him. He knew who they were and called their names and

---

\* The events Diaz described happened on Christmas Eve, 1921. No one was ever arrested for the murder, according to an account in the *Key West Citizen*, 23 December 1977.

† Stetson Kennedy, *I Rode with the Ku Klux Klan* (London, 1954); *Jim Crow Guide to the U.S.A.* (London, 1959).

cursed them for horrible deaths in revenge. He shot the Klan leader himself, one man was blowed up by dynamite when he was working on the bridges, another got caught in the Mattecumbe hurricane, one was ground to pieces under his boat when it went on a reef, and another went fishing and never came back. Isleno's curse killed them all. It's killing another with tuberculosis right now.

I guess I can tell the story as good as anybody. Isleno was a good friend to me; he was a good friend to everybody. He was a Spaniard from the Canary Islands: that's why we called him Isleno. He owned a little coffee shop and had a good business, but he was one of those men what likes to spend their money for a good time, drinking and all that. But he never caused nobody no trouble; all he did was to be happy and enjoy life. Isleno began living with a brown—a mulatto girl. We called her Rosita Negra. They lived in a room right in back of the coffee shop. People talked about his living with a brown, but nobody didn't really think much about it. I think a man's got a right to live with any kind of woman he wants to. If he wants to live with a brown, that ain't nobody's business but his own.

Almost anybody in town can tell you who the Klan members are. I know all them fellows. I think if a man has anything against another man he ought to go up to his face and tell him about it, and not get a whole crowd of men together and hide their faces in pillowcases. Some of the very ones that hung Isleno, I've seen em in Negro jungle houses myself. They try to hide their faces when they see me but I go right up to em and say, "Whacha say, old boy? What're you doing here?" They all jump the fence and put horns on their wives every chance they get. That's what makes me so mad, them men killed Isleno for doing the same thing they do. Only difference was Isleno didn't try to hide it. The Klan sent Isleno a warning to get Rosita out of the house. But Isleno wasn't afraid of nobody. He was a big man, strong as an ox. When he got that warning he just started keeping his gun under the counter of his shop.

Then one night—it was Christmas Eve—about twenty of the Ku Klux Klan came marching down from Duval Street, all dressed in white robes with hoods over their faces and carrying guns and torches. They marched straight for Isleno's shop. He was in bed with Rosita when somebody came to warn him. He ran for his gun, but somebody had already stolen it.

By that time the Klansmen were grabbing him. He put up an awful fight, but they tied him and dragged him to the beach, stripped him, and beat him till his kidneys burst. Isleno fought so hard he got free of the ropes and tore the masks off half a dozen of the men. He cursed them all, swore he'd be revenged and that they'd all die horrible deaths. They beat him some more until he was unconscious, and then hung him up in a tree. He was left for dead but he came to his senses and got loose from the rope somehow, and walked all the way back to his coffee shop. The next morning when I heard Isleno was at his shop I went to see him. His back was a pitiful sight! It looked just like one of those red cube steaks that has been all diced up to make it tender. It was a shame the way they had beat that man! He was in bed and suffering something terrible from the pain of his busted kidney. There was a lot of his friends there to see him, but I couldn't stand it and left.

About twelve o'clock Mr. Ostrom, a leader of the Klan and a very prominent man—was walking past the Cuban Club with his arms full of groceries he was taking home for Christmas dinner. When he stopped across the alley Isleno came out, his pants all bloody in front, and with a revolver in his hand. He shot Mr. Ostrom in the belly five times, and he fell on the sidewalk, begging Isleno not to shoot again.

But Isleno stood there and put five more bullets in the gun and shot Mr. Ostrom five more times. Then he climbed up in the attic of a vacant house and barricaded himself in. The police and the sheriff and the deputies and the National Guards surrounded the place, but Isleno kept them back with his shooting. The sheriff asked him to surrender, but Isleno said he would surrender only to the military commander who was stationed here.

The military man came and promised Isleno protection. When Isleno surrendered, the sheriff promised the military man to protect Isleno if he would turn him over to his custody. So the sheriff took Isleno upstairs in the jail where they beat him some more. After he was unconscious they grabbed him by the heels and dragged him down those iron steps, his head cracking like an egg on every step.

They tied a rope around his neck and pulled his body through the streets behind an automobile and down to the beach. Isleno was already plenty dead, but they hung his body up in a palm tree where it stayed I don't know how long till the buzzards and smell got so bad they had to cut it down.

Stetson Kennedy
*Key West, Florida*
1939

# Rich Knox

When Rich Knox told his story of a fire that got out of hand, he was talking to someone he'd known for years. Genevieve Chandler had lived in Murrells Inlet, South Carolina, for a quarter of a century when she began collecting Gullah folklore and stories like Knox's for the Federal Writers' Project. Gullah is a dialect spoken by rural blacks along the southern coast of the United States. Although she is white, Chandler was fluent in Gullah and had a remarkable ability to record verbatim the rapid, informal speech she heard around her.

A faithful transcription of the vivid Gullah dialect can be somewhat difficult to follow; readers may find that speaking the words aloud helps recapture the striking texture of the language and makes it easier to understand.

Gracious! I been in jail! I been there so many times! Bubba put me there for setting fire in my own field. All that burn was mine. He did have a row of tater plant on my side, and the fire scorch off the leaves.

How come the fire got out, I was burnin up a snake in a hole. Snake run in a stump-hole. I set the thing a-fire. Tryin to burn him out. Wind was breezin up. Fire got way from me. Burn over the whole field. Didn't get nowhere's on nobody else land. And here he lawin me for burnin my own land! Say I'm sottin him a-fire and all that.

Who was the man stood my bond? Lemme see. Andrew Johnson and Bill Oliver gone my bond on a five-hundred-dollar bond till trial at court. Neither one have witness but the family—the first startin of it.

The first startin, one time my wife in the house with a child—one of her chillun—child just bout a week old, and she couldn't get out. And I got in hearin o the house, and I hear there cussin and goin on. And I know that nobody but Bubba and I think I best go back till leven o'clock. And way here leven o'clock here he come, bush ax over his shoulder, dammin and hellin. Dammin and hellin! Dammin and hellin like he was "Mister Big Jim." And my old lady right in bed!

When I walk up, my mother she was there, and all the yard full up with chillun. And it made me sorter mad. So I gone on in my house, and when I come to the door here I have a pistol in my hand. And he offer the bush hook, and cuss all different kind o cuss. He say: "Here I come to find out, people tryin to burn me out!"

And I tell him: "I burnin in my *own* field!"

And I throwed the pistol on him. I sorta aggravate. And here he drawd the bush ax on me! I say: "I blow the heart out you body!"

Then he beg: "Oh, don't shoot! Oh, don't shoot me!" And he grab his bush ax and sail on back home.

Next day Boy come by, and see me grubbin stumps. He say: "Man, how you out here workin? Ain't you know Bubba got a warrant for you? Got out *three* warrant! Sault and Battery, tent to kill, and conceal weapon."

You know, fore they stop, they fine me twenty dollars for puttin out fire! I knocked all that out—and then turn round and make him pay half of *all* the fee! Make him pay five dollars more than I pay. I went to town and got me a surveyor and that surveyor charge me fifteen dollars a day. Showed Bubba he *lawed* me for my own things!

Tell you just what I done. I cross indite him, and tear the thing up. Put the place up for sale. And that make em all come to me to squash the thing up. Drop the case. I had done find a man to buy the place in. Then Uncle William gone to Bubba and warn him: "You don't know what kind o trouble this boy stirrin here."

Next thing I hear, Bubba huntin a lawyer! And next news, here he come. They all tell him he better compromise. Compromise the thing. It natural fire will get way with people some time.

I have one these water tanks on my back that time o that big woods fire. Had the fire all out but a little place on the shingle. And here they huntin me, and huntin me bout witness for that same fire. Man come to me, and try to make me tangle the thing up. Woods cot fire, surrounded the house, and I fought till it stifle me. Mr. Wilson most fall in the fire. That day I learn a lesson o fire.

The very next day I fight woods fire my last time. Man put a fire out at a stump. Then he gone and leave the stump burnin. Come on through the bay. Cut it off from John house and I secure Aunt Havillah. Secure her that day. I fight fire! Fight! Help save all that man pine tree. I got enough o fire fightin. I come out the woods after dark, and all who see me say: "Gracious Granny! You sho got red eyes! You look bad."

And I say, "I feel like I look." And I went home and tell fire good-bye. It burn Uncle William grape vine, sot his roof a-fire, burn all his kindlin, and burn his timber.

Why I through with woods' fire? That man what own all that big woods—all them big pine tree—told his fire-line man to pay all that help—all that gang o men who fought fire. The watchman stopped me and give me a twenty-five cents. I say, "What this for?"

He said, "Fightin fire."

And I told him, "Mister, you keep that."

Genevieve W. Chandler
*Murrells Inlet, South Carolina*
*n.d.*

# Lloyd Green*

*Lloyd Green, a Pullman porter just off work, told Ralph Ellison his story at Eddie's Bar on St. Nicholas Avenue in Harlem. Green's mixed feelings about New York suggested a theme that absorbed Ellison: he hoped to document the changes in the black experience when millions of blacks moved from southern farms to northern cities in the early twentieth century. Ellison included Green's repeated refrain in his novel Invisible Man: Mary Rambo advises the hero, "Don't let this Harlem git you. I'm in New York, but New York ain't in me, understand what I mean? Don't git corrupted."†*

I'm in New York, but New York ain't in me. You understand? I'm in New York, but New York ain't in me. What do I mean? Listen. I'm from Jacksonville, Florida. Been in New York twenty-five years. I'm a New Yorker! But I'm in New York and New York ain't in me. Yuh understand? Naw, naw, you don't get me. What do they do? Take Lenox Avenue. Take Seventh Avenue. Take Sugar Hill! Pimps. Numbers. Cheating these poor people outa what they got. Shooting, cutting, backbiting, all them things. Yuh see? Yuh see what I mean? *I'm* in New York, but *New York ain't in me!* Don't laugh, don't laugh. I'm laughing but I don't mean it; it ain't funny. Yuh see. I'm on Sugar Hill, but Sugar Hill ain't on me.

I come here twenty-five years ago. Bright lights, pretty women.

---

\* Fictitious name.

† Ralph Ellison, *Invisible Man* (New York, 1952; reprinted 1972), p. 249.

*Pullman porter, Union Station, Chicago, 1943. Photograph by Jack Delano.*

More space to move around. Son, if I had-a got New York in me I'd a-been dead a long time ago. What happened the other night? Yuh heard about the shooting up here in the Hill. Take that boy. I knowed him! Anybody been around this Hill knows him, n they know he went to a bad man. What'd he do? Now mind yuh now, his brother's a big shot. Makes plenty money. Got a big car an a fine office. But *he* comes up on this Hill tearin up people's property if they don't pay him protection. Last night he walks into this wop's place up the street n tries to tear it up. Now yuh know that's a bad man, gonna tear up the wop's place. Well, he stepped out the door n a bunch of them wops showed up in a car n tried to blow him away. *He* had too much New York. I'm in New York, yuh see? But New York ain't in me! Hell yes, he went and got too much New York, yuh understand what I tryin to tell yuh?

I been in New York twenty-five years! But I ain't never bothered nobody. Ain't never done nothin to nobody. I ain't no bad fellow. Shore I drink. I like good whiskey. I drinks but I ain't drunk. Yuh think I'm drunk? I don't *talk* drunk do I? I drinking n I got money in mah pockets. But I ain't throwing ma money away. Hell, I talking sense, ain't I? Yuh heard me way in yonder didn't yuh? Yuh came to me, heard me. I didn't have to come after yuh, did I? If I hada been talking foolishness yuh wouldn't a paid me no mind. Hell, I know I'm right. I got something to say. I got something to say n I ain't no preacher neither. I'm drinking. I likes to drink. It's good for mah stomach. *Good* whiskey's good for anybody's stomach. Look at the bottle. Mount Vernon! Good whiskey. What did the saint say? He said a little spirits is good for the stomach, good to warm the spirit. Now where did that come from? Yuh don't know, yuh too young. Yuh young Negroes don't know the Bible. Don't laugh, don't laugh. Look here, I'll tell you somethin:

> Some folks drinks to cut the fool,
> But some folks drinks to think.

I drinks to think.

Ralph Ellison
*New York City*
1939

# Bernice Gore*

*The rent parties Bernice Gore described flourished in Harlem in the 1920s, a response to the high rents and low wages blacks faced when they arrived in New York City. Around the time the rent was due, neighbors were invited to a get-together with music, food, and corn liquor and charged an entrance fee of fifteen cents or a quarter. On Saturday night, Federal Writer Frank Byrd recalls, "you couldn't walk down Lenox Avenue without hearing music from a dozen rent parties."†*

When I first came to New York from Bermuda, I thought rent parties were disgraceful. I couldn't understand how any self-respecting person could bear them, but when my husband, who was a Pullman porter,

---

* Fictitious name.
† Interview with Frank Byrd, April 1978.

ran off and left me with a sixty-dollar-a-month apartment on my hands and no job, I soon learned, like everyone else, to rent my rooms out and throw these Saturday get-togethers.

I had two roomers, a colored boy and a white girl named Leroy and Hazel, who first gave me the idea. They offered to run the parties for me if we'd split fifty-fifty. I had nothing to lose, so that's how we started.

We bought corn liquor by the gallon and sold it for fifty cents a small pitcher. Leroy also ran a poker and black jack game in the little bedroom off the kitchen. On these two games alone, I've seen him take in as much as twenty-eight dollars in one night. Well, you can see why I didn't want to give it up once we had started. Especially since I could only make six or seven dollars at most as a part-time domestic.

The games paid us both so well, in fact, that we soon made gambling our specialty. Everybody liked it, and our profit was more that way, so our place soon became the hangout of all those party-goers who liked to mix a little gambling with their drinking and dancing.

And with all these young studs with plenty of cash in their pockets out to find a little mischief, we soon learned not to leave things to chance. Instead, Hazel and I would go out and get acquainted with good-looking young fellows sitting alone in the back of gin mills looking as if they would like a good time but had nobody to take them out. We'd give them our cards and tell them to drop around to the house. Well, wherever there are pretty women you'll soon have a pack of men.

So we taught the girls how to wheedle free drinks and food out of the men. If they got them to spend more than usual, we'd give them a little percentage or a nice little present like a pair of stockings or vanity case or something. Most of the time, though, we didn't have to give them a thing. They were all out looking for a little fun, and when they came to our house they could have it for nothing instead of going to the gin mills where they'd have to pay for their own drinks.

And we rented rooms, sometimes overnight and sometimes for just a little while during the party. I have to admit that, at first, I was a little shocked at the utter boldness of it, but Leroy and Hazel seemed to think nothing of it, so I let it go. Besides, it meant extra money—and extra money was what I needed.

I soon took another hint from Hazel and made even more. I used to notice that Leroy would bring home some of his friends and, after they'd have a few drinks, leave them alone in the room with Hazel. I wasn't sure that what I was thinking was so until Hazel told me herself. It happened one day when an extra man came along and there was no one to take care of him. Hazel asked me if I would do it. I thought about it for a while, then made up my mind to do it.

That was the last of day-work for me. I figured that I was a fool to go out and break my back scrubbing floors, washing, ironing, and cooking, when I could earn three day's pay, or more, in fifteen minutes, and when I began to understand how Hazel got all those fine dresses and good-looking furs. From then on, it was strictly a business with me. I decided that if it was as easy as that, it was the life for me.

The landlord's agent had been making sweet speeches to me for a long time and I began to figure out how I could get around paying the rent. Well, I got around it, but that didn't stop me from giving rent parties. Everything I made then was gravy: clean, clear profit for little Bernice. I even broke off with Leroy and Hazel. She began to get jealous and catty, and I think he was holding out on profits from the game. Anyway, we split up and I got an "old man" of my own to help me run the house. When he took things over he even stopped girls from going into the rooms with the men unless we were getting half of what they made, and the men still had to pay for the rooms. I've seen some of those girls make enough on Saturday night to buy themselves an entirely new outfit for Sunday, including fur coat. They'd catch some sucker, like a Pullman porter or longshoreman who had been lucky in a game, and have him jim-clean before the night was over. Naturally, I got my cut.

It was a good racket while it lasted, but it's shot to pieces now.

Frank Byrd
*New York City*
1938

# Jim Barber

*Jim Barber's anti-white sentiments were widely shared in Harlem when he was interviewed by Ralph Ellison. The white merchants of 125th Street—among them the furniture store owner Barber mentioned—were particularly resented because they refused to hire blacks for any but the most menial jobs. Black responses to this discrimination ranged from boycotts ("Don't Buy Where You Can't Work") to the 1935 riot that left millions of dollars of property damage.*

I was sitting up on the bandstand drumming, trying to make myself some beat-up change. Wasn't such a crowd in the place that night, just a bunch of them beer drinkers. I was looking down at em dancing and wishing that things would liven up. Then a man come up and give me *four* dollars just to sing one number. Well, I was singing for that man. I was really laying it Jack, just like Marian Anderson. What the hell are you talking about; I'd sing all night after that cat done give me four bucks; that's almost a fin! But this is what brings you down. One a these bums come up to the stand and says to the banjo player: "If you monkeys don't play some music, I'm gonna throw you outa de jernt."

Man, I quit singing and looked at that sonofabitch. Then I got mad. I said: "Where the goddamn hell you come from, you gonna throw somebody outa *this* band? How you get so bad? Why you poor Brooklyn motherfrigger, I'll wreck this goddamn place with you."

Man, he looked at me. I said: "Dont look at me goddamnit, I mean what I say!"

By this time everybody is standing around listening. I said: "I oughta snatch your goddamn head off. Oh, I know the rest'll try to gang me. But they won't get me before I get to you. You crummy bastard."

Then man, I make a break for my pocket, like I was pulling my gun. Ha, Ha, goddamn! You oughta seen em fall back from this cat. This bum had on glasses and you oughta seen him holding up his hands and gitting outa my way. Then the boss came up running and put the sonofabitch out into the street and told me to get back to work. Hell, I scared the hell out of that bastard. A poor sonofabitch! Drinking beer and coming up talking to us like that! You see he thought cause we was black he could talk like he wanted to. In a nightclub and drinking beer! I fixed him. I bet he won't try that no more.

Man, a poor white man is a bring-down. He ain't got nothing. He can't get nothing. And he thinks cause he's white he's got to impress you cause you black.

Then some of em comes up and try to be your friend. Like the other night, I'm up on the stand drumming and singing, trying to make myself some change. I was worried. I got a big old boy, damn near big as me, and every time I look up he's got to have something. Well, the other night I hadn't made a damn thing. And I was sitting there drumming when one of these bums what hangs around the place, one a these slap-happy jitterbugs, comes up to me and says: "You stink!"

Now you know that made me mad before I even knowed what he was talking about. A white cat coming up to me talking about I stink! I said: "What you talking about? What you mean I stink?"

He said: "You ain't a good fellow like the other cats. You won't take me up to Harlem and show me around."

I said: "Hell yes, mammydodger, I stink! If that's what you mean I'm gon always stink. You'll never catch me carrying a bunch of you poor sonsabitches up there. What the hell you gonna do when you get up there? You ain't got nothing. Hell, you poor as I am. I don't see you coming down to Harlem to carry me up to show me the Bronx. You damn right I stink."

Man, he just looks at me now and says: "Jack, you sho a funny cat."

Can you beat that? He oughta know I ain't got no use for him. *Damn!*

Another one comes up to me—another one a these beer-drinking bums—and says: "I want to go up to your house sometime."

I said: "Fo what! Now you tell me fo what!" I said: "What-in-the-world do you want to come up to *my* place for? You ain't got nothing and I sho ain't got nothing. What's a poor colored cat and a poor white cat gonna do together? You ain't got nothing cause you too dumb to get it. And I ain't got nothing cause I'm black. I guess you got your little ol skin, that's the reason? I'm supposed to feel good cause you walk in my house and sit in my chairs? Hell, that skin ain't no more good to you than mine is to me. You cain't marry one a Du Pont's daughters, and I know damn well I cain't. So what the hell you gon do up to my place?"

Aw man, I have to get these white cats told. They think you supposed to feel good cause they friendly to you. Boy I don't fool with em. They just the reason why I cain't get ahead now. They try to get all a man's money. That's just the reason why I found me a place up the street here. Got two rooms in a private house with a private bath. These other cats go down to Ludwig Bauman's [a furniture store on 125th Street] and give him all their money so they can meet you on the street and say: "Oh you *must* come up to my apartment sometimes. Oh yes, yes, I have some lovely furniture. You just must come up sometime." You know, man, they want to show off. But me, I done got wise. I'm getting my stuff outa junk shops, second-hand stores, anywhere, I ain't giving these Jews my money. Like the chicks. I used to get my check and go out with the boys and pick up some of these fine-feathered chicks. You know the light chicks with the fine hair. We'd go out making all the gin mills, buying liquor. I'd take me to a room and have a ball. Then I'd wake up in the morning with all my beat-up change gone and I'd have to face my wife and tell her some deep lie that she didn't believe. I don't do that no more. Now I give most of my money to my wife. And I put the rest on the numbers. And when I see the fine chicks I tell em they have to wait till the numbers jumps out.

See this bag? I got me a head a cabbage and two ears a corn. I'm going up here and get me a side a bacon. When I get home, gonna cook the cabbage and bacon, gonna make me some corn fritters and set back in my twenty-five-dollars-a-month room and eat my fritters and cabbage and tell the Jews to forgit it! Jack, I'm just sitting back waiting, cause soon things is gonna narrow down to the fine point. Hitler's gonna reach in a few months and grab and then things'll start. All the white folks'll be killing off one another. And I hope they do a good job! Then there won't be nobody left but Sam. Then we'll be fighting it out among ourselves. That'll be a funky fight. Aw hell yes! When Negroes start running things I think I'll have to get off the earth before it's too late!

Ralph Ellison
*New York City*
1939

# Eli Luster*

*The sinking of the Titanic, it seemed to Eli Luster, was an act of divine justice against white people. Since the luxury liner had barred black passengers from its ill-fated maiden voyage, the sea disaster was a common theme in black song and toasts. Eli Luster expressed his apocalyptic visions and class antagonisms in a vivid rhetorical style that is still common in Harlem today, according to Ralph Ellison.*

It's too bad about them two submarines. They can experiment an everything, but they cain't go but so far. Then God steps in. Them fellows is trying to make something what'll stay down. They said they'd done it, but look what happened. Take back in 1912. They built a ship called the *Titanic*. Think they built it over in England; I think that was where it was built. Anyway, they said it couldn't sink. It was for all the big rich folks: John Jacob Astor—all the big aristocrats. Nothing the

---

* Fictitious name.

color of this could git on the boat. Naw suh! Didn't want nothing look like me on it. One girl went down to go with her madam and they told her she couldn't go. They didn't want nothing look like this on there. They told the madam, "You can go, but she cain't." The girl's madam got mad and told em if the girl didn't go she wasn't going. And she didn't neither. Yessuh, she stayed right here.

Well, they got this big boat on the way over to England.* They said she couldn't sink—that was man talking. It was so big they tell me that was elevators in it like across yonder in that building. Had the richest folks in the world on it just having a big tune. Got over near England, almost ready to dock, and ups an hits an iceberg, and sank! That was the boat they said was so big it couldn't sink. They didn't want nothing look like this on it, no sir! And don't you think that woman wasn't glad she stuck by that girl. She was plenty glad. Man can go only so far. Then God steps in. Sho, they can experiment around. They can do a heap. They can even make a man. But they cain't make him breathe. Why the other day I was down on 125th Street and Eighth Avenue. They got one of them malted milk places. Well, suh, they got a cow on the counter. It looks like a real cow. Got hair. I was standing there looking and the doggone thing moved its head and wagged its tail; man done even made a cow. But, they had to do it with electricity.

God's the only one can give life. God made all this, and he made it for everybody. And he made it equal. This breeze and these green leaves out here is for everybody. The same sun's shining down on everybody. This breeze comes from God and man can't do nothing about it. I breathe the same air old man Ford and old man Rockefeller breathe. They got all the money and I ain't got nothing, but they got to breathe the same air I do.

Man cain't make no man. Less see now: this heah's nineteen-hundred-and-twenty-nine.† For nineteen hundred years man's had things his way. He's been running the world to suit hisself. It's just like your father owned that building over there and told you you could live in it if you didn't do certain things. And then you did what he told you not to. And he finds out and says, "Go on, you can have the whole building, I won't have nothing else to do with it. You can turn it upside-down if you want to." Well, that was the way it was in the world. Adam an Eve sinned in the Garden and God left the world to itself. Men been running it like they want to. They been running it like they want

---

* The *Titanic* was sailing toward the United States when it sank.
† It was 1939.

to for nineteen hundred years. Rich folks done took all the land. They
got all the money. Men down to the City Hall making fifty thousand
dollars a year and nothing like this cain't even scrub the marble floors
or polish the brass what they got down there.

Old man Ford and J. P. Morgan got all the money and folks in
this part cain't even get on relief. But you just watch: the Lawd made
all men equal and pretty soon now it's gonna be that way again. I'm a
man. I breathe the same air old man Ford breathes cause God made
man equal. God formed man in his own image. He made Adam out
of the earth; not like this concrete we sitting on, but out of dirt, clay.
Like you seen a kid making a snowman. He'll git him a stick and make
the arms. And he'll git another stick and make for his neck; and so on,
just like we got bones. That was the way God made man. Made him
outa clay and in his own image: that was the way he made Adam. One
drop of God's blood made all the nations in the world: Africans, Ger-
mans, Chinamen, Jews, Indians; all come from one drop of God's
blood. God took something outa Adam and made woman, he made
Eve. The preachers tell a lie and say it was his rib. But they have to
lie, I guess. They didn't do nothing but sit back in the shed and let
you do all the work anyway. But God went into Adam and took something out and made Eve. That's the Scriptures; it said he took *something*. I cain't remember the exact words, but it said he took *something*
and it didn't say nothing bout no rib. Eve started having children. Some
of em was black and some of em was white. But they was all equal.
God didn't know no color; we all the same. All he want from man is
this heart thumping the blood. Them what take advantage of skin like
this got to come by God. They gonna pay.

They tell me bout George Washington. He was the first president
this country ever had. First thing I heard was he said to keep us look
like this down in the cornfield. He tole em, "Don't let em have no guns.
You ain't to let em have no knife. Don't let em have nothing." He tole
em if they wanted to have a strong nation to keep us down. He said
if ever they git guns in they hands they'll rise up and take the land;
don't let em have nothing. But he didn't say nothing about no pick
and ax!

They been carrying out what he said. God didn't say nothing. That
was just man's idea and here in this country they been carrying out
what old man George Washington said. But God's time is coming.
Today you hear all these folks got millions of dollars talking bout God.
They ain't fooling nobody, though. They even got IN GOD WE TRUST
on all the silver money. But it don't mean nothing. This sun and air
is God's. It don't belong to nobody and cain't no few get it all to

theyself. People around this park can have all they want. But you wait. God's gonna straighten it all out.

Look at the dust blowing in the wind. That's the way all the money they got gonna be. You see things, folks they call white, but man ain't got no idea of how white God gon make things. Money won't be worth no more'n that dust blowing on the ground. Won't be no men down to Washington making fifty thousand dollars a week and folks cain't hardly make eighteen dollars a month. Everybody'll be equal, in God's time. Won't be no old man Rockefeller, no suh! Today you cain't even buy a job if you had the money to do it with. Won't be nothing like that then. He'll let loose and something'll slip down here and them what done took advantage of everything'll be floating down the river. You'll go over to the North River, and over to the East River, and you'll see em all floating along, and the river'll be full and they won't know what struck em. The Lawd's gonna have his day.

They'll be a war. But it won't be no more wars like the World War. It won't bother me and you. Won't really be no war. It'll be the wicked killing the wicked! The war like the World War'll never be again. They fooled now. They building navies and buying guns. But don't you worry, it'll be just the wicked killing out the wicked. It's coming; God's time is coming and it's coming soon!

Ralph Ellison
*New York City*
1939

# Afterword

The unpublished Federal Writers' Project manuscripts have had a peripatetic history since the Project was dismantled. When it became obvious in 1940 that the Project's days were numbered, an effort was made to salvage what had been collected. State directors were instructed to send copies of all work to the national office in Washington, D.C. The vast quantity of material was deposited with the Library of Congress, which established an Editorial Project to "collect, preserve and organize for use" the FWP manuscripts. Little headway had been made on this task, however, by the time the funds ran out in 1941. Subsequently, the administrative records discovered among the Writers' Project papers were transferred to the National Archives, where they were soon organized and made accessible to the public.

The FWP manuscripts that remained at the Library of Congress fared less well. One portion was crated, shoved from alcove to alcove, and finally relegated to a warehouse outside Washington. These records consist largely of reports and material left over from the preparation of the state and local guidebooks. In addition, the Library of Congress has FWP holdings in its main collection, in the Manuscript Division, and in the Folk Song Archive. In addition to the books published by the Project, the main collection contains numerous mimeographed FWP booklets. Most of this material pertains to local history and includes such items as reports on a Montana copper camp, a Wisconsin circus, and a West Virginia hollow.

The Manuscript Division houses work that was nearly completed at the time the Project ended. This includes an anthology of fictionalized life histories called *Men at Work*, edited and with an introduction by Harold Rosenberg, as well as a manuscript of food lore called *America Eats*, which has been drawn upon frequently by researchers. There is a guide to the FWP material in the Manuscript Division. It is accessible and easy to use, though it includes only a fraction of the Library's Writers' Project holdings. The condition and extent of the major collection of FWP manuscripts—those in the Folk Song Archive—have been described in the introduction to this book.

There are also numerous state repositories of Writers' Project papers. When the Project was disbanded, compliance with the directive to forward all manuscripts to Washington proved uneven. Most of the life histories in the southern region, for example, remained there and are now deposited in the Southern Historical Collection of the University of North Carolina. In addition, some of the work sent on to the national office was later returned for deposit in assorted state libraries, archives, and historical societies. The fate of this material has varied from state to state: Some state depositories have done an excellent job of cataloguing and maintaining their FWP collections; in other instances material has been lost or destroyed. Some of the most interesting material collected by the Chicago Writers' Project, for example, has never been traced and probably was among papers destroyed a dozen years ago.

During the postwar years, the political climate of McCarthyism "drove the memory of the Writers' Project deep into the shade," as Jerre Mangione has written.* Recently, however, there has been increased interest among scholars and the general public in the achievements of the New Deal arts projects. Activities are now under way that will make the wealth of unpublished Writers' Project material more readily available. The Library of Congress has begun to review and process its FWP holdings. The warehoused material, currently being organized, will be substantially ready for use in 1981. And as an outgrowth of the research carried out for *First-Person America*, there now exists a rough inventory of the holdings of the Folk Song Archive. In addition, the Library's collection of slave narratives gathered by the Writers' Project recently has been catalogued under the direction of O. Mervene Couch of the University of the District of Columbia.

Other ongoing projects involve material outside the Library of Congress. Jerrold Hirsch is indexing the FWP life-history narratives at the University of North Carolina's Southern Historical Collection. A survey of state depositories of Federal Writers' Project material has been undertaken by Robert L. Carter of the University of Indiana and myself. There are also numerous plans on local and state levels to organize and publish Writers' Project manuscripts.

These projects to make FWP material more accessible to scholars coincide with heightened interest in all the Federal arts projects. The past few years have seen revivals of plays written for the Federal Theater Project as well as exhibitions of paintings and posters done for the Fed-

* Jerre Mangione, *The Dream and the Deal: The Federal Writers' Project, 1935–1943* (Boston, 1972), p. 366.

eral Art Project. A documentary film on all the arts projects has recently been completed for airing on the Public Broadcasting System. The life-history narratives in *First-Person America* have been dramatized in a six-part series by WGBH (Boston) for National Public Radio.

These recent activities testify to the continuing worth of the New Deal arts projects. The Federal Writers' Project cost the government $27 million—only one-fifth of 1 percent of all WPA expenditures. The Project's value as a relief measure and the excellent books it produced justified its existence. But in the rich vein of unpublished material, the Writers' Project also left a forgotten legacy—one that is only now beginning to be appreciated.

A. B.
*Cambridge, Massachusetts*
*March 1980*

NOTES
INTERVIEWS
BIBLIOGRAPHY
INDEX

# Notes

1. Walter Benjamin, *Illuminations* (New York, 1969), pp. 86–7.

2. William Stott, *Documentary Expression and Thirties America* (New York, 1973), p. 204.

3. Henry Alsberg, speech at the second Congress of American Writers, held contained in *The Writer in a Changing World*, Henry Hart, ed. (New York, 1937), p. 242.

4. Stott, *Documentary Expression*, p. 203.

5. Benjamin A. Botkin, "We Called It 'Living Lore,'" *New York Folklore Quarterly* XIV (Autumn 1958): 198.

6. Quoted in Benjamin A. Botkin, "Living Lore on the New York City Writers' Project," *New York Folklore Quarterly* II (November 1946): 256.

7. Benjamin A. Botkin, speech at the third Congress of American Writers held in New York in 1939. The papers and speeches of the third Congress are contained in *Fighting Words*, Donald Ogden Stewart, ed., (New York, 1940), p. 14.

8. Ibid., p. 12.

9. Ibid., p. 191.

10. Morton Royse to Archibald MacLeish, June 7, 1940, Federal Writers' Project Files, Records of the Work Projects Administration, National Archives, Washington, D.C.

11. Botkin, "We Called It 'Living Lore,'" p. 192.

12. These ideas are discussed by Mara Liasson in "The Federal Writers' Project and the Folklore of Cultural Pluralism," B.A. thesis, Brown University (1977), pp. 20–24; see also Marshall Berman, review, *The New York Times Book Review*, 24 March 1974, pp. 1–3.

13. Stephen Wise to David Niles, January 24, 1939, quoted in "The Federal Writers' Project: A Study in Government Patronage of the Arts," Monty Noam Penkower, Ph.D. dissertation, Columbia University (1970).

14. Botkin speech, contained in *Fighting Words*, p. 12.

15. Ibid., p. 12.

16. Benjamin A. Botkin, *Lay My Burden Down: A Folk History of Slavery* (Chicago, 1945), p. xii.

17. Benjamin A. Botkin, *Manual for Folklore Studies* (1938), Federal Writers' Project Materials, Archive of Folk Song, Library of Congress, Washington, D.C.

18. Stetson Kennedy to Ann Banks, 2 September 1978.

19. Interview with Frank Byrd by Ann Banks, April 1978.

20. Interview with Jack Conroy by Ann Banks, February 1978.

21. Interview with Ralph Ellison by Ann Banks, December 1977.

22. Interview with Betty Burke by Ann Banks, February 1978.

23. Stetson Kennedy to Ann Banks.

24. For a detailed account of black writers on the FWP see Jerre Mangione, *The Dream and the Deal: The Federal Writers' Project 1935–1943* (New York, 1972), Chapter 7.

25. Interview with Ralph Ellison.

26. Henry Alsberg, speech at the second Congress of American Writers, contained in *The Writer in a Changing World*, Henry Hart, ed., p. 245.

27. This point is made in *New Deal for Art*, Marlene Park and Gerald E. Markowitz (Hamilton, New York, 1977), pp. 7–13.

28. Daniel Aaron, "Guidebooks and Meal Tickets," *Times Literary Supplement*, 28 July 1978, p. 837.

29. Mangione, *The Dream and the Deal*, p. 255.

30. Quoted in *The Federal Writers' Project: A Study in Government Patronage of the Arts*, Monty Noam Penkower (Urbana, Ill., 1977), p. 243.

31. Botkin, "We Called it 'Living Lore,' " p. 196.

32. Alfred Kazin, *Starting Out in The Thirties* (Boston, 1962), p. 15.

33. Botkin, speech contained in *Fighting Words*, p. 13.

34. Interview with Ralph Ellison.

35. Botkin, speech contained in *Fighting Words*, p. 14.

36. Interview with Ralph Ellison.

37. Botkin, *Lay My Burden Down*, p. xiii.

38. Henry Mayhew, *London Labour and the London Poor* (New York, 1968), p. xv. Mayhew's work was originally published in London in 1861.

39. Benjamin, *Illuminations*, p. 92.

40. Liasson, "The Folklore of Cultural Pluralism," p. 177.

41. Quoted in Botkin, *Lay My Burden Down*, p. xiv.

42. "Staff Conference in Industrial Folklore" (13 July 1939), typewritten memorandum, Federal Writers' Project Materials, Archive of Folk Song, Library of Congress, Washington, D.C.

43. Prospectus for the "Yankee Folk" anthology, undated, typewritten memorandum, Federal Writers' Project Materials, Archive of Folk Song, Library of Congress, Washington, D.C.

44. Instructions to Federal Writers in the New England Region (11 December 1939), typewritten memorandum, Vermont Historical Society, Montpelier, Vt.

45. For a detailed discussion of this idea, see Alfred H. Jones, "The Search for a Usable American Past in the New Deal Era," *American Quarterly* 23 (December 1971): 710–24.

46. John Dos Passos, *The Ground We Stand On* (New York, 1941), p. 3.

47. Ibid., p. 3.

48. Benjamin A. Botkin, "WPA and Folklore Research: Bread and Song," *Southern Folklore Quarterly* III (March 1939): 10.

49. Benjamin A. Botkin, "Applied Folklore: Creating Understanding Through Folklore," *Southern Folklore Quarterly* XVII (September 1953): 203.

50. Studs Terkel, *Hard Times: An Oral History of the Great Depression* (New York, 1970), p. 17.

# Interviews

# Bibliography

The readings listed below constitute a partial list of sources consulted in the course of preparing this anthology. Specific references in the general introduction may be found in the Notes section. For an overview of the general literature on the 1930s, there are excellent bibliographical essays in Richard Pells's *Radical Visions and American Dreams* and William Stott's *Documentary Expression and Thirties America*. In addition, *Such As Us*, edited by Tom Terrill and Jerrold Hirsch, contains a bibliographical essay that is especially useful for readers interested in learning more about the Federal Writers' Project and oral history.

## INTRODUCTION: PAGES xi–xxv

Aaron, Daniel. *Writers on the Left*. New York, 1961.

Benjamin, Walter. *Illuminations*. New York, 1968.

Botkin, Benjamin A., ed. *Lay My Burden Down: A Folk History of Slavery*. Chicago, 1945.

Couch, William T., ed. *These Are Our Lives*. Chapel Hill, N.C., 1939.

Dos Passos, John. *The Ground We Stand On*. New York, 1941.

Hart, Henry, ed. *The Writer in a Changing World*. New York, 1937.

Kazin, Alfred. *Starting Out in the Thirties*. Boston, 1965.

Mangione, Jerre. *The Dream and the Deal: The Federal Writers' Project 1935–1943*. New York, 1972.

Mayhew, Henry. *London Labour and the London Poor*. London, 1861; reprinted New York, 1968.

McDonald, William F. *The Federal Relief Administration and the Arts*. Columbus, Ohio, 1969.

Park, Marlene, and Markowitz, Gerald E. *New Deal for Art*. Hamilton, N.Y., 1977.

Pells, Richard H. *Radical Visions and American Dreams: Culture and Social Thought in the Depression Years*. New York, 1974.

Penkower, Monty Noam. *The Federal Writers' Project: A Study in Government Patronage of the Arts*. Urbana, Ill., 1977.

Perdue, Charles. *Weevils in the Wheat: Interviews with Virginia Ex-Slaves.* Charlottesville, Va., 1976.

Rawick, George P. *From Sundown to Sunup: The Making of the Black Community.* Westport, Conn., 1972.

Stewart, Donald Ogden, ed. *Fighting Words.* New York, 1940.

Stott, William. *Documentary Expression and Thirties America.* New York, 1973.

Susman, Warren, ed. *Culture and Commitment 1929–1945.* New York, 1973.

Swados, Harvey, ed. *The American Writer and the Great Depression.* Indianapolis, 1966.

Terkel, Studs. *Hard Times: An Oral History of the Great Depression.* New York, 1970.

Terrill, Tom, and Hirsch, Jerrold. *Such as Us: Southern Voices of the Thirties.* Chapel Hill, N.C., 1978.

Yetman, Norman R. *Voices from Slavery.* New York, 1970.

### ARTICLES AND PAPERS

Aaron, Daniel. "Guidebooks and Meal Tickets." *Times Literary Supplement,* 28 July 1978, p. 837.

Botkin, Benjamin A. "WPA and Folklore Research: 'Bread and Song.'" *Southern Folklore Quarterly* III (March 1939): 7–14.

———. "Living Lore on the New York City Writers' Project." *New York Folklore Quarterly* II (November 1946): 252.

———. "We Called it 'Living Lore.'" *New York Folklore Quarterly* XIV (Autumn 1958): 189–201.

———. "Applied Folklore: Creating Understanding Through Folklore." *Southern Folklore Quarterly* XVII (September 1953): 199.

Cantwell, Robert. "America and the Writers' Project." *New Republic,* 26 April 1939, p. 323.

DeVoto, Bernard. "The Writers Project." *Harper's,* January 1942, pp. 221–24.

Fox, Daniel M. "The Achievement of the Federal Writers' Project." *American Quarterly* 13, no. 1 (Spring 1961), pp. 3–19.

Frisch, Michael. "Oral History and Hard Times." *The Oral History Review,* 1979, pp. 70–79.

Hirsch, Jerrold. "Ethnic Pluralism and the Federal Writers' Project," paper presented before the American Society for Ethnohistory, Chicago, October 1977.

Jones, Alfred H. "The Search for a Usable American Past in the New Deal Era." *American Quarterly* 23, no. 4 (December 1971); pp. 710–24.

Mangione, Jerre. "Federal Writers' Project." *New York Times,* 18 May 1969, VII, p. 2.

"What the Writers Wrote." *New Republic,* 1 September 1937, p. 89.

MANUSCRIPT COLLECTIONS AND MISCELLANEOUS SOURCES

Bourne, Frances T. "Report and Recommendation for Disposition of Records of the Federal Writers' Project." Library of Congress, Washington, D.C., July 29, 1949.
Federal Writers' Project Files, Manuscript Division. South Caroliniana Library, University of South Carolina, Columbia, S.C.
Liasson, Mara. "The Federal Writers' Project and the Folklore of Cultural Pluralism." B.A. thesis, Brown University, 1977.
Records of the Work Projects Administration, Federal Writers' Project. National Archives, Washington, D.C.
U.S. Work Projects Administration Collection, Manuscript Collection. Library of Congress, Washington, D.C.
Vermont Works Progress Administration Writers' Project files. Vermont Historical Society, Montpelier, Vt.
Work Projects Administration Federal Writers' Project Materials. Archive of Folk Song, Library of Congress, Washington, D.C.


OLD TIMES: PAGES 3–26

Keleher, William A. *Violence in Lincoln County, 1869–1881.* Albuquerque N.M., 1957.
Mainardi, Patricia. "Quilts: The Great American Art." *Radical America* 7:36–68.


IMMIGRANT LIVES: PAGES 29–47

Clark, Jane Perry. *Deportation of Aliens from the United States to Europe.* New York, 1931.
Dunwell, Steve. *The Run of the Mill.* Boston, 1978.
Hareven, Tamara K., and Langenbach, Randolph. *Amoskeag: Life and Work in an American Factory City.* New York, 1978.
Hemingway, Ernest. *To Have and Have Not.* New York, 1937.
Hoff, Rhoda. *America's Immigrants: Adventures in Eyewitness History.* New York, 1967.
Howe, Irving. *World of Our Fathers.* New York, 1976.
Kraus, Michael. *Immigration: The American Mosaic.* Princeton, N.J., 1966.


THE YARDS: PAGES 51–71

Bracey, John H., Jr.; Meier, August; and Rudwick, Elliott. *Black Workers and Organized Labor.* Belmont, Calif., 1971.

Brody, David. *The Butcher Workmen: A Study of Unionization.* Cambridge, Mass., 1964.

Franklin, John Hope. *From Slavery to Freedom: A History of American Negroes.* New York, 1956.

Galenson, Walter. *The CIO Challenge to the AFL: A History of the American Labor Movement, 1935–1941.* Cambridge, Mass., 1960.

Lynd, Alice, and Lynd, Staughton. *Rank and File: Personal Histories of Working Class Organizers.* Boston, 1973.

Sinclair, Upton. *The Jungle.* New York, 1906.


INDUSTRIAL LORE: PAGES 75–92


Chatterton, Wayne, and Cox, Martha Heasley. *Nelson Algren.* Boston, 1975.

Conroy, Jack. *The Disinherited.* New York, 1933.

Donahue, H. E. F. *Conversations with Nelson Algren.* New York, 1964.

*Maine: A Guide "Down East."* (American Guide Series) Boston, 1937.

*New York City Guide.* (American Guide Series) New York, 1939.

*Oklahoma: A Guide to the Sooner State.* (American Guide Series) Norman, Okla., 1942.

Ware, Norman J. *Labor in Modern Industrial Society.* New York, 1935.


MONUMENTAL STONE: PAGES 95–119


*Barre, Vermont Historical Booklet, 1780–1970.* Barre, Vermont Heritage Festival, 1970.

Colodny, Roby. "Labor in Barre: 1900–1941," *Vermont's Untold History.* Burlington, Vt., 1976.

Demers, Paul. "Labor and the Social Relations of the Granite Industry in Barre." Unpublished B.A. thesis, Goddard College, 1974.

Fenwick, Carroll, ed. *Barre in Retrospect, 1776–1976.* Barre, Vermont: Friends of the Aldrich Public Library, 1975.

*Granite Artists and Their Work.* Barre, Vt., 1978.

Tomasi, Mari. *Like Lesser Gods.* Milwaukee, 1949.

Tomasi, Mari. "The Italian Story in Vermont." *Vermont History* 28, no. 1 (January 1960).

*Vermont: A Guide to the Green Mountain State.* (American Guide Series) New York, 1937.


RANK AND FILE: PAGES 123–135


Bernstein, Irving. *The Turbulent Years: A History of the American Worker, 1933–1941.* Boston, 1970.

"The Book of the Amalgamated in New York, 1914–1940." Presented to the Twenty-fifth Anniversary Convention of the Amalgamated Clothing Workers of America, New York, 1940.

Galster, Augusta Emile. *The Labor Movement in the Shoe Industry*. New York, 1924.

Laslett, John H. M. *Labor and the Left: A Study of Socialist and Radical Influences in the American Labor Movement, 1881–1924*. New York, 1970.

Morris, James O. *Conflict Within the AFL: A Study of Craft Versus Industrial Unionism, 1901–1938*. Ithaca, N.Y., 1958.


## TOBACCO PEOPLE: PAGES 139–159

Janiewski, Dolores. "Race, Class and the Sexual Division of Labor: The Difficulties of Collective Action in Durham During the 1930s." (Paper delivered at the Fourth Berkshire Conference on the History of Women, Mt. Holyoke, Mass., August 24, 1978.)

———. "Sisters Under the Skin?: The Conflict between Race and Class among Female Tobacco Workers in Durham, North Carolina." (Paper delivered at the Thirteenth National Colloquium on Oral History, Savannah, Ga., October 21, 1978.)

Nourse, Edwin G., et al. *Three years of Agricultural Adjustment Administration*. Washington, D.C., 1937.

"People in Tobacco." Series B, Group 3, U.S. Works Progress Administration Collection. Library of Congress Manuscript Collection, Washington, D.C.

Tennant, Richard B. *The American Cigarette Industry*. New Haven, 1950.

Tilley, Nannie May. *Bright-Tobacco Industry, 1860–1929*. Chapel Hill, N.C., 1948.


## WOMEN ON WORK: PAGES 163–180

Algren, Nelson. *A Walk on the Wild Side*. New York, 1956.

Baker, Elizabeth Faulkner. *Technology and Women's Work*. New York, 1964.

Baxandall, Rosalyn; Gordon, Linda; and Reverby, Susan. *America's Working Women: A Documentary History—1600 to the Present*. New York, 1976.

Kennedy, Stetson. *Palmetto Country*. New York, 1942.

*North Carolina: A Guide to the Old North State*. (American Guide Series) Chapel Hill, N.C., 1939.

Smuts, Robert W. *Women and Work in America*. New York, 1959.

## TROUPERS AND PITCHMEN: PAGES 183–213

Brown, Lorraine, and O'Conner, John, eds. *Free, Adult, Uncensored: The Living History of the Federal Theatre Project.* Washington, D.C., 1978.

Burns, George. *I Love Her, That's Why.* New York, 1955.

DiMeglio, John. *Vaudeville, U.S.A.* Bowling Green, Ohio, 1973.

Fox, Charles Phillip, and Parkinson, Tom. *The Circus in America.* Waukesha, Wis., 1969.

Gilbert, Douglas. *American Vaudeville.* New York, 1949.

Howe, Irving. *World of our Fathers.* New York, 1976.

Laurie, Joe Jr. *Vaudeville.* New York, 1953.

Slout, William Lawrence. *Theatre in a Tent: The Development of a Provincial Entertainment.* Bowling Green, Ohio, 1972.

Webber, Malcolm. *Medicine Show.* Caldwell, Idaho, 1941.

Young, James Harvey. *The Medical Messiahs: A Social History of Health Quackery in Twentieth-Century America.* Princeton, N.J., 1967.

## THE JAZZ LANGUAGE: PAGES 217–233

Leonard Feather, ed. *Encyclopedia of Jazz.* New York, 1960.

Hentoff, Nat, and Shapiro, Nat, eds. *Hear Me Talkin' to Ya.* New York, 1955; reprinted 1966.

Hobson, Wilder. *American Jazz Music.* New York, 1939; reprinted 1976.

Panassie, Hugues. *Hot Jazz.* New York, 1936.

## TESTIFYING: PAGES 237–260

"Collecting Gullah Folklore." *Southern Exposure* 5 (1977), pp. 119–21.

Ellison, Ralph. *Invisible Man.* New York, 1947.

*Florida: A Guide to the Southernmost State.* (American Guide Series) New York, 1939.

Foner, Eric, comp. *America's Black Past: A Reader in Afro-American History.* New York, 1970.

Franklin, John Hope. *From Slavery to Freedom.* New York, 1956.

Kennedy, Stetson. *Palmetto Country.* New York, 1942.

Oakley, Giles. *The Devil's Music: A History of the Blues.* New York, 1976.

# Index

## About the Author

ANN BANKS lives in New York City. Her work on the Federal Writers' Project was supported by grants from the Rockefeller Foundation and the Ford Foundation, and she served as executive editor of a six-part series based on *First-Person America* produced for National Public Radio.